# SMASH!

# SMASH!

## GREEN DAY, THE OFFSPRING, BAD RELIGION, NOFX, AND THE '90S PUNK EXPLOSION

## IAN WINWOOD

DA CAPO PRESS

Da Capo Press
Hachette Book Group
1290 Avenue of the Americas, New York, NY 10104
dacapopress.com
@DaCapoPress, @DaCapoPR

Printed in the United States of America
First Edition: November 2018

Published by Da Capo Press, an imprint of Perseus Books, LLC, a subsidiary of
Hachette Book Group, Inc. The Da Capo Press name and logo are trademarks
of the Hachette Book Group.

The Hachette Speakers Bureau provides a wide range of authors for speaking
events. To find out more, go to www.hachettespeakersbureau.com or call (866)
376-6591.

The publisher is not responsible for websites (or their content) that are not
owned by the publisher.

Editorial production by Christine Marra, Marrathon Production Services.
www.marrathoneditorial.org

Book design by Jane Raese
Set in 10-point LinoLetter

Library of Congress Control Number: 2018958066

ISBN 978-0-306-90274-1 (hardcover); ISBN 978-0-306-90273-4 (ebook)

LSC-C

10   9   8   7   6   5   4   3   2   1

TO DAN SILVER AND FRANK TURNER,
COMRADES IN PUNK

# CONTENTS

# SOMETHING'S ODD, I FEEL LIKE I'M GOD

"What is this free hippie love shit?" asks Billie Joe Armstrong, his voice a mixture of mischief and malice. A sky-blue, sticker-strewn Fernandes Stratocaster guitar hangs low at his waist. Everywhere he looks his life is changing with great speed. The twenty-two-year-old regards the audience heaving before him and offers a greeting.

"How you doing, you rich motherfuckers?"

It is August 14, 1994, a Sunday afternoon, a supposedly summer's day in upstate New York. Half a million people have descended on Winston Farm in Saugerties to commemorate, and hopefully celebrate, the twenty-fifth anniversary of the now folkloric Woodstock Music and Art Fair. It was at this event that four hundred thousand people gathered to see bands such as The Who, Santana and the Jimi Hendrix Experience, and hear The warning to give a wide berth to "the brown acid." A quarter of a century on, at Woodstock '94 the appetite was more amphetamine than hallucinogen. In the dog days of summer, bands such as Metallica, Nine Inch Nails and Red Hot Chili Peppers were on-site to trample on any notions of peace and love.

In case you were wondering, the answer to Billie Joe Armstrong's impolite enquiry was "Yeah, not so good."

Considering the scene of rural misery stretched out before him, Armstrong's words were not emollient. From the lip of the stage to the flat of the horizon, people stood soaked in rain and slurry. The sight resembled a refugee camp, only with four-dollar bottles of water instead of worldly possessions. With crashing predictability, as Woodstock '94 began, so, too, did the rain. On the border that separates the torrential from the unmanageable, for three days a dishwater sky threw its very worst onto the campers below. In an interview from this sorry site to a radio station in Sydney, the Australian journalist Andrew Mueller described the scene in one word: "shithouse."

"I hope it rains so much you all get stuck," announced bassist Mike Dirnt as if fingering the trigger of a gun.

This was the summer that saw the second coming of punk rock. In the United States, certainly, this arrival was a spectacle witnessed by an audience far in excess of that which lent an ear in the direction of the Ramones in 1976. A generation on, the new breed's two biggest bands, Green Day and The Offspring, were legitimate mainstream concerns. Each band's third album, *Dookie* and *Smash* respectively, had attained platinum status, and would go on to sell many multiples more. And while the disdain of audiences old enough to have witnessed the events of 1976 firsthand—"That's not punk!" was the phrase that most commonly greeted these arrivistes from the generation that followed—fell like drizzle, for millions of younger listeners the Class of '94 were the real thing. In other words, they *were* the real thing.

Billie Joe Armstrong inhabited a world where he could be found "smoking my inspiration." Eighteen years after the Sex Pistols' Johnny Rotten had announced, "I don't work, I just speed," in 1994 only the drug of choice had changed.

While punk rock as heard in 1994 had its army of older detractors dismissive of what they regarded as a sanitized sound and safe parameters, at Winston Farm the scene was one of authentic chaos. For many an older head, chaos was the genre's key currency. It was chaos that John Lydon, the onetime Johnny Rotten, summoned at the Ritz in New York in 1980, when his band Public Image Ltd. performed behind a curtain, as he goaded the audience to riot by repeating the words "silly fucking audience" over and over again (duly, they obliged). That same year, it was chaos that spilled out onto the thoroughfares of Times Square following a series of dangerously oversold shows by The Clash.

The scene at Winston Farm, though, was chaos on an epic and dangerous scale. With gleeful abandon, Green Day provided the avenue through which an already testy and volatile crowd could express its frustrations. Billie Joe Armstrong would later opine that "I don't think we played that well" at Woodstock '94, as if this was somehow the point. By the time the trio had begun to slog their way through the normally definitive groove of "When I Come Around," the sky was filled with clumps of mud launched toward the stage. By the end of the song, the platform on which Green Day were by now attempting to perform resembled a painting by Jackson Pollock. Amid scenes that were by turns farcical and fearsome, stagehands attempted to cover the stage in sheets of plastic. In an equally futile gesture, Billie Joe Armstrong abandoned his guitar in order to return at least a few clumps of mud in the direction from whence they came, all the while singing the words and the melody to Twisted Sister's pleasingly brainless anthem of bedroom rebellion, "We're Not Gonna to Take It."

"Look at me, I'm a fucking idiot," he announced, describing either the people in the audience or himself, or possibly both.

After forty-five febrile minutes, Green Day left the stage. In attempting to do so, Mike Dirnt was tackled by a security guard.

The collision sheared his front teeth. Prior to his band's arrival that Sunday afternoon, Billie Joe Armstrong's greatest concern was that the slurry at his feet would ruin his box-fresh pair of black Converse. Such thoughts now seemed many miles removed. Leaving behind a stage in a state of some destruction, Green Day were expedited from Woodstock '94 by helicopter, a mode of transport of which the frontman was terrified.

"Woodstock ['94] was about the closest thing to anarchy I've ever seen in my whole life," Armstrong told the author in 2004. "And I didn't like it one bit."

This, though, was also beside the point. Spearheading a new breed of punk rockers, in upstate New York Green Day had orchestrated a riot; a riot of their own.

The one thing on which the dozens of people interviewed for this book are all agreed is the fact that up until 1994, any musician who decided to form a punk rock band was making a poor career choice. Metal bands made money. Hip-hop collectives made money. Country singers made money. But for many of its practitioners, punk rock did not guarantee a living.

Today it seems strange to write such a paragraph. Following the release of *Dookie* and *Smash*, anyone forming a punk band did so with the knowledge that it was possible to become wealthy. It may have taken eighteen years, but suddenly, and forever, the game had changed. Despite this, few writers have attempted to grapple at any great length with the significance and achievements of what Bad Religion singer Greg Graffin describes as "the democratization of punk." This book is an attempt to right this wrong.

Punk rock groups are easy to form and there are hundreds of them. Because of this, many books about underground music are little more than a compendium of band names floating on the page without much context. To the best of my ability, I have avoided batching acts together in lists for no reason other than to acknowledge their existence. Unless a group serves the story, they're not getting past the door. In choosing this course of action, many fine bands have been overlooked, particularly T.S.O.L., the Adolescents and Fugazi. Similarly, any reader hoping to find within these pages an encyclopedic take on every American punk rock hotbed from the period in question would do well to look elsewhere. But be assured, the decision to favor depth over breadth is deliberate.

I have also opted not to step into the debate as to whether Nirvana were or were not a punk rock band. The fact that they never explicitly defined themselves as such is good enough for me. And, anyway, the story of what happened up in the Pacific Northwest has been told many times, often very well. In other words, it has been given the credit it deserves.

The groups that serve this story are the ones who at the time defined themselves as being punk rock, and in fact still do. If it's possible for a tale featuring many millionaires who enjoy enduring careers to be a story about underdogs, this is that story. If this sounds unlikely, then consider this: prior to Green Day and The Offspring, the idea that in the United States a band could become famous by playing punk rock music was *unthinkable*.

With the exception of the dependably elusive Rancid, every person with whom I hoped to speak has made himself or herself available, often numerous times. All did so free of charge. The overwhelming majority of quotes that feature in this book come from interviews specific to the project. Other quotes are from interviews with the author for magazine features written in years past, and are identified as such. In a handful of cases, quotes from other sources have been used—usually from *Rolling Stone,* the *New York Times* and the *Los Angeles Times*—each of which is attributed to the source material. My gratitude for the many people who spoke with me for this project is sincere. The book would exist without them, but it would be unreadable, not to mention unpublished.

Any factual errors contained within are my own.

*Ian Winwood*
Camden Town, London
Spring 2018

The only thing that punk rock should ever really mean
is not sitting around and waiting for the lights to go green

—*Try This at Home*, Frank Turner

# WE'RE DESPERATE, GET USED TO IT

In terms of placing their boots on the ground, it is The Damned who can be credited as having had the most influence on American punk rock. Today this accolade tends to be shared by the Sex Pistols and The Clash, but it was The Damned who were the first English band of their kind to cross the Atlantic and bring their brand of loveable chaos to audiences in San Francisco, Los Angeles, Boston and New York. The impact of these appearances was felt with particular force in LA, whose punk community had been slow to start and reluctant to cohere.

"Anticipation ran high because since their first album had come out in February [*Damned Damned Damned*] The Damned had usurped The Clash as our favorite English band," recalled the LA scene "face" Pleasant Gehman in John Doe's book *Under the Big Black Sun: A Personal History of L.A. Punk*. "[The night] The Damned played the Starwood [was] a pure revelation and also sort of legitimized the LA punk scene."

The gestation of punk took place in an echo chamber that spanned the Atlantic Ocean. At a pivotal Ramones concert at the Roundhouse in London's Camden Town in 1976, guitarist

Johnny Ramone advised the members of nascent English punk bands to practice their craft with fearlessness and with haste. It was The Damned who heeded this advice with the greatest gusto. The group played their first concert the very next night. In issuing "New Rose" as a seven-inch single later that year, they became the authors of English punk rock's first release.

By way of repaying the favor done for them by Johnny Ramone, The Damned were soon inspiring rooms full of American punks. At the Starwood club, the London band asked their audience for spare change and were duly showered with dimes and quarters. This painful onslaught was at least an improvement on the torrents of spit that would rain on them wherever they played in Britain. After and between sets, singer Dave Vanian, guitarist Brian James, bassist Captain Sensible and drummer Rat Scabies posed for Polaroid pictures with their American fans, sometimes charging ten or twenty dollars for the privilege.

As well as their music, The Damned brought to Los Angeles notions of independence. Unlike the Pistols and The Clash, the band were not signed to a major label. Both "New Rose" and *Damned Damned Damned* emerged on the English imprint Stiff Records, a company the business model of which might generously be described as "affordable." So dire were the label's financial straits that two weeks after making The Damned's first album, producer Nick Lowe recycled the master tape by recording Elvis Costello's "My Aim Is True" on it. On another occasion, The Damned arrived at the label's London office demanding money, only to be taken outside by owner Dave Robinson and challenged to a fight. The company also printed up T-shirts bearing the slogan "If it ain't Stiff it ain't worth a fuck."

As if to underscore The Damned's status as Los Angeles's international punk band of choice, Dave Vanian was the cover star of the somewhat short-lived scene magazine *Slash* (Johnny Rotten would not make page one until issue number three). A year after *Slash* first hit record shops and newsstands, the publication expanded to include a record label of the same name. This imprint would go on to release albums by LA punk greats X, the Germs and Fear, among others.

Over in Long Beach, in 1979 Black Flag guitarist Greg Ginn released his band's debut EP, *Nervous Breakdown*, on his own record label, SST (Solid State Transmitters). Realizing that few labels would touch his fearsome band, Ginn instead decided to look in the phone book for a pressing plant and from there decided to fly solo. Independence coursed through his and Black Flag's veins to a masochistic degree. As with the Ramones, the band toured only in a van, at times listening to ZZ Top's blockbusting *Eliminator* album over and over again. They traveled in a state of penury so acute that its members were reduced to subsisting on white bread and dog food molded into the shape of a baseball and eaten with the speed of a fastball. Until the band's demise in 1986, Black Flag released a series of increasingly strange albums on SST. A thuggish Los Angeles Police Department (LAPD) regularly broke up their concerts for no reason other than the sport of it.

"It's funny, but when I talk to kids now I tell them that punk was actually dangerous in the 1980s," says Dexter Holland, frontman with Orange County's most popular band, The Offspring. "You think it's fun now to have blue hair, but in 1984 having blue hair would have gotten you beaten up."

The nihilism and violence of Los Angeles and neighboring Orange County was hard won. Punk gatherings were notoriously bothersome affairs. At an X concert an audience member was stabbed in the back in the literal sense for no apparent reason. Trouble also attached itself to Venice Beach's Suicidal Tendencies. The band's shape-shifting self-titled debut album suffered the indignity of being voted the worst of 1982 by LA's most influential punk magazine, *Flipside*, who were left aghast at its brazen mixture of punk and metal. At the time, the only people who seemed able to stand "ST" were an army of fight-happy pseudo-gangbangers known as the Suicidals.

"The violence at the shows of that time hasn't been exaggerated," says Fat Mike, bandleader with one of the city's most enduring bands, NOFX. "If anything, it's been *under*represented. It's kind of why we went. You think you're indestructible, even though at a show with five hundred people there would be ten or twenty big fights. I remember me and my friend going to a show and he got a drink from the water fountain and some guys just shoved his head into it and knocked out some of his teeth. Another friend got a broken bottle in his mouth, which actually only resulted in three chipped teeth. And I was at a Dickies show at a little club and someone I knew stabbed my friend and we had to rush him to hospital. He almost died. So when it comes to the violence of that time, there really is no exaggeration."

With fingers twitching on their standard-issue billy clubs, by far the greatest threat to the city's punk fraternity came from the LAPD. The force was led by its unsmiling commissioner, Daryl Gates, yet to be forced out of his post following riots that engulfed the city in 1992. "Gates basically hated every kind of minority, even punks," recalls Dexter Holland. Quick to fall in line, officers at street level took this antipathy and converted it into physical force. Concerts were regularly disrupted and audience members beaten. Riots took place at shows by Black Flag and the Ramones. Cops mounted on horses broke up a set by the always antagonistic Fear at the LA street festival, at which yet another riot ensued. A performance by the dependably provocative Dead Kennedys at the Longshoremen's Hall in the industrial neighborhood of Wilmington culminated in police officers surrounding and entering the building and ordering everyone to leave.

"I remember hiding under a table while this was going on," recalls the then seventeen-year-old Dexter Holland. "My friends

and I were naïve enough to think, 'Well, we haven't done anything wrong so they won't bother us.' Then suddenly tear gas
was going off. I don't know if you've ever seen a tear gas canis-
ter, but when it hits the floor it kind of makes this hissing sound.
I remember thinking, 'Oh, I've never smelled tear gas, so I better go and check it out.' So that wasn't very nice. Then I made
my way to one of the exits, which was of course packed with
people trying to get out. Even though there was nowhere to go,
I remember a cop screaming at me, 'Get the fuck out of here!' I
got hit by a billy club so hard that I thought I'd broken my arm.
It hurt like hell. Maybe that's why after that, suddenly I didn't
like cops."

Part of the DNA of the first wave of Southern Californian
punk rock was made up of the kind of energy that lives in the
shadows. "I'm gonna go out / get something for my head / if I
keep on doing this / I'm gonna end up dead," announced Black
Flag's first singer, Keith Morris, on "Gimmie Gimmie Gimmie"
as the band clatter behind him like a dining set in a spin dryer.
Morris left the band in its early stages as Greg Ginn began to
flex his dictatorial muscle. Fueled by alcohol and cocaine, Morris then formed the influential Circle Jerks. On the band's debut
album, on the fifteen-minute and twenty-five-second *Group Sex*
he gleefully announced that "I was so wasted . . . I was out of my
head." Elsewhere, Orange County's dysfunctional Social Distortion sang of a misfit girl who "shoots methedrine" and "has sex
at fifteen." Fear were more provocative still. "Steal the money
from your mom / buy a gun," sang the soulfully voiced Lee Ving
on "We Destroy the Family." The band also boasted political tendencies that might diplomatically be described as hawkish. "Ha-
tred is purity / weakness is disease / we will bury you," was the
promise made on "Foreign Policy." These last four words echoed
the threat made by Russian premier Nikita Khrushchev in an
address to Western ambassadors at the Polish embassy in Mos-
cow in 1956, in the early days of the nuclear age.

Of all the Southern California punk bands from this period, it is X that are the best. The group formed in 1977 after bassist and co-vocalist John Doe and guitarist Billy Zoom recruited Doe's poet partner Exene Cervenka and drummer DJ Bonebrake. X had a gift for sniffing the turbulent and fetid air that enveloped them and transposing it into songs the claustrophobia of which bordered on the oppressive. They were by a distance the most artful and substantial of early-day Angelino punk bands.

"X was actually the first punk show I ever went to," remembers Fat Mike. "It was at the Whisky [a Go Go] in Hollywood. I was fourteen years old. My friend actually tricked me into going by telling me that we were going to the movies. But for me, it changed everything. The energy of the music, the way that the people in the crowd were dressed and how they looked . . . I just thought, 'I don't know what this is but I know that I want to be a part of it.'"

In 1980, the group released *Los Angeles*, their debut album, a nine-song collection the tautness of which is exhausting. It is a record thick with dislocation. The title track was inspired by a friend of the band's, Farrah Fawcett Minor, who left LA for England in order to pursue Captain Sensible of The Damned. In the song, the decision to head east is motivated by a deep disillusionment with the city. "She had to leave Los Angeles" sings Doe, "[because] she'd started to hate every nigger and Jew / every Mexican that gave her a lot of shit / every homosexual and the idle rich." This, clearly, is language in its most reductive form. In lesser hands it would be construed as the view of its writers rather than those of the character about whom they sing. The morality of X's early body of work draws its strength from the atonality with which it's delivered. The listener is free to do with the information whatever he or she chooses. X aren't interested in explaining the difference between right and wrong. Their songs are littered with drifting people searching for a foothold. But in Los Angeles, "the days change at night / change in an instant."

"X is the band that has defined the Los Angeles punk scene, and there isn't a lot of room for compromise in what they sing about—or much room to breathe," writes Greil Marcus in *In the Fascist Bathroom*. He adds that "X's vision isn't fragmented, it's not secondhand, and its ambition is to discredit any vision that suggests there's more to life than X says there is."

The world of chaos and danger inhabited by LA punk was saved from becoming a half-remembered oral history by the filmmaker Penelope Spheeris. A onetime writer for the sitcom *Roseanne*, Spheeris's first foray into documentary features resulted in a picture that in 2016 was selected for preservation in the US National Film Registry by the Library of Congress as being "culturally, historically or aesthetically significant." *The Decline of Western Civilization* is a hundred-minute picture that profiles X, Fear, Black Flag, Circle Jerks, Germs, Alice Bag Band and Catholic Discipline. Concert footage is interspersed with segments of informal interviews. The words of fans and supporters of the movement also feature. The film is sufficiently bracing that shortly after its release in the summer of 1981, Daryl Gates penned an open letter demanding that it never again be shown in Los Angeles. Prior to its first public airing, a trailer clip warned potential viewers to "see it in a theater where you can't get hurt." This advice was only partial hyperbole.

"I'd never seen it with an audience, so we screened it and this woman stands up [at the end] and the very first question she asks was 'How can you live with yourself when you are glorifying these heathens?'" recalled Penelope Spheeris some years later. "That was the first thing I heard! . . . But if you do something that's really criticized, it might not be [seen] that way thirty or forty years later."

*The Decline of Western Civilization*'s ability to shock is only partly attributable to the physical and musical violence it displays. More remarkable still is the film's tone of unending nihilism. Virtually everything framed by the camera seems dislocated or dazed. The lives on display are distant and separate, not just from everyday society but from *anything at all*.

No one more fully embodies this than Darby Crash, the frontman with the Germs. Born Jan Paul Beahm, Crash was in fact a gentle and kind presence. As a child his mother bought him a typewriter on which he would compose poetry for days at a time, sequestered in a bedroom from which he would emerge only to eat meals. When the Germs first began playing in Los Angeles, other bands such as X declined to take them seriously. They did so with good reason—the Germs couldn't play. Darby Crash would attempt to disguise this by deliberately injuring himself onstage.

"How is it you keep getting hurt?" asks Penelope Spheeris in *The Decline of Western Civilization*'s starkest scene.

"Well, first I did it on purpose to keep from getting bored," is his answer.

"What's the worst you ever got hurt?" she asks.

"The Whisky [a Go Go]. I cut my foot open."

"What happened?"

"I came down the stairs kind of to do an encore and jumped on half a broken glass . . . [I] had to get, like, thirty stitches."

As he speaks, it is obvious that Darby Crash is a wreck. By 1980, he was in hock to heroin to a terrible degree. No longer creative and no longer productive, his world was closing in around him. At half past ten on the night of December 7, he and his friend Casey Cola were refused entry to a party in Bel Air. The pair headed to the punk club Hong Kong Café to see a set by the band Sexsick. A call was made to a member of Circle One, the Germs' tight group of mostly female fans, by an acquaintance who had encountered Crash that evening and had been told of his plan to kill himself. The caller was told not to worry as this kind of talk was not unusual. Further and stronger protestations were met with the words "Relax. Go home and get some rest. Everything's gonna be fine."

That same night, Darby Crash bought four hundred dollars' worth of heroin. Returning to the garage of Casey Cola's parents' house in which the pair were living, the singer injected his girlfriend with a nonlethal dose. He then introduced into his own bloodstream a quantity strong enough to have killed four people. When Cola awoke on the floor at noon the next day, her partner lay dead beside her. She would later reveal that the pair's intention was to commit joint suicide, but that at the last moment Crash had spared her life. Less than twenty-four hours later, outside the Dakota building in Manhattan, Mark Chapman drew a gun and assassinated John Lennon. With this, the story of the final hours of Darby Crash was blown from the sky.

It couldn't last, and it didn't. The sheer energy and combustibility of LA punk featured structural deficiencies that were too profound to overcome. This was also the case five hours north in San Francisco and the East Bay. Many acts died a prompt death, or else transformed themselves in unconvincing ways. Most had little choice. Any band that announces its presence with music comprised of fury, nihilism and force will quickly find itself in a cul-de-sac from which only the most imaginative will emerge. The number of American punk groups that managed to do so was vanishingly small.

"A lot of these bands changed their sound," says Billie Joe Armstrong. "Basically, they compromised. And a lot of people talk about these bands now as if they're gods. But the truth is— and I'm loath to use this term—but a lot of these bands sold out."

Come the second half of the 1980s, punk bands were in such a hurry to sell out that it seems incredible that they'd ever bought in, in the first place. In 1985, Fear followed up *The Record* with *More Beer*, a sophomore set the banality of which is hinted at by its title. It featured unacceptable lyrics such as "strangle me a bitch, gonna leave her in a ditch" and a sound so tepid that one could replicate it by placing a seashell to one's ear. In the same year, Circle Jerks released the woeful *Wonderful*. A fraudulent attempt to find a wider audience, the album's chances of success were no better than finding a pot of gold at the end of a rainbow spray-painted on a toilet wall.

For punk rock, winter was coming. Up in San Francisco, the Dead Kennedys disbanded in sinister circumstances after letters of complaint were sent to the censorial pressure group PMRC (Parents Music Resource Center) and to prosecutors in Los Angeles from a mother whose teenage son had bought a copy of the band's third album, *Frankenchrist*. The parent was upset about an insert of the artist H. R. Giger's *Work 219: Landscape XX*, more commonly known as *Penis Landscape*. The group's four members and others in the chain of distribution were charged with violating the California penal code. Lack of evidence was cited as the reason the charges against each defendant save for frontman Jello Biafra and Michael Bonanno, the former manager of the band's label, Alternative Tentacles, were dropped. The ensuing criminal trial of the two men who remained in the frame resulted in a hung jury, while the Superior Court of Los Angeles struck down the request for a retrial. It is not unreasonable to believe that the state jeopardized the liberty of a band and its associates simply because it could. A lack of corporate muscle made them easy prey. The ordeal left Dead Kennedys exhausted. Within a year they were no more.

"Punk rock was pretty much dead from '84 to '88, '89 even," says Greg Hetson, the former guitarist with Circle Jerks and Bad Religion. "It was sent back underground. Everybody grew their hair long. So many people from the scene were suddenly playing glam rock or speed metal. With the exception of a few bands, everyone had broken up or were evolving into something else. A few bands made it, but there very few of them."

The acute decline of American punk in general and of its Californian branch in particular can be attributed to factors other than the fact that too many of its practitioners lacked the wit with which to execute a second act. External forces were also at work. Elsewhere in California, a movement was emerging that was dismissively known as "thrash metal." Thrash was untamed and feral. Unlike many in the punk rock scene, it was neither self-conscious nor in any way cool. Metallica hinted at the hard rain soon to fall with the release of their debut album, *Kill 'Em All*, in 1983. Three years later, under the tutelage of producer Rick Rubin, Slayer unveiled the gnashing and foaming *Reign in Blood*, an album of such swivel-eyed fury that in an instant it killed the genre it represented stone dead. In the face of this, punk could not compete.

Its lyrics, too, were losing their capacity to shock. By the latter part of the 1980s, rap had commanded the limelight in a way that punk had thus far failed to do. This achievement came not in spite of the movement's refusal to compromise, but *because* of it. Rap stamped on the racial fault line on which America has always trembled. Whereas punks were beaten by police armed with billy clubs, young African Americans were shot to death. Theirs was the sound of a danger so authentic that at times it seemed life threatening. In Compton, N.W.A.—Niggaz Wit Attitudes, to give them their full name—were busy weaponizing music in a way that challenged every order that wasn't brand new. "I'm a young nigga on the warpath / and when I'm finished it's gonna be a bloodbath / of cops dying in LA," announced Ice Cube on the unequivocal "Fuck the Police." By comparison, punk rock was no longer shocking or awesome.

N.W.A.'s debut album, *Straight Outta Compton*, released in 1988, would sell three million copies in the United States alone. This feat was achieved despite the record being issued on an independent label, Ruthless. The group's success did not go unnoticed by one pivotal player in the punk community. In 1988, Brett Gurewitz was the owner of the punk rock label Epitaph as well as the guitarist in Bad Religion. The band he had cofounded as a teenager had not released an album in five years. They had rarely played outside of California and were largely unknown elsewhere in America, let alone the rest of the world. They had sold fewer than twenty thousand records. Even by the standards of 1980s punk rock, the band were second tier.

But to the surprise of everyone, not least themselves, Bad Religion were about to emerge as the saviors of American punk rock.

## CHAPTER ONE

# MORE A QUESTION THAN A CURSE, HOW COULD HELL BE ANY WORSE?

It was in a recording studio above a chemist's shop that Bad Religion were told they weren't very good. After months of practicing, the band entered Studio 9 on the corner of Sunset Boulevard and Western Avenue in Hollywood to lay down the six songs that would comprise their self-titled debut EP. The facility's in-house producer looked them over and asked if they were a power trio. The four members looked at each other and answered, "Sure, why not?" The studio technician listened with growing skepticism as the group ran through their small collection of short songs. With a frown of disapproval he delivered his verdict. The compositions weren't finished, he said. Some of them needed choruses. And where were the guitar solos?

The fact that at this stage in their development Bad Religion were about as capable of executing a guitar solo as they were of playing Chopin's "Sonata no. 2 in B Minor" was beside the point. Between them, Brett Gurewitz and vocalist Greg Graffin had each written three songs that when combined clocked out at a blush over nine minutes. Two of these songs, "Politics" and "World War III," were as fast as anything produced in the name of Southern Californian punk rock. In their eyes, their hirelings' bewilderment at these efforts marked him as being yesterday's man.

Greg Graffin, Brett Gurewitz and bassist Jay Bentley formed Bad Religion in 1980. The trio were students at El Camino High School in Woodland Hills. Gurewitz was seventeen, while Graffin and Bentley were two years his junior. Drummer and fellow student Jay Ziskrout completed the fledgling group's original lineup.

Although they didn't yet know it, Bad Religion had at their disposal a talent that would set them apart from other bands of their kind. An émigré from Wisconsin, as a student at Lake Bluff Elementary school on the north side of Milwaukee, each morning before class Greg Graffin would sing in the school choir. Under the tutelage of teacher Mrs. Jane Perkins, he and his fellow prepubescent choristers would gather in their school's music room and sing songs from the radio and, when in season, Christmas carols. The unforgiving hour at which these gatherings took place was mollified by the fact that the students were given ten minutes in which to play records by the Beatles and Led Zeppelin on the school's superior stereo system. In due course, Mrs. Perkins noticed Graffin's talents and a bursary to a summer music camp in Madison soon followed.

"We were singing songs from Stevie Wonder and James Taylor and we would perform the songs of these artists when the parents came to the concerts," Graffin recalls. "I was often chosen as the soloist, so I'd be singing these songs from the radio with Mrs. Perkins accompanying me on the piano. I never thought of myself as a particularly gifted singer. In fact, I just assumed that everyone could sing the way that I did."

They couldn't. Over time, Graffin's soaring and authoritative voice would become one of Bad Religion's defining characteristics; the band would also learn how to deliver three-part harmonies. This, though, would take time. As heard on their debut EP, the group were just one of many from Los Angeles County whose chief currency was the energy of youth. Their sound was unvarnished and sometimes ungovernable. Musical arrangements didn't exist and their technical chops were no more than rudimentary. What they did have, however, was an instinct for melody that has endured for almost forty years. Even at their most incendiary, Bad Religion's sound is never wholly divorced from pop music.

For Brett Gurewitz, the release of his band's svelte debut recording would change his life in two ways. The first would steer a course toward becoming one of LA punk's most charismatic and interesting writers. ("Brett is probably the most talented songwriter in punk," says Fat Mike, himself no mean composer.) The second would see him develop into an astute businessman, not to mention punk rock's most influential tastemaker.

In 1980, Bad Religion decided to eschew the complications of finding a label on which to release their eponymous debut EP by founding their own. In doing so they avoided the ignominy of being ignored by the majors and the frustrations of signing with a small independent. The label that now housed them was given the name Epitaph, an operation established and owned by Brett Gurewitz. Its first release carried the catalogue number EPI001.

For the start-up capital required to get his record label off the ground, Gurewitz tapped up his dad. Duly, Richard Gurewitz—know to some as "Big Dick"—lent his son fifteen hundred dollars without much hope, one would imagine, of ever seeing a return on his investment. With this, Bad Religion and Epitaph were off to the pressing plant, while "Mr. Brett," as he is some-times known, was on his way to becoming an impresario.

Despite Bad Religion's status as their label's one and only artist lasting for little over a year—Gurewitz's would release the Vandals' *Peace Thru Vandalism* EP in 1982—the company and the band for which it was formed remain synonymous.

In the year following its release, EPI001 sold a modest but not discountable five thousand copies. This tally was aided by Greg Hetson, who as the guitarist with the Circle Jerks occupied a space higher up the punk rock food chain than did anyone in Bad Religion. To this day, this hockey-loving rhythm guitarist remains one of the most recognizable and enduring figures of the LA scene. One night, Greg Graffin and Jay Bentley met Het-son at Oki-Dog, a stay-open-late hot dog joint on Willoughby and Franklin in Hollywood. Graffin had with him a cassette of his band's music that he gave to the guitarist. Along with his thanks, Greg Hetson promised that if he liked what he heard he would make sure it was played on LA's *Rock Radio Show*, broadcast in the vampire hours on the country's most influential radio station, KROQ, on which he was to be a guest that coming weekend. This promise was honored.

"Oki-Dog was this twenty-four-hour place that punks would hang out at after shows," remembers Hetson. "I don't know if Greg believed me when I said I'd get them to play it on the show, but I meant it. That's just the kind of thing that we all did. Ev-eryone had each other's backs. So I gave it to 'ROQ and said, 'This is a new band from the [San Fernando] Valley' and they put it on the air. I think it was a demo tape that probably ended up being their first single. That's how I met them and we just kind of became friends after that."

In order to record the full-length album that would soon fol-low, like many bands of their standing Bad Religion were forced to become creatures of the night. Ten months after the unveil-ing of their debut seven-inch single in January of 1980, that autumn the still-teenage band took a freshly minted collection of songs to Track Record in North Hollywood. Over the course of the next four months they recorded the collection that would emerge, oddly, more than a year later under the title *How Could Hell Be Any Worse?* If this schedule sounds lavish, it wasn't. The studio may have been bona fide to a degree beyond the group's most elaborate dreams, but in recording their album while the rest of city was asleep, the teenagers secured Track Record's services for nigh on nix. And while it's true to say that *How Could Hell Be Any Worse?* was recorded over three months, the sessions comprised short blasts of manic activity rather than a diligent twelve-week slog. The bulk of the album was tracked over just two nights in November of 1980; half of which tracks were mixed during the intervening day.

Following this initial flash of activity, the band departed the studio for their rehearsal room—otherwise known as the "Hell-hole," a fetid space that doubled up as Graffin's mother's ga-rage—in order to write yet more songs. This process was de-layed by a fit of pique from their eighteen-year-old drummer. Irked by the belief that his bandmates were failing to pay due respect to his contribution to the cause, Jay Ziskout gave notice to quit with no notice at all. Such was the speed of his departure that he walked out without his drum set. His replacement was Pete Finestone, a friend who might loosely be described as the band's roadie. Hectic practice sessions followed as the group at-tempted to complete the writing for their album while bringing the playing of their newest member up to code. Bad Religion re-turned to Track Record in January of 1981, and over the course of a weekend completed the twenty-nine minutes and fifty-four seconds of music that would comprise their first twelve-inch vi-nyl release.

To say that *How Could Hell Be Any Worse?* is an improvement on the EP that preceded it is an understatement. It is, for one thing, untypical of similar albums from this period. Generally, punk records from teenage bands who spent their days beneath the sunshine of Southern California tended either to revel in their own brattishness or else try hard, and sometimes very hard, to shock. Bad Religion did neither. If not quite sophisticated, the music is nonetheless both confident and advanced. The band's bold and perhaps reckless decision to produce the record themselves may have harvested mixed results—listened to today, the sound is somewhat swampy—but this instinct for self-reliance would in time serve them well. The album's two best tracks, "We're Only Gonna Die" and "Fuck Armageddon . . . This Is Hell" (a song that is much better than its title suggests), written by Graffin and Gurewitz respectively, are sufficiently innovative as to dispense with the services of a chorus. By now attention was being paid to musical arrangement and song structure. More notable still was the emergence of their vocalist's enduring lyrical style, a humane and sometimes good-humored pessimism far too dignified to ever descend to a hysterical pitch. In the lyrics to "We're Only Gonna Die"—"early man walked away as modern man took control / their minds they weren't the same, to conquer was his goal"—Graffin gives a clue as to the direction his intellectual pursuits were headed. Brett Gurewitz's own lyrical style was also emerging. The obverse of his bandmate's glass-half-empty point of view—in which the glass was often entirely empty, while in some instances there was no glass at all—it would be simplistic to say that the guitarist's words act as a counterbalance to Graffin's intellectualism. But it would not be wholly so. The days when Gurewitz could write a couplet of the quality of "I had a paperback crime running straight down my spine" had yet to arrive, but poetry in its embryonic form does flicker from the album's lyrics. "There are two things you can do, one is turn and fight / the other is to run headlong into the night" are the options made available on "Into the Night."

*How Could Hell Be Any Worse?* looks the part, too. Its back and inner sleeve are adorned by Gustave Doré's illustrations of Dante Alighieri's *Inferno*. The front cover is a monochrome picture of LA's surprisingly drab topography, shot by the noted punk photographer Edward Colver from a vantage point in the Hollywood Hills. The sleeve was issued in fire-truck red and, in the days when LPs were the size of pizza boxes, the overall effect was striking. The title written in capital letters on the album's top right corner is of course youthfully glib. By no measure can Los Angeles be described as "hell." But relatively speaking, the thousands of people hermetically sealed in cars, the paucity of the pedestrian life, the absence of greenery and the city's often melancholic stillness can make Los Angeles seem *hellish*. The fact that it keeps catching fire doesn't help, either. But in ways that don't wholly matter, the title the band bestowed on their debut album tends to present them as hysterical brats unable to distinguish between a place that is sometimes soul sapping and somewhere that is life threatening. (Gurewitz himself would later amend the question posed in 1982 in the rhyming couplet "More a question than a curse / how could hell be any worse?") But the question is not wildly unreasonable. Even in sun-kissed Southern California, a new generation had discovered punk and were using its power as a reaction against the eternal foes of conformity and the threat of a quiet life.

"I think there were a lot of bored middle-class kids who had time on their hands and who hated the image that the powers that be—parents, teachers, society—wanted to put on them," says Noodles, known to his parents as Kevin Wasserman, the guitarist with The Offspring. "It was a reaction against clean-cut kids, good grades, nine-to-five jobs, two point three children, a wife and a white picket fence. That was just bullshit. People would go and work for Boeing, or some other defense contractor, which was a big industry in Orange County, which I think lends itself to a lot of the conservative attitudes here. And people just wanted to rebel against that. It's just not how real people are. Punk rock in Southern California may not have come from the poverty that you hear The Clash talk about. It was different from that. And it didn't come from playing shows on the Bowery [the site of the punk club CBGB]. But punk rock here did play in very poor parts of the city. You weren't allowed to play the upscale clubs that had dress codes and girls in thongs serving drinks. Punk rock was relegated to the back-alley clubs. Or you would hire VFW halls in the middle of the desert. A lot of times the bands would be playing in burned-out warehouses in LA. So we did have that element of punk rock as well. But, yeah, a lot of the kids who were playing in bands grew up in really middle-class suburbs."

If Bad Religion's first twenty songs offered a glimpse of the towering influence its creators would in time exert, it *was* only a glimpse. But from these tiny acorns all manner of things would grow. In 1982, the band could at least content themselves with the knowledge that a copy of *How Could Hell Be Any Worse?* had taken up residence in the homes of ten thousand listeners. The group may not have been on their way to the top, but at least they were on their way to *somewhere*.

This forward momentum lasted for precisely twenty-two months and eleven days. On November 30, 1983, Bad Religion put their name to an album that is now regarded by those who know it, or at least know of it, as being one of the most peculiar releases ever unveiled by a punk rock group. *Into the Unknown* is a soupy, keyboard-heavy curiosity that would be entirely dis-countable were it not for its loveable precocity. A wordy oddness that its authors continue to embrace is also appealing. Not un-predictably, in 1983 the album's waiting public either failed to understand what it was Bad Religion were trying to convey in such snappy songs as "Time and Disregard" (Part 1, Part II, Part III, Part IV), or else couldn't stand it. The punk magazine *Max-imumrocknroll* wrote of the record, "Into the Unknown and out of the window." In a spirit of droll consolation, Greg Hetson half attempted to comfort Greg Graffin with the words "Fuck 'em if they can't take a joke."

"The punk scene at [that] time wasn't very attractive to us," says Graffin. "The drugs and violence had taken their toll, which were things that never interested me anyway. I was always in Bad Religion for the music. When we started playing punk it was a thriving social scene. It was a feeling that you were part of something . . . But from 1983 to 1987 the punk scene was completely dismantled. At best it was a loose conglomerate of various types of people who were interested in various types of music. And there was no central meeting point for the punk scene anymore. The police had closed down a lot of places because of the violence and the drugs. It was hard even to *play* in a punk band. Consequently, Bad Religion didn't have a central focus at that time and I think that's manifested in [*Into the Unknown*] itself. It wasn't a focused album; it was all over the place. It's easy to write it off as being just an attempt at a new style of music. But if you look at it in the context of two songwriters [Greg Graffin and Brett Gurewitz] who really loved music and felt free to experiment, it makes a lot more sense."

Asked today, Mr. Brett will say that Epitaph printed ten thousand copies of *Into the Unknown*, of which they sold none. This seems statistically unlikely, but popular lore does have it that many, many thousands of copies ended up piled high in Jay Bentley's garage. As if this weren't odd enough, the fact that at the time Bentley was no longer a member of the band makes it only more so. The only time Bad Religion have played any songs from *Into the Unknown* live was at a concert attended by thirty people at the Mabuhay Gardens club in San Francisco. Realizing that punk rock shows at the time were drawing crowds of similar numbers even at venues such as the now venerated Cathay de Grande in Hollywood, Graffin began to lose faith. He was also fully cognizant of the fact that no one cared about Bad

Religion's curious new album. The decision was made to leave Los Angeles for his home state and a place at the University of Wisconsin. By doing so, for the next five years the band in which he performed fell into a slumberous state from which they would only occasionally emerge.

**N**o one could have predicted that by effectively ceasing to exist, Bad Religion were opting for the wisest career choice available to them. Between the end of 1982 and the spring of 1987, the group played live fewer than *twenty* times. A creature of near total hibernation, this slumber was so profound that between November of 1982 and September of 1988 just five songs were recorded, one of which was an old song (a retooled version of the eponymous track from their eponymous debut EP). When in February of 1985, Bad Religion reconvened to record what would be for many the reassuringly titled *Back to the Known* EP, only two of its members, Greg Graffin and Pete Finestone, had survived from the group's earlier incarnations. Standing in for Jay Bentley was Tim Gallegos of Wasted Youth, while Greg Hetson deputized for Brett Gurewitz on guitar. Not entirely absent from the band, however, along with Graffin, Mr. Brett produced the ten-minute EP.

Following its release on Epitaph in April of 1985, Bad Religion performed precisely one concert in support of *Back to the Known*. Among the four new tracks premiered that night was "Along the Way," a highly contagious song that would remain part of their live set well into the twenty-first century. But stymied by its creator's lack of profile and barely in possession of a pulse, the group's third release sold just five thousand copies. All around them, in Los Angeles and anywhere near it, punk rock was packing up its tent. By now Greg Graffin was a full-time student at the University of California, Los Angeles (UCLA). Jay

Bentley repaired and restored motorcycles and also, improbably, found work as a film stuntman. Brett Gurewitz, meanwhile, was spending more time in a recording studio than he ever did as a member of Bad Religion. Deciding to dedicate himself fully to this pursuit, Gurewitz moved from the San Fernando Valley to Hollywood. After completing a course at recording school, he then opened his own studio, Westbeach Recorders. It was at this modest facility that he would make his bones as an engineer and producer in what might reasonably be described as guerrilla music-making.

"Everything was fast back then because that's the only way we had to get things done," he remembers. "A lot of the bands I was working with had no budget, so they'd come to me and say, 'We've got three hundred dollars and we want to make a record.' And I'd say, 'Okay, well for three hundred bucks I can give you two ten-hour days in the studio.' So they would come in and of course I'd end up giving them two sixteen-hour days because that's how long it would take to get the record done. We'd be leaving the studio as the sun was coming up. I'd do whatever I had to do to finish it. I was trying to make a living, but it was really, really tough. It really was hand to mouth. I was selling time for fifteen dollars an hour, for which you got me and you got the recording studio. It was hard to live that way, even though I was working eighty- or ninety-hour weeks. Even then, I was still barely scraping by. So basically I learned how to make records that sounded really good, and I learned how to make them fast."

It's worth noting that none of these albums or EPs by artists as diverse as Keith Levine from Public Image Ltd. and Tom Morello's pre–Rage Against the Machine band, Lock Up, were issued on Gurewitz's label. Like the band it had been formed to serve, Epitaph Records was packed in mothballs as tightly as were Bad Religion. Between the release of Thelonius Monster's *Baby You're Bumming My Life in a Supreme Fashion* on

New Year's Day of 1986 and *Head First* by Little Kings exactly three years later, Epitaph unveiled just one record. Fortunately for them, it would be an album that caused an earthquake.

The genesis of Bad Religion's third album, *Suffer*, sprung from a conversation between Greg Graffin and Greg Hetson. With Graffin buried deep in his studies, Hetson believed that the now only very occasional singer had lost sight of the fact that a small but patient audience had kept faith with his hibernating band. "You should play some shows," he was told, "it might be fun." Implicit in this suggestion was the notion that the guitarist was also offering his own services to the cause. In doing this he turned this "you" into a "we" that endured for more than twenty-five years. Before you could say "That's a wrap," Jay Bentley returned from whichever burning building he was about to leap out of and once more strapped on the bass guitar. Finally, Graffin picked up the phone and called the other half of Bad Religion's songwriting team, who, as it happened, hadn't written a song for more than four years.

The news was in: Bad Religion had been invited to play at the newly opened 924 Gilman Street club up in the Bay Area city of Berkeley. The band were traveling north in a van; would Brett care to join them and play guitar? This was all it took to cement the band's first classic lineup, a personnel that would record the albums *Suffer, No Control* and *Against the Grain*, a triumvirate sometimes known as the "Holy Trinity." To Gurewitz's acute surprise, the trip north up Interstate 5 was a success, and one from which the band returned to Los Angeles fortified and enthused. Talk turned to the possibility of writing new songs and of recording a new record.

"I wasn't expecting much [from the visit to San Francisco]," he says. "I was expecting it to be a very small show. So I drove up with the guys and it was bonkers. It was a completely packed room. Kids were hanging off the rafters, going nuts, singing every word to the songs. And I remember thinking to myself,

'Wow, I really was not expecting that in the slightest.' So some of the guys in the band were saying that it seemed like we were more popular than we ever were. I think this was the result of us going away for a little while, which is kind of weird. That's not how things are supposed to work. Maybe Greg [Graffin] realized what was happening, but I really wasn't aware that there was so much interest in the band."

By 1987, Bad Religion had gained a reputation, burnished a reputation, besmirched a reputation and then gone to sleep. The average age of its members was just twenty-four. At this point in the career of most groups, the fuel that keeps the show on the road is esprit de corps. Young acts are united in the aim of capturing the attention of the entire world. But where other bands were hungry, Bad Religion were merely peckish. The decision to record *Suffer* was not motivated by the fact that the group had nothing better to do, or because its members clung to their union as if it were a security blanket without which their lives would lack definition. Along with the fact that in 1987 Bad Religion's personnel had things in their lives other than their band—in fact, at this point the band was probably the *least* important thing in each of their lives—the music they regrouped to play all but guaranteed that they wouldn't get anywhere. As Greg Hetson says, "At this time there was really nobody putting out punk music because there was really no market for it. The only exception, really, was Brett and Epitaph. My hat goes off to him for that, for sure."

"Basically the guys decided to make another record and they said, 'Okay, well, we'll start writing songs and we'll record them and then when it's finished we'll release it on Epitaph,'" remembers Gurewitz. "To be honest with you, I was really keen on that. Over the previous four years I'd spent probably ten thousand hours in the studio. My life was nothing but recording. I was doing rock music, I was doing country music, I was doing Sunset Strip metal bands, I was doing downtown art bands; I was doing all kinds of bands. So I spent several years really developing my recording skills and I'd become really good at it. So the idea of bringing my prodigious recording experience to Bad Religion and making an album that sounded really good was really exciting to me. I'd never been able to do that before. So we decided to do it on Epitaph. I thought, 'Well, I'll reboot the label and just like the first [EP] my own band can be my first release.' So that was the genesis of really trying to have a label and making a go of it. Also, part of it was the fact that I thought I could write some pretty good Bad Religion songs."

Surely much to Mrs. Graffin's relief, her son and his friends had left the Hellhole in favor of Uncle's, a rehearsal space in the San Fernando Valley. Here the group would meet once a week. At each session, Graffin and Gurewitz would arrive with one new song each that they would then teach the rest of the band how to play. Seven days later, two more songs would be added to their repertoire. With metronomic regularity—two, four, six, eight—fresh material was amassed. The fact that this bounty amounted to barely half an hour's worth of music was irrelevant. Its strength and quality were what mattered.

As sluggish and sedated as they may once have been, by 1988 Bad Religion were a band with a purpose. At Uncle's, the fifteen songs that would comprise *Suffer* were practiced to the point of precision. With the exception of the nascent vocal harmonies for which the group would soon be known—the "oozin' aahs," as they are sometimes called—and the odd guitar solo, such as they were, *Suffer* was transported from rehearsal space to recording studio without a trace of a footprint. The album was transposed to tape and mixed at Westbeach Recorders in seven days. By the standards to which Brett Gurewitz had grown accustomed, this timetable was expansive to the point of indulgence. While the production details on the record sleeve credit the entire band, it was their recently returned guitarist's years of experience recording acts who had neither a pot in which to piss nor a window out of which to throw it that gave the album its bite. Suddenly, a harvest was about to be reaped from what had appeared for the longest time to be a fruitless pursuit. The dray-horse shifts of Brett Gurewitz's severe apprenticeship now arced toward one point: *Suffer*.

"There was a good vibe around us when we made that record," he recalls. "The band hadn't been hanging out regularly. Greg [Graffin] had been in college, so that relationships felt fresh again. The spirit of it was a lot of fun. There's something about that in the recording itself. It's very spontaneous. But at the same time the album has good fidelity. It has good balance; it has a good sound. Especially compared to the punk albums from the LA hardcore scene that had come out previously, it sounds *loud*."

It is worth remembering that when *Suffer* was released *almost no one was listening*. It was the work of a band the copybook of which was blotted. It represented a genre of music that appeared dead. It was released on a label whose most successful release had emerged six years earlier and had sold ten thousand copies, and even that was by the same band. In terms of a bet for success, the album's odds were so long that any bookmaker in town would have let a gambler name their own odds. Yet despite no one really knowing it, American punk rock was in the market for a record to fill the vacuum that threatened its existence. If it didn't seem obvious at the time, it does now: *Suffer* was the only game in town.

It remains a fantastic record. The qualities attributed to it by Brett Gurewitz are correct, but more than this it bears the kind of magic ignited at the intersection of timing and execution. A priest had been summoned to the bedside of a genre that was not expected to rise from its hospital bed. Bad Religion arrived with a defibrillator and 50 cc's of adrenaline. What's more, they came alone.

*Suffer* is best viewed as a seamless piece of music of a dependably high quality out of which particular high points emerge. Those impartial to its charms might wonder why almost every song begins with a single beat from a snare drum, or why in terms of musical arrangements the album is deficient to the point of being remedial. But this is to miss the point. What matters is the grace with which Bad Religion harness an energy that is both exhilarating and tightly controlled. What counts is an ear for melody and songwriting so fundamental that one can imagine many of the songs being played in numerous musical styles. In one of the true tests of all guitar-and-song-based music—is this material sufficiently strong as to stand tall when played and sung acoustically?—*Suffer* aces the paper.

It is the performance by Greg Graffin that is most impressive. On earlier Bad Religion recordings the singer was at a loss as how best to deliver the tunes he knew how to carry. By 1988, raw potential had developed into tasteful execution. *Suffer* is the first time that Graffin unveiled a genuine talent for phrasing, the most undervalued weapon in a vocalist's armory. This he uses to deliver words that stand so far apart from what the majority of punk bands had until this point delivered as to be remarkable. Many groups of Bad Religion's stripe had written strong lyrics, but this strength was usually derived from their alignment to the violence of the music on which they are carried. If this music is removed, the lyric fails. The Sex Pistols are an exception to this rule, as are X. Elsewhere, the pickings are slim. This trap is one into which even the most revered groups can fall. The Clash may have sighed with joy at a couplet such as "every cheap hood strikes a bargain with the world / [but] ends up making payments on a sofa or a girl" from "Death or Glory." But this fleetness of foot does not make it to the end of the song. "He who fucks nuns will later join the church" is a perceptive enough point, but it is tin-eared.

On *Suffer*, Bad Religion had higher minds to fry. Where other bands ranted hysterically about living at the end of days—about which they were always wrong, clearly—Graffin used historical and scientific precedents to point out the failings of his species. "The masses of humanity, still clinging to their dignity / the masses of humanity have always, always had to suffer," he sings on the album's title track. Elsewhere, the unsustainability of an economic system that in a world of finite resources values growth over all else is explored on the song "How Much Is Enough?" written by Brett Gurewitz. "When will mankind finally come to realize / that his surfeit has become his demise?" he asks. Best of all is "Forbidden Beat"—a rare example of the band's two songwriters sharing a credit—a rhythm that "thunders away at first light of each day as the simpleton lifestyle evolves / but soon enters dusk as the last surrey rusts and a new day upon us results."

"We were on tour in Europe when I first heard *Suffer*," remembers NOFX's Fat Mike. "It was [the group] the Yeastie Girls who played it for me. It was just amazing. The songs, the sound, everything about it. Really, there's nothing like it. The lyrics are smart, the harmonies are great, the melodies are great. It was— what?—twenty-odd minutes of pure joy. The tour we were on was terrible, and then on the last day I heard *Suffer*; and suddenly I realized, 'Oh right, of course, punk rock is great . . .' Before *Suffer* it felt like my band was kind of out there on our own. We weren't, but that's how it felt; and I'm sure that that's what it felt like for other bands, too. But then *Suffer* came out and everyone who heard it knew that it was special and that it could keep the scene alive."

Opinions regarding the immediate impact made by the album remain a matter of dispute, not least among the people who made it. Greg Graffin once told the author that on the US tour in support of *Suffer*, which also happened to be the band's first tour worthy of the name, a good night constituted a crowd of a hundred and fifty people. On a bad night this number could be as low as twenty. Greg Hetson remembers *Suffer* being entangled by distribution problems that delayed the album's release by a week or more. In the meantime, the band played to a hundred people in a venue in Cincinnati built for almost ten times this number. "The album didn't really take off straight away," he recalls. "It really didn't. For maybe ten days after its release, we didn't even have an album to sell. You couldn't find it in the stores. It wasn't an overnight sensation by any means."

"To the extent that it was possible for something to be an instant sensation in 1988, *Suffer* was truly an instant sensation" is how Brett Gurewitz remembers things. "Nobody could say enough good things about the record. Not only that, but the distributors were ordering copies from me, and then ordering more straight away. The reviews were very positive. The band became very in demand for playing live. The record was not just selling in LA, but it was also selling extremely well in northern Europe—with the exception of England, which has always been a bit insular. People over there thought that the kind of music we were playing was over, and I kind of got that because in the US people thought the same thing, and I was one of them. But *Suffer* has a very particular relationship with punk and with what punk means. People were buying it and asking us to come and play. It became a true sensation."

*Suffer* sold ten thousand copies in its first six months, a figure unlikely to have widened the eyes of New Kids on the Block. During its initial run, sales duly doubled, then trebled. Germany in particular took a tumble for the band, as, in fewer numbers, did audiences in southern European countries such as Spain and Italy. *Suffer* was also garlanded with praise in many of the right places. Los Angeles's *Flipside* and *Maximumrocknroll* in San Francisco both judged the album as the best of the year. This was at a time "when music journalism still mattered," as

Greg Graffin kindly puts it. The latter magazine also placed the band on its cover.

"It was very gratifying to have the two most important taste-makers of the day deem *Suffer* to be an important album," says Graffin. "That was very satisfying to me. But of course I didn't think that this would mean that the album would become as eternally cited as it is today. I did view it as being a feather in my cap, but I didn't think of it as being particularly important. But I think I can speak for me and Brett when I say that we were both trying to write music that had an original and distinct quality. I'd say that we were still finding that originality and that on *Suffer* we hadn't found it yet. But I do think it's funny that while we were in the process of becoming something [worthwhile] we created something of lasting importance. You never know what's going to work until you try it. And I do think there's a real freedom of expression that comes through on *Suffer*."

I n the spring of 1980, Bad Religion made their live debut at a party at a warehouse. The father of a local punk owned a food import business, the key to which she managed to finagle. Its doors were then opened to two hundred teenagers, numerous kegs of beer and two noisy bands. The headliner that evening was Social Distortion.

Led by songwriter and frontman Mike Ness, "Social D," as they are often known, were formed in 1978 in the town of Fullerton in Orange County. Equipped with half a voice and an insatiable appetite for self-destruction, Ness's musical and personal deficiencies were offset by a natural talent and an understanding of music beyond the boundaries of punk's well-guarded walls. With time he would take from the genre the parts to which he felt suited and easily leave the rest behind. In later years, the band would go on to find significant success, a prospect that at the time would have seemed utterly inconceivable to anyone who remembers the frontman in the first half of the 1980s. But Mike Ness isn't one of these people. Today there are weeks and months from this period for which he cannot account.

The frontman pulled himself together in the autumn of 1985, the point from which no drugs or alcohol have entered his system. Today he puts one in mind of a punk rock Mickey Rourke. Like so many others in the scene, Ness formed his band as an outlet through which to rage against all that was good and decent, including much that was good and decent within himself. In his years spent navigating the fast lane, he placed the air-cushioned sole of a Dr. Martens boot on the pedal and floored it.

"Technically, I should be dead or in prison because that's the way I was going," he says. "My epitaph should have amounted to a paragraph in an underground fanzine. 'Mike Ness, singer with Social Distortion, overdoses in a hotel room.' 'Mike Ness was shot and killed after running his mouth off in a bar on the wrong side of town.' But from the start my circumstances were tough. I grew up in an alcoholic home. My father was somewhat of a tyrant and it was his way or the highway. After my parents finally divorced, when I was living with my mom things just got worse. Her alcoholism brought a lot of shame and insecurity. It really wasn't a very good childhood."

Moving out of the family home, Ness rented a one-room apartment in Fullerton. Like a gravitational force field, this address sucked the energies of the local punk community toward it. Unlikely to land a spot at the Ideal Home Exhibition, these living quarters were immortalized by another esteemed Orange County group, the Adolescents, on "Kids of the Black Hole." "Kids in a fast lane living for today / no rules to abide by and no one to obey / sex drugs and fun is their only thought and care / another swig of brew, another overnight affair," sings frontman Tony Reflex. If this sounds like fun, which of course it does, consider also that behind this door lay a "house of the filthy, [a] house not a home / [a] house of destruction where the lurkers roamed."

With just two singles and three songs in the public domain, in 1982 Social Distortion left Orange County for a nationwide tour with LA's Youth Brigade. The two bands traveled on a bus. Today a tour bus is a mobile home containing three television sets, berths for up to eighteen people, three lounges, a kitchen and a toilet. This was not the kind of bus on which Mike Ness and his friends traveled the country on the Another State of Mind tour. Instead they rode aboard a school bus. It wasn't just any school bus, either; it was a school bus that kept breaking down. The passengers slept at the rear on mattresses of uncertain provenance. In circumstances that might generously be described as trying, after more than a thousand miles on a journey that featured fistfights, euphoria and disillusionment, the tour imploded in Washington, DC, a three-day drive from Southern California. Social Distortion were sufficiently displeased with their lot that they immediately broke up, albeit temporarily.

The fact that this youthful misadventure was filmed and released as a full-length feature means that none of the stories from the tour are folkloric. *Another State of Mind* may not have attained the status or reputation of *The Decline of Western Civilization*, but it does provide a bracing insight into the bonhomie and brutality of what would come to be known in punk rock circles as the "DIY ethic." The film is also notable for its footage of Mike Ness sitting on a porch writing the song that gave the documentary its name. "Another State of Mind" remains one of the best-remembered tracks from Social Distortion's debut album, *Mommy's Little Monster*, released the following year.

"That tour was both a success and a failure," says Ness. "What can I say? I was young and I had fun, so for me it was a success. I was doing what I wanted to do, and seeing parts of the country that I'd never seen before; plus we got to play pretty much every night. What you have to remember is that I was practically homeless at the time, so the longer I stayed out there the longer I didn't have to go back and deal with shit going on back here. Things were pretty bad with me in those days, what with my alcoholism. But things got a lot worse when I got home."

Barely out of his teens, in 1982 Mike Ness had terrible taste in role models. Maneuvering himself out of the deep shadows cast by his dysfunctional family home, the twenty-year-old instead looked for guidance from such stable and reliable figures as Sid Vicious, who died in 1979 from a heroin overdose; Johnny Thunders, who would subsequently die from a heroin overdose; and Keith Richards, for whom it is a miracle that he didn't die from a heroin overdose. Predictably, in the late 1970s and early 1980s, "dope" left its bloody fingerprints all over the LA punk scene, most notably in the death of Darby Crash. Brett Gurewitz would also fall under the spell cast by a needle and a spoon, not to mention a number of other hard drugs. But of all the artists who lived to tell their tales of addiction and chaos, few were as reckless as Mike Ness.

"It was horrible," remembers Jim Guerinot, who in 1983 made the surely unwise decision to become the manager of Social Distortion. "It was really me and Dennis [Danell, Social D's rhythm guitarist] at the time because Dennis was my running buddy. He and I weren't saints by any measure, but we weren't junkies either. But Mike would call and you'd just let it go to the answering machine because you did not want to pick up the phone. Every time he called it would be because he needed to get money for dope. He would hawk the band's gear when they weren't around. He would hawk *other* bands' gear when *they* weren't around. He was always stealing stuff. He was just a pain in the ass who was best avoided. I remember being at a party with him and having to knock down a door because he OD'd in the other room. He was facedown in a cat box. The paramedics had to come and hit him with adrenaline like the way Eric Stoltz did with Uma Thurman in *Pulp Fiction*. I remember my girlfriend's brother was a lawyer and he would represent him for free because, you know, he was in jail a lot of the time. Back then he could make things very hard."

Mike Ness's most infamous hour came when 1985 was barely an hour old. Today Cathay de Grande is known as the Argyle, a "cocktail den" and nightclub for the pretty young things of Hollywood. But in the 1980s it was a punk club with a fearsome reputation for violence and shady behavior. On the night in question, the Cathay was the venue at which Social Distortion would play in the new year. When a club employee offered to pay the group with two grams of china-white heroin, Mike Ness agreed without first seeking his bandmates' permission. For Ness this was an opportunity to cut out the middleman—"It saved me the job of stopping off at my dealer's place on my way home," he says—while for the other three members of the group it was just cause to give notice to quit with immediate effect.

But whereas once Mike Ness would think nothing of tapping his left arm with his right hand so as to raise a vein into which he could inject heroin, today he conducts the interview for this book en route to the gym. (Others in the band's orbit have been less fortunate. In a disquieting incident, the group's former drummer, Casey Royer, was arrested in Orange County after an alleged overdose in front of his twelve-year-old son.) In the days and weeks after cleaning up his life, Ness moved in with Jim Guerinot. In doing so he proved that though now a roughly sketched picture of health, the habits of sloth were proving hard to shake. "Even with him clean, things didn't get much better," says the manager. "I had this big water jug that I'd throw all my change into, which was something I'd done since I was a little kid. But out of this Mike would siphon off anything that wasn't a penny. I'd go to the jar 'cos I had no money and there'd be nothing but [copper] coins in there."

Guerinot told his unwanted guest that his landlord had caught wind of his presence and from this point on he would be expected to contribute his share of the now doubled rent. The story may have been a fiction, but it worked. "Boom! He was gone. I got rid of him!" By now Social Distortion had reformed, at least after a fashion. The band functioned to a point but remained a part-time concern that didn't make money. By 1987, Ness had learned a trade. He was now a house painter, a job he hated and at which he was no good. At the end of each working day, he would spend five or six hours at the Casbah Recording Studio in Fullerton laying down the tracks for what would become Social Distortion's second album, the once prophetically titled *Prison Bound*.

"It's amazing how much energy you have when you stop chasing drugs and committing petty crimes," he says. "I used to spend my whole day doing these things. It was amazing to me how much energy I suddenly had. I was fortunate that I was able to put that energy into my music. Finally, and somehow, I developed a work ethic."

One often overlooked aspect of being a junkie is that junkies are boring. As the fearsome addiction takes hold, life is distilled down to just one aspect: finding the money with which to buy drugs. "Mike went from being the guy you wouldn't want around, because like any junkie what he would do is rip my shit off and be a pain in the ass," says Guerinot, "but once he got clean he was really fun to have around. He suddenly became a great and really sweet guy."

Released in January of 1988, *Prison Bound* introduced itself to the world with no fanfare at all. Yet despite the ten-song set's failure to trouble the *Billboard* Hot 200 album chart, or, indeed, any chart anywhere in the world, it did draw up the blueprints of what is now recognized as being Social Distortion's signature sound: a mixture of punk and classic rock, country, blues and even rockabilly. With an inherent energy and Mike Ness's sneering voice oscillating on the note, the band need not have worried that they were shedding their punk rock carapace. In doing so their music was gaining a universal quality. In a parallel universe, it was even possible to imagine the songs on *Prison Bound* becoming *hits*.

Then as now, KROQ was California's most influential radio station. This in turn made it the most influential music broadcaster in the United States. If KROQ sneezed, America caught a cold. But by 1988 the station's DJs were more likely to say "fuck" on the air than they were to play a song by a punk band. It came, then, as an enormous surprise to Mike Ness when one morning while driving to work he heard his own voice singing back at him. With X floundering, with Bad Religion not yet emerged from hibernation, KROQ picked a song from a band that it seemed no one cared about, written by a house painter who just three years earlier seemed determined to kill himself, and played it on the air. This the station did many times.

It would of course be wrong to say that up until this point Mike Ness couldn't get himself arrested because he had, many times. But, really, Social Distortion's curriculum vitae was that of a middling local punk group. Their debut album was good, but not great. Their leader's burgeoning drug habit meant that live appearances were restricted mostly to Southern California. Although Ness could spit and sneer as well as anyone—as he had with his warning "run and hide when I'm on the street / your fears and your tears, I'll taunt you in your sleep" on 1983's "The Creeps (I Just Want to Give You)"—there was little that was remarkable from Social D's earlier days. But as the 1990s neared, an authorial voice emerged from the band's standard-issue exoskeleton. Mike Ness's songs featured a roll call of characters markedly down on their luck. There were drifters, loners and losers driving around in beaten-up cars looking for an easy dollar and a woman with smiling eyes who would break their heart. By now, Mike Ness sounded older and wiser than his years. He was no longer a punk with a point to prove; he was a man who knew how to take, as well as how to give, a beating.

Like the Pogues, Social Distortion took the template of punk and from it found new ways of expression. Ness seemed at one with his vignettes about people in neighborhoods that were some way from being described as "emerging." The band even covered Johnny Cash's "Ring of Fire" long before the man in black became the hipster's country star of choice.

Social Distortion themselves could hardly have been any less fashionable had they appeared wearing double-denim. As if their presence on KROQ wasn't unlikely enough, the band then signed their names on a major label recording contract. With the exception of X's unsuccessful alliance with Elektra more than five years earlier, they were the first of the Southern Californian punk rock groups to do so.

"Think about it," says Jim Guerinot. "'Prison Bound,' a song released on an independent label, goes to number one on KROQ and this leads to Social Distortion signing a deal with Epic Records, who the band are familiar with because that's the label that put out albums by The Clash. It's really a very unlikely story. And when they sign to Epic, there's no backlash; and the reason that there's no backlash is because there's no *anything*. Nobody's listening. Nobody cares. But Social Distortion at this point had begun to step away from the rest of their peers, whether it be Bad Religion or T.S.O.L. Even X, who I revered to a high degree, were not getting their videos played on MTV."

"At that time punk was a four-letter word," says Mike Ness. "It had a stigma behind it. I remember being on a major label being great because I got to quit my day job and I got an advance. I was able to buy a house and to go on the road full time. But it was frustrating because, frankly, the record label had signed Pearl Jam and Michael Jackson and that was where all their money was going. They were, like, 'Well, we're not going to put a whole lot into Social Distortion' because they didn't know what to do with us. Theoretically they thought we could be played on the radio right after Tom Petty, and we could have.

But no one knew how to do that because nobody knew anything about the band. I remember having art meetings about the record covers with these middle-aged people, and I was, like, 'Do you even know what this movement was about?' So it was frustrating. But I don't regret the three or four records that we made with the major label because I think it did bring a different kind of credibility to the band. It was the credibility of 'Hey, these guys are worth signing. These guys are a real band.' And that was very validating for us. It made us want to work harder."

Social Distortion's first two albums for Epic—1990's *Social Distortion* and 1992's *Somewhere Between Heaven and Hell*—would each be awarded gold discs for sales in the United States in excess of half a million copies. With this, the band became the first American punk rock act to successfully hitch their wagon to the major label gravy train. They wouldn't be the last.

## CHAPTER TWO

# THERE WAS ALWAYS AN URGE, A NEED TO BELONG

It seems fitting that one of the engines of Bay Area punk rock was born and raised in the Motor City. As a child, Lawrence Livermore would walk the streets of Detroit listening with a fearful fascination as the heaviest of heavy industries pounded all around him. Born in 1947, Livermore knew by instinct that a life working as a rivethead at a plant that made cars for General Motors, Ford or Chrysler was not a fate for which he was destined. He quotes the actress Lily Tomlin, who when asked at what point she decided she wanted to leave Detroit answered, "As soon as I realized where I was." Livermore claims to have reached this conclusion by the age of five.

Long before the dawning of the twenty-first century, the word "Detroit" had become shorthand for the depths to which Washington, DC, would allow what was once one of the most vibrant and powerful cities in the United States to fall. "Leave Detroit out of this," said Moe Szyslak, the barman in *The Simpsons*. "Those folks are living in Mad Max times." In 1967, the city succumbed to a racially defined five-day riot that would leave forty-three people dead and two thousand buildings destroyed. It was also the year that Livermore started sniffing glue. He progressed to LSD and, in for a penny in for a pound, duly became a hippie. He subsisted on cheese sandwiches and spent many hours handing out flowers to strangers. Satellite-high, he would accost passersby in the street and rave at them about the attainment of universal harmony and world peace. One night, two cops with their guns drawn emerged from bushes and arrested him. Finding himself before a judge, he was offered two choices: a lengthy spell in prison or a suspended sentence contingent on him securing a steady full-time job.

Livermore chose the latter, and landed much the same kind of gig as he might have been given in the Big House. He now spent his days smashing rocks with a jackhammer. This was at Zug Island, a foundry on the south side of Detroit. In time the young worker was promoted from breaking rocks in the hot sun, not to mention the frigid snow, on a slag heap, to a coke oven the flames of which illuminated the city to the north. By now a highflyer in the nonrenewable fuel racket, Livermore was duly promoted again. His task now was to keep watch on the oven's temperature and pressure gauges lest they blow up and kill everyone at the plant. He undertook this serious job with the sense of purpose it required—he did it high on mescaline and LSD while reading a weathered paperback of Fyodor Dostoevksy's *Crime and Punishment* that he didn't understand.

If listening to good music and not reading great books had taught the young Lawrence Livermore anything, it was that there is a feeling people get when they look to the West that is too strong for many to ignore. The twenty-year-old's boots may have been planted on the terra firma of the not-yet-turned-to-rust belt of the American Midwest, but his eyes were trained on California. He listened to the Doors, who told him that "the west is the best / get here and we'll do the rest." (Here Jim Morrison's words would prove prophetic; he eventually moved east to Paris and died in the bath.) Whatever this meant, he was in.

Today Lawrence Livermore is one of several polymaths interviewed for this book. At seventy years old his mind weaves like a drunk driver on a motorway between topics as varied as Chinese history, Fulham Football Club, baseball, hippies and punk. He has swapped coasts and now lives in the New York borough of Queens. He jousts on Twitter, helps with the etymology of early photographs of Green Day and, via Facebook, asks if any friends might care to help him celebrate his birthday by circumnavigating the island of Manhattan on foot. As is the case with many people whose words helped to write this story, he is also generous with his time.

Back in the 1960s, however, Lawrence Livermore sounds like a young man not overburdened with wisdom. To prepare for his journey to the Pacific coast, Livermore sold the motorbike by which he had defined himself in Detroit and bought a Volkswagen van of questionable durability. His other worldly possessions were given either to friends or to the trash collectors. En route to his new home, and without actually having yet set foot in California, he was pulled over by two officers from the San Diego Police Department who, after finding the two Benzedrine pills he'd brought along for the journey, handcuffed him to their cruiser. He was left to languish in county jail for two days. On his release, he realized that the long arm of the law also had sticky fingers. The cops had taken all but thirty-five dollars of the money he'd saved with which to begin his new life. His rations amounted to a single packet of brown rice.

In Northern California, Livermore occupied himself with activities typical of the time and place. Some of these pursuits were fully subversive. While not a member of the White Panther Party, he was nonetheless close enough to the group to experience its machinations firsthand. With a provocative manifesto that demanded freedom from "the vicious pig power structure and their mad dog lackeys," not to mention "the freedom of all prisoners held in federal, state, country and city jails," Livermore enjoyed a crow's-nest view of how easily rhetoric slips from cup to lip. The White Panther Party implored their followers to abstain from drugs, yet one of its key architects, John Sinclair, shoveled down drugs in the same way he devoured *The Anarchist Cookbook*. "Do as I say, not as I do" was the gist of his reply to the charge of hypocrisy.

By the time Ronald Reagan was starting his second term as the fortieth president of the United States, Lawrence Livermore had had enough of pretty much everything. Eschewing the commander in chief's blueprint for American renewal—a curious mixture of bare-knuckled neoliberalism and a sinister, folksy paternalism—he decided to live more or less off-grid. With his partner, Anne, he set up home in the tiny community of Spy Rock in California's Mendocino County, almost two hundred miles north of the Bay Area. The winters were as frigid as the summers were remorseless. Financial straits were often so dire that he had to make calculations as to whether he had enough gas in his car's tank to get him to the nearest shop and back. To the extent that she tended to half a dozen marijuana plants, Anne was the gardener of the house. Save for the fact that people no longer found themselves under arrest for making wine, rural Northern California was the Napa Valley of pot production. Come harvest time, each year federal helicopters would shatter the tranquility of the boondocks, not to mention the nerves of every illicit farmer in the region. Despite sharing his home with a stash that could not be seen from the air, this Mr. Small of pot producers still fretted at the prospect of a visit from the Man.

Livermore describes 1985 as being the worst year of his life. Deciding to get his midlife crisis out of the way early, he became a bandleader of sorts and formed the Lookouts. The group were a power trio comprised of two people. He was joined by a bass player, twenty-four years his junior, who went by the virtually unbeatable punk rock nom de plume "Kain Kong." The only thing for which the Lookouts wanted—aside, that is, from an audience—was a drummer.

As it happened, the solution to this problem lived just a mile away—or, as the people of Spy Rock know it, right next door. Livermore's closest neighbors were Frank Wright II and his wife, Linda. Following the husband's honorable discharge from the US Army, the family moved to California and set up home in Mendocino County. But while Frank may have chosen a life not free from the trappings of the hippie ideal, at his core he was a rowdy and forthright man. Despite not being the kind of person to whom Lawrence Livermore would normally gravitate, up in the mountains of Spy Rock one made the best of one's surroundings, and that included the neighbors.

The Wrights had a son, the lovably unruly Frank Edwin Wright III, who was twelve. The youngest member of the family had a knack for quickly picking up the rudiments of whatever musical instrument on which he laid his prepubescent hands. This talent, however, was never married to its essential life partner, perseverance. But seeing as the pickings for musicians in and around Spy Rock were slim, Lawrence Livermore decided that the drummer for the Lookouts should be a hyperactive child who by all accounts appears to have been nothing less than Bart Simpson made flesh. His recruitment of Frank Edwin III came with the blessing of the boy's mother and father.

"The environment that he grew up in and that I was living in was very unusual," says Livermore. "In a way life was about surviving in an environment that was completely alien. Put it this way: the idea of having a punk rock band was not greeted at all favorably by the locals. It was very fortunate, however, that his parents were very open-minded and were willing to let their son try this new activity. He was a very rambunctious child, although I wouldn't say that he was difficult. But with the drums he found something that he was very good at and because of that he liked it, too. I think that along with his parents he'd be the first to admit that [joining the Lookouts] changed his life dramatically.

"His dad was a captain in the US military who'd had some pretty horrendous experiences in the Vietnam War. One of the interesting things about him is that he came from a long line of very strict and almost oppressive military types. But Frank decided that when he had a son he was not going to make the same kind of mistakes that his family had made with him. He was going to be genuine and gentle and open, some might say almost to a fault, because [his son] did run a little bit wild. But the fact is that if Frank had stuck true to his own upbringing and his family tradition, his boy would never have been allowed to play in a punk rock band, or would never have been allowed to play the drums, or would even have been allowed to hang out with me."

Despite having no idea how to play the drums, Lawrence Livermore taught the Lookouts' youngest member how to play. This he did by reducing a kit set up in his home to just a snare drum and bass drum. Sticks in hand, Frank Wright III was asked to keep time with the 1950s standard "At the Hop" by Danny and the Juniors. After this, Livermore cued up "Rock and Roll Is Here to Stay" and instructed his charge to once more keep the beat. He watched in silent wonder as a child who up until that point had never picked up a pair of drumsticks nailed the rhythm with metronomic precision. A thought flashed across his mind: "This might work."

(Not everyone in the Livermore house that day remembers this quite so fondly. At the time the guest room was occupied by Frank Wright III's aunt Olivia, who was visiting from England. She described the music made by her nephew and his young friend as being "an infernal noise." For years afterward she maintained that the sound was "the most god-awful racket I ever heard in my entire life.")

By the time Frank Edwin Wright III left for home, he had landed the gig as the drummer with the Lookouts. To celebrate the arrival of the band's newest and youngest member, Livermore gave him a nickname: "Tre Cool."

**T**he influence that Lawrence Livermore would come to exert on the Northern Californian punk rock scene is remarkable. The fact that his achievements grew from seeds sown in a town that might be described as "one horse" had the locals not eaten it is doubly so. 1985 heralded not just the formation of the Lookouts but also the publication of Livermore's own local newspaper. The *Iron Peak Lookout*'s first issue featured articles about that season's marijuana harvest and the tale of a black bear that found its way into someone's home and somehow managed to drink milk from an upturned refrigerator. Neither of these stories was picked up by the *Washington Post*. As with the band of almost the same name, the *Iron Peak Lookout* was not greeted with total acclaim from its intended readership. By way of retaliation, in time Livermore dropped the first two words of the title and rebranded the publication as a music-based fanzine.

His next writing gig was as a "shitworker" for *Maximumrocknroll*, one of America's most storied and enigmatic publications. Unfailingly militant and proudly, sometimes tediously, independent, "*MRR*," as it is often known, began life in the late seventies as a punk rock radio show on Berkeley's KPFA station. By 1982, the brand, as its founding fathers would never have dreamt of calling it, had expanded to a monthly print edition that endures to this day. Its founder in this format was Tim Yohannan, known not always affectionately as "Chairman Tim," a onetime hippie who forged the magazine in his own image and ruled it without democratic decree. Operated on not-for-profit principles and published on paper of a quality inferior to that of a tea bag, the wordy, black-and-white, easily smudged chronicle represents both the best and the worst of the punk community. Then as now, it is a confusion of dichotomies: internationalist yet isolationist, creative yet conformist, independent but often herdlike in its modes of behavior and outlook. It could by turns be wildly inspiring and irritatingly pious, sometimes in the same sentence. *Maximumrocknroll* refuses to take advertising dollars from any major label or from any company with major label affiliations. Dead to them are any band who signs a deal with one of the Big Three music corporations—Universal Music Group, Sony Music Entertainment and Warner Music Group— or even to a record label whose catalogue is distributed by these companies.

"It was a bit like a cult and I guess in the end that's what freaked me out a bit," remembers Lawrence Livermore. "But unlike most of the people who worked there, I was Tim [Yohannan's] own age. I'd been around the block a few times and I'd seen things like this before. I'd seen cultlike scenes in the 1960s and early '70s. In fact, it reminded me uncannily of the White Panther movement and I'd walked away from that with good reason. I had no desire of subsuming my will to the whims of the Great Leader."

Livermore would begin spending serious hours in the magazine's headquarters, the "Maxipad," a residential property on Clipper Street in San Francisco. This was the house that a number of "shitworkers"—the name given to anyone who put their shoulder to the *Maximumrocknroll* cause—called home. Though laughter could be heard ringing within the walls of number 484, the magazine's founder made sure that no one was left in any doubt about the seriousness of the *MRR* mission. Respite from the ideological oppression came only on the mornings when Yohannon was off-site working at his part-time job. When staffers heard the wheels of his car coming to a stop on the road outside, an ironic cry of "Daddy's home" rang around the house.

For Lawrence Livermore, the realization that he'd had his fill of tub-thumping theocracy came after he received a handwritten note from Chairman Tim. Arriving home one afternoon, he found taped to his door a piece of paper which read: "The up-stairs bathroom and sink need scrubbing. Take care of it." It was only when he was on his knees with a scourer in his hand that Livermore reached his moment of epiphany: there was nothing more that could be wrong with this scenario.

As with their brethren in Southern California, this period was a confusing time for punks in the Bay Area. But whereas bands in Los Angeles whose talents stretched to one album's worth of good ideas became metal bands with no ideas at all, up north the music being made was busy pushing its way toward its logical extremities. Aided and abetted by Jello Biafra and the occasional wisdom and incessant ranting of *Maximumrocknroll*, the genre's ideological template was now etched in stone as if it were tablets from a biblical fable. But while Biafra and *MRR*'s sermons were broadcast from San Francisco, the flock were gathered in the East Bay.

Residents of Oakland and Berkeley have long believed that the City by the Bay looks down on them. If not quite the New-ark to New York's Manhattan Island, the seven square miles of San Francisco is the place that Northern California's opinion formers and tastemakers call home. It is the city in which Joe DiMaggio married Marilyn Monroe. The intersection of Haight and Ashbury Streets in the city's Upper Haight was the epicen-ter and birthplace of the hippie movement. It has the City Lights bookshop at which Allen Ginsberg read his grandly controver-sial and much revered Beat poem "Howl." It had Candlestick Park, the stadium at which in 1966 the Beatles performed their last concert before a paying audience, and in which the glam-orous Giants and 49ers played baseball and American football respectively.

In the mid-1980s, the East Bay had little to compare to these dazzling jewels. Berkeley is home to a fine university, UC Berke-ley, and Oakland has the often successful Athletics baseball team. But even the A's play in a brutalist stadium with all the character of a municipal car park. Compared with the glamour at the other end of the Bay Bridge, the East Bay is a blot on an earthquake-prone landscape.

With tours of duty in a declining Detroit and Spy Rock behind him, the surprise is not that Lawrence Livermore moved to the East Bay but that it took him so long. With the division of time beginning to weigh in favor of the city, he was approached by Dave Dictor, mainstay of the no-shit-taken hardcore band MDC, who at the time were the biggest fish in the small pond of Bay Area punk. Dictor had a proposition that would benefit both men. In order to keep a roof above his head, the singer needed to find at least two new people to move into the house in which he lived, and he needed them fast. If this offer seemed too good to be true, it was. When Dictor said "house," he meant a two-bedroom apartment; when he said "two-bedroom apartment," he meant a place that originally had two bedrooms that had since been subdivided into four. The dwelling was known as the "Rathouse."

"Everyone had moved out of the house, and for good reason," remembers Livermore. "As I would learn, Dave was difficult to live with. But I did need a place to stay, as did two of my friends, so we moved in straight away. This was when I was still living in the mountains. But with things starting to happen in the Bay Area I wanted to have a base down there. So for two hundred dollars a month I was able to rent a room . . . it ended up being a very chaotic environment."

Then as now, Lawrence Livermore had yet to find a pie into which he didn't want to plant a finger. After moving to the city, he then enrolled in college. As well as this he continued to publish *Lookout*, while the band of almost the same name was able to put down roots in the fertile soil of the East Bay rather than the barren ground of Mendocino County. It is for this reason

that the Rathouse occupies a place of significance in this story—
it was the place from which Tre Cool made his bones in the big
city. He was thirteen years old.

"Tre has recollections of coming out there when he was [a
young teenager] when the Lookouts played their first shows in
the Bay Area," says Livermore. "He got to meet Dave Dictor and
was quite impressed with him, as most thirteen-year-olds would
be. But although it was a neat little scene, at that time it really
was the dying embers of punk in San Francisco."

With the drummer still years away from the age at which
he could legally drive, Tre Cool would spend nights at the Rathouse. "I didn't need drugs because I was high on people," he
told the author in 2004. From this base he would make his first
appearances in live venues in and around the Bay Area. If MDC
were on tour, he would sleep in Dave Dictor's bed.

"It was great but he never changed his sheets," remembers
the drummer.

Every scene needs a focal point and the Bay Area was about
to get one. The urban centers of Northern California had a
number of clubs at which punk bands could play, places such
as Mabuhay Gardens, Ruthie's Inn and the Stone. But each of
these establishments represented just that: the establishment.
They served alcohol. They had age restrictions. They had owners who were known to become jittery at the prospect of concerts culminating in their property being razed to the ground.

The Alternative Music Foundation, as it is never known, or
924 Gilman Street, as it is sometimes known, or Gilman, as it
would become known, opened on New Year's Eve 1986. Today
there is spirited debate as to who can claim credit for the idea
of opening the Bay Area's first bespoke punk club, but what is
beyond dispute is that Tim Yohannon played a pivotal role in

establishing a space that is open to all and in which the only thing not tolerated is intolerance. In 1986, *Maximumrocknroll*'s not-for-profit "business model" meant that the publication had amassed a sizeable war chest. One assumes that this bounty was held in escrow on the off chance that an anarchist revolution might break out from sea to shining sea in the United States. Failing that, a punk club would do.

It is testament to Gilman's durability that its doors remain open to this day. Thirty-two years ago Tim Yohannon kicked in ten thousand dollars with which to transform a good idea into an active operation. This figure would rise to something in the region of forty thousand dollars by the time the club was in a shape fit to accommodate paying customers. Often, electricians, plumbers and carpenters would arrive to help without needing to be asked. Until the final evening of 1986, a space that was now a club on a nonresidential street in Berkeley had never before staged a concert. Everything needed doing. Toilets required installation, a stage had to be built, fire exits had to be made fit for purpose. Without all of these things, 924 Gilman Street would not have received the city permits that would keep its benefactors out of jail. As it was, the authorities signed off on the paperwork just hours before the venue opened its doors for the first time.

"Basically, Gilman Street is a little black box," says Veronica Irwin, a student at UC Berkeley and one of the club's latter-day volunteers. Like every other person who has put in a shift at the communitarian venue, she did so without pay. "There's no sign outside announcing what it is. In fact, the first time I went there I thought, 'Where the hell am I?' From the outside it's just a brick building. There's a painted sign that says 'The Caning Shop,' so obviously it used to be something else. It wasn't intended to be a venue. So you go in and it's all black with the graffiti that's accumulated since the eighties, from little tags to huge murals, some of which are beautiful and some of which are really disturbing. There's a huge one of a pregnant woman with a fetus that is just super disturbing. There's a wooden ceiling with a bunch of ladders, almost like a fire-wing, which doesn't look too secure. On one side there's a bunch of bathrooms that are not gender specific, which is something they're very adamant about. And there's a little stage in the back corner, which I suppose was built by someone when the club opened. But the whole place looks like it was never meant to be a venue. It's really, really bare bones."

The policies of Gilman Street are established at monthly meetings that all volunteers are invited to attend. On the first weekend of each month, between fifteen and forty people will arrive with topics to discuss and grievances to air. The club is directly democratic, and any band that wishes to appear on its stage must first be granted committee approval before being allowed to do so. Any group signed to a major label is automatically prohibited from adding a night at Gilman to its touring itinerary. Discussions between politically minded activists regarding what is and what is not acceptable in their shared space are frequent. The nearest thing to an ultimate sanction is an "86," named in honor of the year the club first opened its doors. This sanction can be imposed on temporary terms, just as it can be awarded for all manner of infractions, some of which are clearer than others. Technically, patrons are not permitted to drink within a two-block radius of Gilman's doors. A list of the club's ten fundamental rules (or, if you prefer, commandments) can be found in the venue itself as well as on its official website. A membership fee costs two dollars.

"Basically it's things like no drinking, no violence, no drugs, no stage diving, no sexism, no homophobia," says Veronica Irwin. "The list is written in stenciled graffiti writing which is written about two or three feet wide. The membership card is kind of what keeps the club going [financially] and on top of that people pay the ticket price for the show itself, which compared to other places is cheap. Oh, and people aren't allowed to bring dogs." For enquiring minds that want to know exactly what type of person would bring a dog to a punk rock show, Irwin has the answer. "Gilman has a lot of people that are called the 'Gilman Rats,' which is meant as an endearing term, and a lot of them have dogs. These kids are younger and some of them lead pretty ordinary lives. But some of them suffer from addiction or come from families that suffer from addiction. Also, some of them are out of school or are homeless; they left school early because they couldn't take it anymore. It's a very ragamuffin group of young people, some of whom do have dogs. And if you get a bunch of kids moshing around, you don't really want to throw a dog into the mix."

Naturally, Lawrence Livermore was one of 924 Gilman Street's principal architects. The man who is fast emerging as the Forrest Gump of our story says that "you'd be hard pressed to get me to say anything negative about the place. It's one of the more brilliant social enterprises I've been involved with in my life." But Livermore does note that "like all small and insular societies things do tend to get overdramatized at times and people do tend to take things too much to heart." His most nagging concern is that "nothing lasts forever. Gilman Street has clocked up more than thirty years now, but because of the changing music scene and the gentrification of the area [around it], I don't know how much longer it can survive."

It is of course easy to laugh at the thought of forty volunteers arguing on a Saturday morning over the suitability of a band based on something said in an interview or an ambiguous couplet on a lyric sheet. It's just as easy to laugh at a level of bureaucracy that ensures a turning circle like that of an oil tanker. But perhaps a wry and affectionate chuckle would serve a better purpose. After all, anyone who disapproves of Gilman's list of rules and sanctions can avoid them simply by attending concerts *at almost every other club in the world*.

"Gilman was my first real taste of what it was like to be a punk," remembers Billie Joe Armstrong. "It wasn't just about music; it was also about a community and a movement. Every single weirdo and nerd and punk around the Bay Area would be there, and it was great. The shows were [for people of] all ages. I wanted to go to gigs at other places when I was fifteen but I couldn't because the entry was for people aged twenty-one or over, or it was eighteen-year-olds and over. But Gilman was run by kids and I could get in without someone scamming a ticket for me. A community was being built with great music and artists and bands and fanzine editors and people who were getting exposed to the world of politics. Gilman was the first time I learned anything in my life. Before Gilman, everything I'd learned up until that point was bullshit. It was a place that you could go and talk about things like racism, sexism and homophobia. Whenever you went there was always a conversation taking place."

During this febrile period Lawrence Livermore decided to found his own record label, and there are no cash prizes for guessing the name he decided to give it. The man who fronted the Lookouts and who produced a fanzine called *Lookout* founded Lookout Records in 1987 as a somewhat functioning company with fellow Bay Area punk enthusiast David Hayes. Before this, Livermore had used the name as the imprint on which his band's album, *One Planet One People*, was released; once this was done he had no plans to issue any other material in the company's name. But the notion that the music being made by Bay Area bands with whom he was friends was better than most of the albums being released at this time was tugging hard at his sleeve. The trouble was that no one took these bands seriously.

Livermore would walk around enthusing to anyone who cared to listen, and many more who did not, about the quality of the music being made right under their ears. "People would laugh at me and call me names," he remembers. Undeterred, he realized "that if I wanted to hear some decent records, I was going to have to make them myself."

Much to Lawrence Livermore's surprise, it turns out that this task wasn't much more complicated than issuing a fanzine. In 1986, the fabulously named the Mr. T Experience, a punk group from Berkeley, had issued their own album, *Everybody's Entitled to Their Own Opinion*, under their own steam. Livermore gave them a ring and asked if they'd kindly hand over the contact details of the people who had produced, engineered, mixed and mastered the LP. He then called these people and asked if they'd be willing to work with the groups he hoped would comprise Lookout Records' earliest catalogue. With these elements in place, the label duly issued four seven-inch EPs by the bands Operation Ivy, Crimpshrine, Corrupted Morals and Isocracy. The cost of this enterprise was four thousand dollars, every cent of which was plundered from what remained of Livermore's savings. "I guess it was a pretty idiotic thing to do," he says.

He was clear that his intention was to release records, not to sign bands. None of Lookout's artists were actually contracted to his label, a business model that would endure throughout his decade-long tenure. The company's first four seven-inch singles were sold for two dollars a copy. Once the costs of recording and pressing had been recouped, the artist received sixty percent of the profits. By contrast, a band on a major label will take a cut of between twelve and twenty percent of the retail price of each record they sell. Measured in terms of album sales, the model used by Lookout works out at something like a dollar more per record.

Despite the fact that in time the independent imprint would sell LPs in enormous quantities, the company's office was a single rented room in a house in Berkeley. Lawrence Livermore lived next door, also in one room, the rent for which was ninety-eight dollars a month. This would be his address until he moved to England in 1997 (although flush with success, in 1994 he did move into a larger room next door, at the cost of two hundred bucks per calendar month). Twenty years later, Livermore is sitting with the author in the Spread Eagle pub in Camden Town two days after Christmas. Drinking black Americano coffee with no sugar, he seems bemused by the idea that anyone would think of this as an ascetic existence. He seems fully flummoxed by the notion that no other owner of a significantly successful record label would choose to live this way. "It took me quite a while to adjust to the idea that I could spend money like a normal person instead of living in a little hovel," he says.

"When we first started doing this type of music, the term 'pop-punk' wasn't used that often," he says of the sound for which Lookout Records would become best known. "I suppose it had a brief phase in the days of the Buzzcocks and so on, but it kind of faded away. So when Lookout got going in the late eighties, we were just putting out local music from our scene. It was only a few years later that people started generalizing it as pop-punk. It was at the same time that people started criticizing and complaining that this kind of music was ruining the punk scene. I took a bit of umbrage at that, and I was a bit bewildered as well. The derivation of 'pop' comes from *populus*, which means 'people.' So do the people who were complaining hate other people, or what? What's wrong with people liking your music? And that continues to be my viewpoint to this day. The moment that something becomes remotely popular, someone is going to say, 'Oh, that's no good, that's awful.' Or they'll say, 'Oh, the wrong people are liking this.' I never set out to be a pop-punk label, but when people started characterizing it as such I thought, 'Okay, if you want to call us that then I guess we are.' And I didn't mind a bit."

On Lookout Records' early-day roster, it was Operation Ivy who stood first among equals. It is even reasonable to suppose that without them the label's catalogue would consist only of its namesake group's first album. Like so many others, Lawrence Livermore was captivated by Op Ivy's live show, and its hectic and heated amalgamation of punk and ska. The idea of launching a label had been sitting idly in his head for a while, but it was this, he says, "that pushed me over the edge." He realized he'd been dithering long enough. "I thought, 'This is one of the greatest things I've ever seen in my life. Obviously this music has to be recorded for posterity.'" Livermore approached the band and told them he would like to release an EP under their name. Their response was more a concern for their friend's sanity than a whoop of joy. It wasn't that the group didn't want to put out a record, they told him, it was just that they couldn't imagine selling as many as a *thousand* copies.

O peration Ivy's genealogy can be traced back to the early 1980s. Tim Armstrong and Matt Freeman were casual friends who lived in Albany, a town that borders Berkeley on its northernmost frontier. The distance between the two places is short enough that after shows at Gilman Street many punks would walk to Albany to buy deep-fried treats from the town's all-night donut shop. But while Berkeley was a college town with plenty of sharp edges, its upstairs neighbor was suburban. The collars of the shirts worn by its residents were blue, and starched. For adolescents in the market for diversity and danger, the best view was to the south.

Tim Armstrong and Matt Freeman were two school friends who were both drawn to Berkeley, but whose experiences of the city were different. Armstrong would gambol along the artery that is Telegraph Avenue with his older brother and his friends as they shopped for records. These bigger kids nicknamed him "Tagalong" and would introduce him to the music of The Clash and The Specials. Conversely, Freeman's father was a police officer who instilled in his son the knowledge that Berkeley had a mean streak.

The pair came together in earnest in 1983, when they combined as entrants in their school's talent and variety show. Tim played guitar, while Matt played bass. They called their act Cougar Follies and their set included a ramshackle cover of Elvis Presley's "Blue Suede Shoes." It was hardly a surprise that the band failed to win any prizes that day, but Cougar Follies' one and only live appearance is notable for being the first time that Tim Armstrong and Matt Freeman played together onstage. Come their senior year, the pair had decided to commit themselves seriously to making music. By this point the guitarist had already been in a punk band, C.O.D., and in joining forces with his school friend he was now in his second. The group called itself Basic Radio. Following a year of fruitless rehearsals, the pair were brought closer together by a mutual disdain for bandmates who weren't taking the cause as seriously as they were. In an interview with Lawrence Livermore, Armstrong remembers saying to his friend, "This is bullshit, these kids are fucking knuckleheads, what are we gonna do? And it was like our first band meeting, the first time we became a team."

Tim Armstrong knew a kid from North Berkeley named Jesse Michaels who had been a member of a group called S.A.G. The pair bumped into each other at the Berkeley Bay Area Rapid Transit (BART) station and discussed the idea of forming a band. Potential influences were batted around, names such as The Specials, The Beat, Stiff Little Fingers and the Ramones. To complete the lineup, the trio recruited Dave Mello, a drummer who could barely keep a beat and who thought nothing of ignoring punk rock's dress code by playing with two bass drums, an aesthetic faux pas that was quickly corrected by Matt Freeman. Almost as quickly the bassist helped Mello find his musical chops. Freeman had learned from instrumental music class at Albany High that the best way of learning to play along with a drummer and thus locking together a band's most important ingredient, its rhythm section, was to play with his back against the bass drum. This technique taught the young musician how to play in time with the beat and left him with welts across his back. Duly fortified, the band began writing music while Jesse Michaels penned lyrics. They called themselves Operation Ivy, a name cribbed from two multimegaton thermonuclear bomb tests staged by the US government in the 1950s. Tim Armstrong also decided that from this point forth he wished to be known by the nickname "Lint."

The band's first gig took place at Dave Mello's home; their second was held at 924 Gilman Street. The members of Operation Ivy were well known to the faces at Gilman. Tim Armstrong and Matt Freeman, certainly, could be counted on to attend far more shows than they missed. Each Monday morning, Freeman would arrive in his car and take the rubbish bagged up from the weekend's happenings to the Berkeley dump, for which he was rewarded with free admission to a show of his choosing. At their first appearance onstage at the club, Operation Ivy supported MDC, a band the powers of whom were by then acutely on the wane. Despite few people outside of the East Bay knowing anything about them, the support act quickly became the band of choice for the patrons of 924 Gilman Street. Many was the time the four members would arrive at the club thinking they were there to spectate only to discover that their band's name had been written on the board that announced the evening's entertainment.

Without a blueprint and without much precedent, in the spring of 1988 Operation Ivy became the first band of the Gilman Street generation to head out on a nationwide tour. They had a plan of sorts, and an EP—*Hectic*, released that year—to their name. One thing they didn't have was a van. Instead the group traveled in a 1969 Chrysler Newport. They had no credit cards and virtually no money. For the tour's first seventy-two hours the four heedless young men survived by eating cheese sandwiches while sitting on the bonnet of their car. Their equipment was stored in a box built by Armstrong's father affixed to the Newport's roof. The car's occupants were spared from skidding to their deaths by Freeman's father's insistence on fitting the car with a new set of tires. It was on these wheels that Operation Ivy traveled from the Pacific to the Atlantic Oceans, and then back again. The band estimated that they traveled three thousand miles in their four-door ride. Lawrence Livermore reckons the distance to be twice that.

They were on the road for six weeks. They spent their nights sleeping on the floors of houses inhabited by punks they met in each of the cities they visited. Failing this, they slept beneath the stars. The group spent just one night coddled in motel bedsheets, and did so only after a storm forced them to seek shelter for the evening.

For all its toil, Operation Ivy's journey from the East Bay reaped an unreliable harvest. On some nights the gigs would be full with fans who were familiar with the band's music to the point of word perfection. On other evenings business was slow. In El Paso the band played in someone's living room to an audience of three people. After driving for hours through a storm that would have been much easier to navigate in an ark, in Lexington, Kentucky, they played to four people. Only one of these knew the band's music; the others had simply wandered in from the street.

But by traveling to distant shores, Operation Ivy had become trailblazers for an East Bay scene that had not yet become expansionist. In their absence, the hearts of Berkeley's punks grew fonder, and upon their return the band's popularity had grown exponentially. A homecoming concert at Gilman became the club's biggest draw to date. The crowd was suddenly peppered with kids from the suburbs wanting to see the band play and to perhaps become a part of a small and inclusive community.

But Gilman was a fragile ecosystem. Many of its representatives were made uncomfortable by the presence of outsiders, while others viewed the arrivistes as elements that could bring only harm to their scene. Even the modest success of a previously well-kept secret was enough to raise hackles. While there were those among the East Bay's punk fraternity that were pleased to see Operation Ivy gaining momentum, there were others whose reactions were less generous. Brett Gurewitz's observation that punk bears a reactionary edge were borne out by some members of the band's live audience shouting, "Ska boys!" at them in a manner that didn't always seem good natured.

But those who wish for a scene to continue without change are certain to be complicit in smothering it to death. Genies are not in the habit of returning to a life in a bottle, just as not every new person let in on a secret should be viewed with mistrust. At one Operation Ivy concert Tim Armstrong was approached by a young man unable to gain entry. The kid pleaded his case. "We have the same last name," he said. His name was Billie Joe.

Lawrence Livermore suggested that Operation Ivy capitalize on the relative success of *Hectic* by recording a second EP. This suggestion was demurred with the counteroffer that the time had arrived to record a full-length album. Livermore disagreed, believing it to be too soon for the band to embark on a project of this scale. He was also fretful about finding the money with which to finance such largesse. But the group were disinclined to heed the advice of others, even if this other was a friend. In making their decision, a course had been set from which they refused to deviate. We might as well be hanged for a sheep as for a lamb, the group reasoned, so an album it must be.

The recording of the songs that would comprise *Energy*, Operation Ivy's one and only LP, was arduous. Its sessions occupied the winter of 1988 and then sprawled into the spring of the following year. The band's original idea was to track the songs at an empty Gilman Street and have them engineered by Radley Hirsch, a technician who had manned the venue's sound desk since its earliest days. Lawrence Livermore considered the fact that the group had knocked out the six songs that comprised their *Energy* EP in a single afternoon and asked himself, "How hard can this be?" By doing this, he had spied a beehive of providence and swung at it wildly with a stick.

From the start the process was beset by creative disharmony. Hirsch wanted Matt Freeman to play with a clean sound and through a Marshall amplifier, while the bassist desired a distorted sound through a different amp. A third amp was then suggested, which Freeman didn't like either and which, anyway, was too big to be transported in his car. In choosing to record in a venue rather than a studio, Operation Ivy thought it obvious that the sound they were looking for should be as live and as undiluted as possible. But here they were spending weeks on a single song, overdubbing parts time and again. Because of this, the one crucial and intangible ingredient of all debut punk albums—vibe—was absent from the start. Lookout's cofounder, David Hayes, who had traveled with Operation Ivy on their six-week US tour, stopped by to ask them if they were really fully committed to making an album. Fried and snow-blind, by this point the band were no longer sure.

The only way to escape from the corner into which Operation Ivy had painted themselves was to start again. As the band packed up their equipment and departed for the Sound and Vision recording studio in San Francisco, Radley Hirsch was told that his services were no longer required. Now under the guidance of producer Kevin Army, the group quickly transformed themselves from a wheezing nag into an unstoppable force. Within a week they had tracked each one of *Energy*'s nineteen songs. So focused were the sessions that even when ravenous the musicians refused to take breaks that would allow them to go out and buy food. The solution to what had become a com-plicated problem was found by becoming *uncomplicated*. But evidence of the grind of making Operation Ivy's debut album did exist. In its original form, the song "Freeze Up" featured the lyric "It's 1988, stand up and take a look around." By the time the track was released, this date had been put forward by a year.

*Energy* has on its conscience the fact that it helped inspire a generation of American ska-punk bands few of whom were fit for purpose. (This rule does have exceptions, of which LA's the Interrupters are one.) But as with *Suffer, Energy* would play a pivotal role in revitalizing the scene it represented. "Truly those two records reenergized the punk scene in America and really kick-started what we know now as the nineties punk explosion," says Brett Gurewitz. "Bad Religion and Operation Ivy were the two bands that lit the fuse."

Over time, the East Bay group's record would sell more than a million copies. But at the time of its release in May of 1989, only lunatics would have predicted this level of success.

Operation Ivy may not have been alone in merging ska with punk rock—credit must also go to New England's Mighty Mighty Bosstones—but the vim with which they did so gave the enter-prise a revolutionary edge. The music was more than an Ameri-can love letter to English groups such as The Specials, The Beat and the Selecter, just as it is more than a fawn in the direction of thumping hardcore. *Energy* is well written and finely executed. It also rather cutely revels in its own stereotypes. In a fit of delib-erate double negatives, on the song "Knowledge," later covered by Green Day, Jesse Michaels sings with glee that "all I know is that I don't know / all I know is that I don't know nothing."

In its first year of release, *Energy* sold two thousand copies. Despite this apparently lowly figure, Lookout Records were pleased with the album's performance. "We thought that it was very, very good," remembers Lawrence Livermore, "which for those days it was." But in the face of their hushed success,

Operation Ivy were beginning to fracture. For one thing, the band's reputation as the Gilman generation's most consistent and powerful live act was taking a beating from one of its own. Livermore remembers one experience about which he still speaks with regret. With some difficulty, he had convinced a group of journalists from San Francisco to cross the water to the East Bay, a place they regarded as being unworthy of investigation, to see Operation Ivy perform at the Crossed Wagon Club. Livermore's experience of "every single [one of the band's shows] being astounding" seemed so dependable that he felt certain that they would prove a hit with his guests. You'll be glad that you came, he told them; this is going to be amazing, he said. Come the evening's end, however, he was left feeling mortified and let down.

"What I didn't know is that things had already started to go downhill for [Tim Armstrong]," he says. "On the night I invited the journalists over, the band were starting to attract attention from people outside of the scene. But [Tim] showed up drunk and basically wrecked the show. It was just embarrassing. Me asking these writers to the gig was me saying, 'Hey, what's going on in the East Bay is really worth looking at.' And they were, like, 'Huh? This is just a mess. This is just chaos.' I shouted at him very strongly afterwards, saying, 'How dare you do this?' I was mostly embarrassed, but I was also really concerned about him as well. I think that after years and years of struggle he had a hard time dealing with it suddenly being obvious that people really liked his band and were appreciative of what he was doing. He won't be the first or the last artist to deal with that kind of pressure by drinking and drugging too much."

That day, Tim Armstrong had invested a lot of energy in getting drunk. Alcohol was taken on Telegraph Avenue and then on the roof of the nearby Barrington Hall student housing cooperative in Berkeley. By show time the musician could scarcely stand up, let alone play a set. On the pavement outside after the show a furious Lawrence Livermore told Armstrong that his drinking was no longer cute. He was presented with a list of people Livermore had known whose lives had been ended by drink and drugs. He listened as the older man asked him how he dared take both his talent and the opportunities it afforded him and throw them away simply for the sake of getting drunk. He was reminded that millions of kids would give anything to possess his kind of talent, yet here he was giving it to the fire as if it were nothing more than a bad joke. Tim Armstrong was so dumbfounded by the livid honesty with which Livermore spoke that years later he could recall the tirade's every word. It would, though, be some time before he heeded its warnings.

By now things were changing. Lawrence Livermore's belief that the music emanating from the East Bay and the community that nurtured it deserved wider attention was fast becoming realized. Kids from all over the United States were descending on 924 Gilman Street, viewing it not as a working cooperative but as a shrine. The local band Sweet Baby became the first of their peers to sign a major label recording contract, a move that did not end well. Standing on shifting sands, many of the scene's founding fathers saw its energies changing and becoming darker. Believing that Gilman Street had lost its feeling of being a family, Tim Yohannan decided to stop funding the club. The venue briefly closed before an ad hoc committee raised enough money for its doors to open once again, much to the astonishment of all. Suddenly the club had proved that it could do more than exist—it could also *endure*. Lawrence Livermore describes the operation as being one of the few working examples of anarchist principles in action, not to mention one of its longest running.

But if 924 Gilman Street survived, Operation Ivy did not. On May 28, 1989, the group played the club for the final time. The booking was intended to be both a concert and a release party for their greatly delayed debut album. But by the time the late-spring evening arrived, the band had decided that their work on this earth was done. Like The Smiths' *Strangeways Here We Come, Energy* became one of the few box-fresh studio albums released by a band that no longer existed.

Even those who considered themselves a part of Op Ivy's inner circle were left agog by a decision they did not see coming. As Tim Armstrong tells it, the event was notable for its lack of drama. One day he and Jesse Michaels were on Telegraph Avenue drinking the beers that Armstrong had just bought. The pair were sitting on a volleyball court talking about music and about their band. According to Armstrong, as their words unfolded, it became clear to both men that by this point Operation Ivy was no longer the same thing it had been at the start of its life and that its existence was no longer cherished. He gives short shrift to the idea that it was Michael's decision to leave that caused the breakage. Instead, he recounts the meeting as a consensual agreement that his and Jesse Michaels's hearts were no longer committed to their cause. Over warming beers in Coyne Court, both men decided to allow their creation to die.

Lawrence Livermore remembers things differently. He accepts that Armstrong and Michaels may have shared drinks while sitting on a volleyball court, with the result of this meeting being that Op Ivy existed no more. But he insists that the singer took the decision to resign from the group unilaterally, thus causing it to fold. He remembers opening the front door of a house in which he was staying at the time and seeing Tim Armstrong and Matt Freeman standing at the threshold, bereft. "Our band just broke up," they told him. "They were really upset," he recalls. The three men walked the border between Oakland and Berkeley for miles as one half of what was no longer Operation Ivy tried to come to terms with the events of the day.

"It was like they had post-traumatic stress disorder," he says.

"The upsetting thing to me was that the band wasn't going to exist anymore and that two of my friends, Tim and Matt, were extremely upset because this was their life," he continues. "When they came over to tell me, they were just devastated. I just walked around for hours with them trying to put it in a better light. But it was just impossible. I can't really contradict [Tim's version of events] but all I know is that they came to the house that night and said, 'Jesse doesn't want to be in Operation Ivy anymore and we're breaking up.' I've quizzed him several times since then and he just denies that. The official party line is that they mutually broke up, but my take on it, as well as that of several other people who were close with them, is that it didn't happen that way. Jesse was from a different background from them. They were working class and everything was about playing music. That had been their lifelong goal since they were small children. Jesse was more of a . . . I hesitate to call him a dilettante because he's still a working artist today, although he does painting and writing. But his attitude was 'Oh, I'll try being in a band; I'll see if this is fun. Oh, it's not fun anymore so I'll do something different.' It's the privilege of being from a middle-class background. But Tim and Matt could not comprehend why someone would do that. Being working class myself, I related to that. I thought, 'Why would you give up the opportunity of doing something great?' This was in the final stages of their record. I think we were working on the artwork."

"From start to finish the whole Operation Ivy story lasted only two years, from May of 1987 to May of 1989," he says. "It came and went like a comet streaking overhead. They broke up virtually the minute the album came out."

Come the evening of May 28, word had leaked that Op Ivy's show at Gilman Street would be the last time that anyone would see them live. (Although contrary to the received wisdom, this was not the case; the band actually played for the last time at a party the following afternoon.) The occasion was marked by the transformation of Gilman into a death trap. Legally the club could accommodate three hundred people, although on the night something like twice this number paid entry. On top of this, both Mike Dirnt and Lawrence Livermore estimate that several hundred more fans managed to cram themselves in to what had become a suffocating and airless room. As a means of negating the conventional divisions that separate performers from their audience, Gilman prided itself on not having dressing rooms or a backstage area. In a venue as packed as a packet of couscous, this presented its own logistical difficulties. As well as Operation Ivy, the evening's three other bands, the Lookouts, Surrogate Brains and Green Day, who opened the show, also had to work out how to get to, and on, the stage.

"That night was bittersweet," says Mike Dirnt. "I mean, it was weird. "No one wanted to believe that it was going to be their last show, but we knew there was a chance that it would be. And they were red hot that night. Anything that grows that fast has to explode. And they were so fucking good. They were the best band in the world at that time. There may never be a better club show than there was that night. And to fit close to a thousand people into Gilman Street was just crazy. I had to stand up against the wall on a table just to see. But you knew you were experiencing something really special . . . It was great to be on the bill, but we all just wanted to see Op Ivy. That's what we were excited about. I don't even remember playing, that's how incredible their performance was. You knew you were somewhere really special and experiencing something that you may never, ever see again."

Almost thirty years on, Operation Ivy's final show in front of a paying audience, or at least in front of an audience some of whom had paid, remains the most celebrated night in the history of Gilman Street. In terms of a memory on which to dine

out, it is better than most. Lawrence Livermore was on hand to
see the Sex Pistols' last ever concert—that is until their nostalgic
reformation in 1996—at San Francisco's Winterland Ballroom
in January 1978. He heard for himself Johnny Rotten's rhetorical final words, the most famous in punk history: "Ever get the
feeling you've been cheated?" In 1973, he was in attendance at
Madison Square Garden as Led Zeppelin shot one of their performances for inclusion in the concert film *The Song Remains
the Same*. But Operation Ivy were one of the Bay Area's own,
and for Livermore this was true in more than one sense.

Asked today to quantify his contribution to 924 Gilman
Street's first wave and all that flowed from it, he seems at a loss
for an answer. He speaks of the success that came the way of his
consistently ramshackle label as if it were a minor achievement
that happened to someone else. Yet in terms of its significance
to the punk cause, Lookout Records stands behind only Epitaph. The only difference is that Brett Gurewitz's label remains
a going concern. But even the extinction of the company Livermore founded doesn't seem to bother him unduly. It is as if it
is for others to gaze with admiration at the wellspring of talent
he helped to divine. While they are doing this, Lawrence Livermore has quietly moved on.

## CHAPTER THREE

# I'M COMING OVER,
# I'M COMING OVER

It's unlikely that anyone in attendance at London's Powerhaus club on the evening of July 7, 1993, realized that they were at an event that would prove to be significant. The author, flush with the money earned from an article in a national magazine that proclaimed American punk rock to be dead, certainly did not. Perhaps in the hope of seeing a ghost, that summer's evening a ticket was secured to watch NOFX and The Offspring play a concert that offered no hint that the dam that separated punk from a broad audience was in any danger of breaking. If anything, the scene looked to be calcifying. In the United Kingdom at least, even the fortunes of California's most popular punk rock group were faltering. That same summer an appearance by Bad Religion at the Town & Country Club in London's Kentish Town attracted barely five hundred people to a venue designed to house four times this number.

Tickets for the night's entertainment at the Powerhaus cost five pounds. Perhaps inevitably, those in attendance interviewed for this book hold differing memories of the evening.

The club was packed to bursting, says one. The room was full, but not prohibitively so, says another. Not a bit of it, says a third, the place was half full at best. Meanwhile, the author can't fully shake the notion that it was The Offspring rather than NOFX who headlined the three-hundred-capacity venue, possibly because just twelve months later their days as a support act would end forever.

Footage from that evening appears to have been shot from the middle of a slam pit. In the days before smartphones made cameramen and -women of us all, in 1993 handheld cameras could be the size of a toilet cistern, and it is a mystery quite how its owner secreted it past the venue's towering security detail. Those "dancing" in front of the stage will surely recall that the Powerhaus saw no need to invest in air conditioning; they might also remember that on this hot summer's night the room smelled of feet. Now on display on YouTube, here The Offspring have been molested by the passage of time. Noodles plays his guitar while shirtless, his hair constrained behind a baseball cap affixed backward. Dexter Holland is in the midst of his less than well advised "cornrow years." His arm's-length hair whips around like untamable strands of fusilli pasta threatening to take out the eyes of anyone who dares to look at it. But despite a look that has aged no better than an episode of *The Fresh Prince of Bel Air*, The Offspring sound good. Even the lo-fi standards of footage so amateurish that it borders on the avant-garde cannot fully obscure the energy and thrust of a song such as "Get It Right."

Their date at the Powerhaus was the first time the Orange County quartet had trodden on England's green and pleasant land. NOFX, on the other hand, were by this point veterans of the European touring circuit. On a previous visit, the band realized that their spiky, funny, irascible and dependably rebellious songs might help them attain a previously unthinkable status.

They might, they realized, be able to make a living from playing music. More unlikely still, it dawned on them that they might make a living from playing music *with each other*.

"I think it was '91 that we came back from a European tour with eight thousand dollars each," remembers Fat Mike. "That was also the year that I graduated from college. My wife at the time, she made nineteen thousand dollars working at a public relations firm. So the band was, like, 'We can do this.' At the time, that sounded crazy. But then again we'd just made eight grand each from a five-week tour, so, you know, it suddenly seemed possible."

To say that the first seven years of NOFX's existence constituted a "career" is to dress the word up in comically loose-fitting clothing. Formed in Los Angeles in 1983 by Fat Mike (Michael John Burkett) and guitarist Eric Melvin, the pair were soon joined by drummer Erik Sandin (nickname: "Smelly"). For five years the band splashed around releasing singles and EPs, none of which were any good, on small independent labels. Their cover artwork featured photos from an S&M session, while titles such as "The P.M.R.C. Can Suck On This" did at least show that they had the good taste to aim their displeasure in a direction likely to cause offence. As with every group featured in this book, NOFX recognized punk rock not as a means to an end but as an end in itself. They were durable, too, and happy to trundle off on no-hoper national tours from which other bands deserted their posts. Even the fact that the number of people attending concerts on their third US tour were fewer than those on their first did not deter them. Given that a young band has got to be going some to see a tiny audience *get smaller*, this is quite something.

"I've got to say, if there's one thing that NOFX is it's that we're the most improved punk band," says Fat Mike.

This is true.

"See, the first Bad Religion seven-inch, which they made after they'd only been together about four months, is great. The

Circle Jerks [first] record is great. The same goes for Social Distortion, for the Adolescents—all great. Our first two records were terrible, with our first one being particularly bad. It took us the first six years of our career, so from 1983 to 1989, until we got to the point where we could claim to be mediocre."

But a mere eight years after forming, NOFX discovered their mojo. The addition of Aaron Abeyta, otherwise known as "El Hefe," on guitar did much to help this cause. Abeyta is a multi-instrumentalist, a graduate of the Berklee College of Music, one of punk rock's finest lead guitarists and the man whose credit on one NOFX album comprised just one word: talent. El Hefe brought a fine ear to the group, not to mention an instinct for musical execution that eclipsed those of his new bandmates by a distance of many galaxies. These qualities married well with Fat Mike's emerging talents as a composer. Contrary as ever, the frontman's ability to craft songs had gone from an anti-talent to its opposite at exactly the point at which most writers realize that the skills they seek will remain forever out of reach. But from a stillborn start the group's leader became good at his job, and then very good indeed.

A number of the band's core constituents point to 1991's *Ribbed* as the point at which NOFX went from ringers to contenders. But it was with the release of their fourth album, *White Trash, Two Heebs And A Bean*, that the group emerged as swans from ducklings that were not just ugly, but deaf as well. The title is indicative of the glee NOFX take in their desire to offend. In 1992, the term "white trash" was reserved for snobs who felt superior to people who happened to have less money than them. A heeb is a Jew. A bean is a Hispanic. Then as now, this is the band's ethnic etymology. As such, the words used to describe it are theirs to reclaim as they wish. It is also worth noting that the album's working title was *White Trash, Two Kykes And A Spic*. In a rare instance of compromise, this option was jettisoned following complaints from a family member.

It remains a fine record, and one that features a number of the band's most fondly remembered songs. Many of the thirteen-track set's purest diamonds are secreted in the finer details. By now Fat Mike was emerging as a superior lyricist with a keen ear for a fine couplet. At one point a character is introduced who "spent fifteen years getting loaded / fifteen years 'til his liver exploded." Elsewhere, a same-sex encounter begins when a disillusioned straight female meets a new friend who "said my name's Louise / now would you take your clothes off please?"

Equally impressive is NOFX's ability to be both serious and humorous, qualities that are at their most effective when combined. On the one hand "Johnny Appleseed" is a deeply loveable two-and-a-half-minute skit about a Mexican American who earns his living as a gardener. There he is "making sure that the garden grows / (yeah, yeah, yeah) watering the yard with the gardening hose." Sung with irrepressible delight by El Hefe, the song stands up to repeated listens even a quarter of a century on. But there is a mischievous and even a subversive edge here. "Johnny Appleseed" is a song about the perceptions of race. In Los Angeles, many, if not all, gardeners are of Mexican descent; ergo, many white Angelinos think of Mexican Americans as hired help. In a brief spoken-word section, a clipped-voiced record executive enthuses about Johnny's marketability to what he surely imagines to be the same suburban demographic that at the time was falling heavily for urban rap music. "He's very hip, very gang, very Hispanic" is the description.

By the time NOFX planted their feet on English soil in the summer of 1993, they had been a fully minted touring band for eight years and visitors to Europe for five of those years. On their earliest US caravans they came home with fifty dollars each. On one tour the band kitty amounted to eighty bucks. By the standards by which they were then operating, this seemed to them to be a fabulous sum of money. But the kitty was kissed goodbye when the van in which they were traveling burst a tire. During these times NOFX really were winging their way around the world. But as Fat Mike says, "It was fine because we didn't know any different and no one bitched about it."

"I got our first tour in '85," he says. "We rode in a station wagon, but there were three of us so that was fine. There was a lot of room to lie down if you wanted to. But our first European tour was done under the worst conditions. We drove around with [support band] Drowning Roses, plus a driver and a tour manager. And we had no trailer. So there were nine people in the van, plus our equipment. We were sitting in there with our knees on our guitars, kind of like you would [when praying] in church for a long, long time. We had one drive from Rome to Munich that took twenty-two hours. So those were the conditions that we drove around a whole continent in. Luckily for us, in Europe there were squats that we could stay at, or else someone's house. But sometimes we did have to drive all night. But, you know, who cares?"

For their visit to Europe in support of *White Trash, Two Heebs And A Bean* NOFX was riding aboard a tour bus. In the context of punk rock, in 1993 this could hardly have been any less exotic were it a Boeing 747 piloted by John Travolta. It is remarkable to recall just how much currency those in the scene invested in the mode of transport utilized by the bands they admired. The gold standard was Operation Ivy and Rancid, both of whom had toured in cars. The latter did so through a frigid European winter in a vehicle with a broken heater. Vans were the most common form of transport; the more people crammed inside, the greater the moral purity. Anyone with ideas above punk's proletarian station rode in a tour bus, a display of bourgeois largesse that in a different age would have seen its inhabitants shot by Bolsheviks.

On Bad Religion's entertaining long-form video "Big Bang," released in 1992, there is an amusing interlude during which

Greg Graffin—posing, one presumes, as a stereotypical fanzine interviewer—quizzes Brett Gurewitz about the band's decision to tour Europe in a bus.

"Why choose a tour bus over small vans, small inconspicuous vans that you could just sneak into the clubs? Is it because of the autograph thing? Do you want to people to recognize that you're popular? What is it?" he asks.

"Well, actually last year we had two beat-up bread trucks that we traveled in, rather than a bus," is the answer. "And actually they cost more money than the bus. So our tour manager . . . got us a bus and we're all quite happy with it."

"So it's cost, then. All you're worried about is the expense?"

Struggling to suppress his laughter, Gurewitz points a metronomic finger at his bandmate and says, "No, mister, I never said that!"

"No, I distinctly heard you say that the only thing you're interested in is making money," says Graffin.

NOFX shared their bus with The Offspring. There were berths for twelve people, and thirteen traveling passengers. Usually it was Noodles who volunteered to sleep on the floor. Fat Mike can't speak highly enough of Noodles. He laughs at how the week before the interview for this book he found himself in a restaurant in Orange County waiting for Eric Melvin. Remembering that this was the neighborhood around which The Offspring guitarist lives, he placed a post on Instagram and suggested he join him. In short order the most famous spectacle-wearer in punk rock came smiling through the door.

As NOFX's tour bus negotiated its way through London's spiderweb streets, a few miles north of the Powerhaus the life of a young London woman was about to change. On the afternoon of the July 7, Chrissie Yiannou didn't know that in just a few hours' time she would be attending her first punk rock show. Were it not for her sister's boyfriend, Chico, stopping by the house and, apropos of nothing, inviting her to a concert at the club on Islington's Liverpool Road, she would not have seen either The Offspring or NOFX that night, and perhaps never would. At the time a metalhead with a fondness for the noisier end of that market, Chrissie said that, yes, she'd love to spend an evening watching bands she didn't know in a club in which condensation dripped from the ceiling. Just hours later, she was left so impressed by NOFX's set that she hustled her way backstage to relay this verdict to the band personally.

"I went to see Fat Mike after the show and said, 'When are you coming back?'" she recalls. "And he said, 'We're never coming back. Never coming back. England hates us.' And I said, 'No, that's not true, it's just that they don't know you. If they knew you it'd be a different story.' Apparently that tour wasn't a success. I remember walking around the Powerhaus and it was quite empty. But I'd loved them so much that I really wanted to see them play live again. So I said, 'If you'll let me I'll book your next [London] show. I'll make sure that everyone knows about it.' And he said, 'Fine. Well, if you do that we'll come back.'"

At the time, Chrissie Yiannou was working without much heart for a small independent music public relations firm. She was being paid a standard wage for a music-business apprentice; in other words, nothing. None of the publications toward which her employer punted bands had heard of NOFX, let alone considered writing about them. When it came to booking a concert, Chrissie knew nothing. But she'd made a verbal commitment in a world where such things mattered as much as mafia oaths. In the days before tightly worded *New Yorker*–length record contracts and lawyers with eyes like a bird of prey's, one's word of honor was a cherry that could be popped only once.

Chrissie Yiannou may have been a punk for no longer than the time it takes to listen to a punk song, but just as quickly she learned two of the movement's most important codas: think on your feet and make something happen. She knew of a large record shop on Berwick Street in Central London—at the time a thoroughfare teeming with such establishments—that smelled of vinyl and in which could be found all manner of homemade punk fanzines. She bought every one and wrote a letter to each of them. I'm putting on a show, she said, a band called NOFX, please come. Two or three months later, each "zine" ran her request. She learned of a company called CNL, based in the East Midlands city of Nottingham that at the time was the only outfit in the country that booked overseas punk acts. She spoke to man called Johnny, the booker who had only recently lost the sleeves of his shirt booking NOFX and The Offspring on the tour that had so inspired the phone call he was now fielding. I don't know, he said, we lost a lot of money that last time we brought the band over.

"He wasn't very confident," Chrissie remembers. "In fact, he wasn't confident at all. But I was, like, 'Please, just let me. I believe in them so much.'"

"Okay, okay. So at which club do you want to book them?"

"The Garage."

"Do you mean the one in London?"

"Yes."

"Erm . . ."

Just a mile from the Powerhaus, the Garage stands on the north side of Highbury Corner in Islington. Today the club has undergone the kind of facelift favored by Joan Rivers, but in 1994 it was a low-ceilinged club that was at least as dark as a coal mine. Its floors were sticky from beer bought at the bar that ran the length of the rear wall. The sound-desk was inside a cage. Behind it, merchandise was sold, sometimes from a suitcase. The toilets smelled as if they might in fact be a secret portal to hell. The stage stood near the foot of two invisible stairs seemingly designed to break the ankles of paying customers. Much to the annoyance of professional concert photographers, the stage was unprotected by security barriers. Anyone who fancied joining a band onstage easily could, and on some nights many did. The Garage distinguished itself from the Powerhaus only in that its capacity was more than twice as large.

With a sound like a washing machine enduring a nervous breakdown, Chrissie Yiannou sent faxes to Fat Mike in which she placed a positive spin on what were fast becoming local difficulties. "Hi, Mike," she'd write, "Great news! We've sold fifty tickets so far!" failing to add that six hundred and fifty tickets remained on sale. She'd tell him that lots of fanzines were hoping to interview him, a revelation about which he seemed pleased, at least to a point. A reply would arrive comprising three words— "Thanks! Love, Fat"—written in a scribble. For these efforts Chrissie was paid not a penny. As show night neared, the pressure began to build.

"I used to wake up in the middle of the night sweating at the thought that no one would turn up," she remembers. "In fact, I used to wake up in the middle of the night sweating at the thought of *the band* not turning up. I don't think I ever really believed that they would come."

In the 1990s, the numbers of people who might attend a concert in any venue smaller than a theater were difficult to predict. Today almost no one will arrive at a gig without first having booked online. In earlier times tickets could only be bought from record shops, or else from the venue itself. If ordered by phone, tickets would then be dispatched by post. One formula for estimating the night's gate was to multiply by three the number of advance tickets sold. The larger percentage was known as the "walk-up." But this method was prone to wild and unpredictable variables—the weather, say, or the night of the week, or a strike on public transport. Yet in the then hard-to-come-by-information age, this was as close as the small-market end of the concert business came to statistical analysis.

On the afternoon of July 1, 1994, the lovely Highbury Fields park at the rear of the Garage's loading doors was littered with punks drinking beer and taking in the air of a fine summer's day. As the shadows lengthened in the evening sun, seven hundred people could be seen queuing along the Holloway Road from the venue's front doors.

"On the day of the show I was so nervous," says Chrissie. "I remember I went to the venue at about three o'clock and there was already a queue. Punks from all over the country were gathered outside. I just couldn't believe it. And that was the beginning of something, when very easily it could have been the end."

NOFX rewarded Yiannou's unpaid efforts in the name of their cause with a paid position as their UK publicist. The Offspring followed suit, as did the entire roster of Epitaph Records. From a spare room in her mother's house, she sat at a black-and-white Brother computer next to a sewing machine and sent CDs to magazines and fanzines across the country. She spoke by phone and via fax to independent artists and to a record label owner whose circumstances were about to change to an extraordinary degree.

Almost by accident, the British conduit through which independent American punk bands would reach the homes of many was open.

U p in the East Bay, Lawrence Livermore was allowing himself a chuckle at the complications of unexpected success. By 1994, Lookout Records had three commercial success stories to its name: *39/Smooth* and *Kerplunk*, the first two albums by Green Day, and Operation Ivy's *Energy*. The two artists had become the capstones against which many of the label's other bands measured themselves. The reason that this pair were the company's most successful acts, and their most successful by a great distance, was because they were better than the rest. But for all its ideals of unity and fraternity, punk rock cannot remove itself fully from human nature. Many bands in each scene were riven by a rivalry that was sometimes good natured and sometimes not. Keen to keep up with the Armstrongs, some of Lookout Records' other artists were making demands of Lawrence Livermore. We want you to spend the same amount of money promoting us as you did promoting Operation Ivy and Green Day, he was told time and again. As if speaking to children, Livermore would answer that the promotional budget for both of these bands combined was "about two hundred dollars."

Lawrence Livermore arrived so early on the scene with Green Day that the band were not yet known by this name. For two years they had been called Sweet Children. The decision to make a change was made after the band realized that the name bore too close a resemblance to a group called Sweet Baby Jesus, who later became Sweet Baby. "For a time I thought Green Day was a terrible name," says Livermore. "I realize now that it's a name that you can grow into and which over time can mean different things. But at the time I thought it was stupid."

When Sweet Children joined the Lookout roster in 1989, its members were even younger than those of Operation Ivy. Billie Joe Armstrong and Mike Dirnt were both just sixteen years old. By this time, Lawrence Livermore's intention of issuing records by bands whose talents might otherwise have gone unnoticed was becoming a reality. His definition of a successful record was one that managed to recoup its costs; anything else was gravy. "I think I had quite a good ear for spotting bands that would be successful in that way," he says. Livermore says that he recognized the talent of a band that in six months' time would become Green Day the first time he heard them. What's more, he recognized that other people would, too.

"I immediately knew that they were special," he says. "I'm probably showing my age here, but I can only compare them to the Beatles. That's what I thought about them. I was seeing them playing in this little cabin by candlelight and I remember thinking, 'This is what it must have been like standing in a room with the Beatles when they were just getting started . . .'

I wouldn't have made this comparison for any other group that I've ever seen. But it's the only one I could make for them. I don't want to make it seem like I was all seeing and that I knew that they were going to be the biggest band in the world or anything. I've made sweeping pronouncements many times in my life and been spectacularly wrong. But there's been a few times when I just quietly knew and didn't shout it to the heavens or anything. And I just quietly knew that they were really astounding and that the music they were making was really good.

"But of course there's always many a slip between cup and lip, and I've seen many good bands that were on their way to great things only for it all to fall apart. And that could have happened to Green Day, because they were only sixteen years old. But I thought, 'They *could* be the next Beatles.' I just kind of knew it on some level."

But while Lawrence Livermore knew this, others as yet did not. The absence of paths beaten to their door meant that when it came to recording music, the band were bereft of options from which they could choose. There was no bidding war. There was only Lawrence Livermore, a good guy with a noble idea and the means of production. So Sweet Children joined forces with Lookout, the record company equivalent of the Battersea Dogs & Cats Home. By the time of the release of their first EP, the four-track *1,000 Hours*, released in April 1989, the band had become Green Day.

"There wasn't a lot of joining [Lookout] in those days," says Livermore. "All of us were outcasts that nobody took seriously. Green Day were so young at the time that the idea of being on a record didn't really compute with them that much. So when I said to them, 'I want to make a record with you guys,' Billie Joe's answer was 'Er, yeah, okay.' And that's all there was to it . . . Nobody else was interested in putting out records by them. I was kind of the crazy guy who was willing to do it."

Billie Joe Armstrong and Mike Dirnt have been friends for more than thirty-five years. The pair first met in the fifth grade after their respective schools merged in the oil refinery town of Rodeo, California. They shared classes in which Mike made Billie laugh. The pair's first conversation in the school canteen was about music. Dirnt could play the piano by ear and was obsessed with the radio. His new friend owned a Fernandes Stratocaster guitar, bought for him by his mother, which he named "Blue" and would play for at least some part of every Green Day concert the band have ever performed. A few months after Mike Dirnt had met his new friend, Billie Joe's father fell ill and did not recover. The son was absent from school for a week or two, but when he returned the bond with his future bandmate grew stronger. Billie was suddenly looking at a life without a father. Mike's parents managed a bar and so were out of the house when he was not. As a result, the pair were left to find their own entertainment. This they did by stealing cassette tapes, firing bottle rockets and speeding down the hills of their hometown strapped inside of shopping trolleys. Billie Joe Armstrong would later remember these times fondly in the song "Outlaws."

As well as this, the two teenagers would sit in each other's bedrooms making mix tapes. During this period Billie Joe was a war zone of anti-fashion. The eldest of five children, his hand-me-downs came not from siblings but from friends. He wore the same school shirt for six consecutive semesters. He had a business-up-top-party-at-the-back mullet. Both he and Mike Dirnt were besotted with the idea of becoming professional musicians. This pursuit fostered in them a keen work ethic, if not at first a reliable sense of direction. According to Lawrence Livermore, the pair spent money making professional-sounding demo tapes of songs that he describes as being "metal tinged," and which he also describes as being "not very good." Billie Joe Armstrong himself is on record as saying that were it not for punk rock, he may well have ended up as a guitarist in a speed-metal band. He escaped this fate with the help of a seven-inch single on which could be heard a song that would prove as important as any in his teenage years.

In the middle part of the 1980s, England's Billy Idol was a superstar the world over. His charismatic sneer was so elastic that Billy Bragg once joked that it could only have been manipulated by a roadie at the side of the stage pulling on a length of fishing wire. In 1976, this platinum-blond-haired Londoner was one of the city's original punks. Yet despite talent and ideas, his band, Generation X, were never really afforded the success or respect their music deserved. But in a bedroom in Rodeo, California, a teenage boy was listening to the particularly English song "Kiss Me Deadly"—"the snooker hall is empty 'cos they're all out playing pool / hustling down the Fulham Road doing deals with Mr. Cool"—and wondering if he, too, could write a song that combined the tunefulness of the original British Invasion with an energy that he had yet to identify as belonging to a genre called punk rock.

In 1987, aged just fifteen, Billie Joe Armstrong and Mike Dirnt formed Sweet Children, perhaps in an attempt to secure copyright on the worst band name of all time. The group played their first show at Rod's Hickory Pit in Vallejo in the autumn of that year. A further six shows appeared on the docket for 1988. By far the most prestigious of these was a booking at 924 Gilman Street in the last week of November. Over the course of the next three months, Sweet Children appeared at Gilman a further three times.

"You have to remember that we got into a band at exactly the same time as we got into punk rock," Billie Joe Armstrong told the author in 2004. "Most bands have two years to get themselves ready, but we didn't do that. For us it was more or less simultaneous."

The final piece of a puzzle that neither Billie nor Mike knew needed solving came in the shape of the hyperactive drum prodigy Tre Cool. In the autumn of 1988, Sweet Children were booked to play in a cabin on the grounds of a house in the Northern California mountains. The outbuilding had no electricity, while the land on which it stood had a padlock on its front gates. The band and their Volkswagen van managed to make their way in—"breaking and entering" being the technical term—and, powered by a generator, played by candlelight to eight people. (This also happened to be the occasion on which Lawrence Livermore saw the group for the first time.) Packing up their equipment for a drive home that while long was at least downhill, they heard a teenager playing on a drum kit in a manner superior enough for the group's two-man string section to widen their eyes in each other's direction. In more than one sense, Tre Cool's timing was perfect.

Sweet Children were beginning to be compromised by structural deficiencies that while not yet critical were nonetheless starting to nag. Their drummer, Al Sobrante, known to his mum as John Kiffmeyer, was the trio's senior member by two years. His organizational skills allowed Billie Joe Armstrong and Mike Dirnt to act like children raised on a diet of methamphetamine and Sunny Delight. Kiffmeyer was the one who had connections to Gilman and who introduced Armstrong and Dirnt to the scene that first defined them. But the drummer saw Green Day as being just one of a number of things that occupied his time. As well as being the band's drummer, he also planned on attending college. He didn't much fancy heading out on the road for the group's first-ever tour. On top of this, his playing was not much more than adequate.

When John Kiffmeyer enrolled at Humboldt State University, Green Day were suddenly in the market for a new beat. In one of the shorter tenures in punk history, for less than a month, Dave EC, the drummer for the fabulously named Wynona Ryders, filled this role. But the union didn't hold and once again Billie Joe Armstrong and Mike Dirnt were on the prowl for a third partner. It is a source of argument between Billie and Lawrence Livermore as to whether or not the guitarist first played with Tre Cool on a guest appearance with the Lookouts in the summer of 1990. What is not in doubt is that the drummer was friendly with the now two-piece Green Day. Billie Joe remembers that the first time he actually met Frank Edwin Wright III he was wearing "this weird old man's plaid suit none of which was color coordinated whatsoever" and a swimming cap. Billie was drinking with a couple of girls who recognized Tre Cool as a member of the Lookouts. After hearing them call his name, the drummer simply turned and bowed, a move the guitarist thought was most impressive. When in November of 1990 Armstrong and Dirnt asked him to join their band, Tre said yes.

It wasn't at first a perfect musical marriage. Like players such as Charlie Watts, Max Weinberg and Pete Thomas, today Tre Cool plays a kit comprised of just five drums. "Five is all you need," he once told the author. At the start of the 1990s, he played a red Pearl kit with bass-drum-mounted double tom-toms and two floor tom-toms. He played with a technique that was youthfully ostentatious. When Mike Dirnt says that their newest recruit's style "was kind of too much," it's difficult not to summon the image of Animal from *The Muppet Show*.

"We were trying to let him figure it out, but really a couple of things had to happen: he had to sort of dumb it down and I had to step up my game," he says. "But the way Tre and I play now is like we share an unspoken language. We can look at each other and just start doing certain things and it will happen."

"Music is Tre's whole life, as it is for Billie and Mike," says Lawrence Livermore. "Even then, that's what he did. That's what he was. He was pretty much a perfect match and I think time has proved that to be correct. But at the time that Tre joined, I didn't really know if it would mesh. I did know that he was good enough technically but I didn't know whether his style would fit with theirs. But when I saw the three of them playing together, it was obvious that they'd moved into a whole new dimension."


I t's feasible to wonder whether without music Billie Armstrong, Mike Dirnt or Tre Cool would have ever made it to Europe. But at a time when few American listeners cared about domestic punk rock, there existed a musical underground railroad that offered beleaguered bands safe passage to foreign countries in which they might glimpse the possibility of a better future.

In the summer of 1989, Bad Religion took an eleven-hour flight from Los Angeles's LAX to Schiphol airport in Amsterdam, to begin a run of nineteen concerts in as many nights. The excursion took in the sights of West Germany, as it then was, the Netherlands, Belgium, Austria, Switzerland, Italy and the United Kingdom. The band traveled on tourist visas and slept in small rooms above the clubs in which they were playing. Failing this, they stayed in squats, one of which was raided by the police at four in the morning. A German driver named Kuxer ferried them around in a van. As well as this, this droll native was happy to disabuse his passengers of the notion that Germans want for a sense of humor. En route to a booking in Berlin, the monolingual Americans watched bemused as their driver spoke with an immigration officer manning a checkpoint at the Berlin Wall. After a volley of crushed vowels, Kuxer returned to his vehicle and with a steel voice told his charges that there was a problem. "He wants all of the Jews out of the van," he said.

"You have to remember that [Bad Religion] weren't enterprising young men even when we were old enough to be," says Greg Graffin. "We just saw [the tour] as an opportunity to go to Europe . . . We were seduced by the idea, so we went over to

Europe and to our great surprise we were able to find an audience . . . I remember we played in Essen, which is in Germany, or West Germany as it was at the time, and the line to get into the venue was around the block. The show was incredibly well attended; it was sold out. And here we were just flabbergasted that these German-speaking people knew all the lyrics. Many of them had homemade T-shirts that not only had the words 'Bad Religion' on them, but also had images of our first album, *How Could Hell Be Any Worse?,* silk-screened onto them. It was very flattering to us that here were these foreign-speaking people who really loved our first album, even though it was by then already six or seven years old."

By dint of having toured Europe with Circle Jerks two years earlier, in the dog days of the summer of 1989, Greg Hetson was Bad Religion's de facto seasoned veteran. Despite an air of impish innocence, the guitarist was experienced enough to know that on the US tour in support of *Suffer*, Bad Religion could count an audience that numbered in the low three figures as significant. He also knew that performing to a smattering of people in a large hall was something the band shouldn't take personally. Hetson's stoic durability had been hard won. He wasn't about to develop a teenage crush at the sweet nothings whispered into his ear by people with exotic accents.

"I remember we were getting all these offers to go and play in Germany, I guess because we were getting [orders for *Suffer*] from over there and the record was taking off," he says. "They were saying 'Come to Germany, come to Europe; you've got to come here, you're really taking off here!' I was thinking, 'Yeah, I don't know.' Because *Suffer* had had a slow start in the US, it was kind of crazy to be a band that couldn't get arrested over here [in the United States] but who were being told that we had to go to Europe. But we arrived in Germany and we were playing these squats and clubs and youth centers, all of which were completely overpacked and where people were overflowing into the streets. I would look out and see people jammed into this space that should have held four hundred people and think, 'What the fuck is this?' At the time the band was pretty much everybody's part-time job and we had no clue of our popularity. It was crazy. It was like Bad Religion mania."

Mike Dirnt likes to joke that the first time Green Day toured Europe was so long ago that he was allowed to smoke on the plane. "How many bands can say they smoked on a flight over to Europe?" he asked the author in 2004. The bassist also believes that "no group should be allowed to make an album until they've toured Europe first." Green Day were afforded the opportunity to do this with the help of three friends of Lawrence Livermore who shared a house in the London borough of Walthamstow. The Londoners—two of whom were English, the third an American—had a van they were willing to lend to visiting bands, or, even, in which they would ferry these bands around Britain and mainland Europe. The only thing required of the musicians themselves was a tourist visa, two or three guitars and a spirit of derring-do.

Green Day made their live European debut on October 25, 1991, with an appearance at the Ostbunker in the German city of Osnabrück. They arrived with armfuls of their own records, which, under questioning from immigration officials, they insisted were gifts for friends. Also on the bill that night were the group S.A.N.E, whom Billie Joe remembers as being "super punk." Despite having been outside the United States for less than forty-eight hours, the singer already had a lowering feeling about the fact that he had thus far failed to score pot. It was with relief that he spied the night's other band backstage engulfed in a cloud of smoke. It was here that Billie Joe Armstrong learned an important lesson regarding cultural traditions. Unlike in the United States, in Europe joints are rolled with tobacco. Begging a toke at the Ostbunker that night made the American feel sick. But it did get him high.

Green Day remained in Europe for almost ten weeks on a tour that seems to have been designed to weed out the weaklings who pay lip service to notions of death or glory. The going was tough to the point of being homicidal. Green Day may not have been the first band to fly east to chance their arm on a continent on which only two countries share a common language, but the circumstances under which they did this seem uncommonly grueling. Still teenagers, the trio played sixty-five concerts in little more than two and a half months, in often frigid weather. But Green Day were no arrivistes. Before disembarking in the Fatherland with jetlag and a German phrase book, in 1991 the band had already played more than a hundred concerts in the United States in places as far-flung as Alabama and Arkansas. They were fluent in the language of self-sufficiency, then as now the mother tongue of punk rock bands in the East Bay. This was not their first time at a rodeo staged far from home. Had it been so, surely they would never have survived it.

"When Green Day toured the UK and Europe the tour was not pleasant," remembers Lawrence Livermore, who joined the band on the tour's eight-date English leg in the deep and dark December of 1991. He arrived red-eyed at Heathrow Airport hefting two boxes of Green Day records. Employing the tactic of talking until the listener loses the will to live, he convinced a customs officer that the albums were not intended for sale in the United Kingdom. "Central heating was not at the time universal, so I remember being cold a lot," he says. "I remember making do. But it was exciting, too. The fact that some kids from our scene, some very young kids, were able to go across the ocean and play in this legendary land of England—that alone was enough. If they'd come over and played one show and had people applaud them and had somehow managed to get home again, I think that would have been considered a big deal."

Culture shocks abounded. For the first time in his life, Billie Joe Armstrong felt like he was becoming an informed citizen.

The band played and slept in numerous squats in which everything seemed to be political. In some cities the debates centered on opposition to local or national government. In others the conversation was about squatters' rights. He learned about socialized medicine free for all at the point of need. He couldn't believe that Europeans could damage themselves at their leisure and that a doctor would fix them without them being presented with a bill. He soaked things up like blotting paper. The band spent so much time in Germany that when they finally did return to California their frontman found that the rhythms of his speech had changed. Friends wondered why he was now speaking very slowly and without his usual accent.

"When we went to Europe we didn't know anything," he says. "And I mean, we didn't know *anything*. We were, like, 'Sure, let's book some shows in Europe!' But when we got [there], suddenly we were nervous. Some of the shows were scary. Suddenly we were playing shows with these other bands who were just tougher than us. I remember one of them was called So Much Hate. I remember that night thinking, 'Right, now we're playing with real punk rock bands.' For lack of a better comparison, I look at it as like when the Beatles were in Hamburg. We had that same communication barrier. We were in the situation where a band on tour has to lose their minds, and be able to find each other to try to make life make sense again. That's why people quit, because they start losing their minds. We felt like we were a bunch of clowns that were in a small car."

On some nights, Green Day would appear onstage wearing lipstick and wigs that they'd found somewhere along the way. Tre Cool would play on kits borrowed from drummers who threatened to kill him were he to change the sets' configurations, even though some of them defied logic. They joked with a woman at the door of a German squat about what she would do if they tried to steal the night's takings, to which she replied, "This" and pulled out a loaded gun. In a snowbound Copenhagen,

Mike Dirnt broke three of his four bass strings while playing to six people. One of these was so drunk that he took this level of destruction to mean the American was the greatest bass player who had ever lived. The band slept the night in the venue while a couple noisily had sex on the stage. Another night was spent sleeping in a storeroom alongside a human head preserved in a jar of formaldehyde. Predictably, their van broke down *all the time*, but only once caught fire. Their amps blew up *the day* they arrived. Such was the squalor in which they were living that Billie Joe contracted lice and had to shave every hair on his body save for that which grew from his head. Offered the opportunity to extend the tour by a further two weeks, the singer remembers thinking, "What's the·stupidest thing we can do? Sure, we'll do that."

"The more things that challenged us, the more I found out what kind of human being I am," he remembers. "It shows what you are willing to risk to get to the next gig. And it never felt like something we shouldn't be doing."

"The amazing thing about that tour is that you can never go back to it," says Mike Dirnt. "That's an experience I'll be able to think back on for the rest of my life. I understand it. If you don't do it before you get famous, you'll never be able to do it. It was one of the biggest learning experiences of my entire life. It was a very formative three months."

For Green Day, arriving in England was a moment of significance. On a later tour, the author remembers being in the band's dressing room in Las Vegas in which five framed photographs were hung on the walls. The images were black-and-white shots of the Beatles, Rolling Stones, Sex Pistols and the Clash; the fifth was a picture of Iggy Pop with fried-egg eyes. The country was also the birthplace of The Who and the Kinks, both adored by Billie Joe Armstrong. As well as this, London was of course the city from which Generation X exploded into life.

It is to be hoped that this wide-eyed sense of musical heritage helped inure Green Day to the fact that their first tour of the United Kingdom was taking them to some of England's least glamorous towns. The band unloaded their gear for a concert in Tunbridge Wells. They appeared on stages in Stoke-on-Trent and Hull. They played in the northern onetime textile town of Huddersfield without knowing that this was the place at which in 1977 the Sex Pistols performed their last concert on British soil for nineteen years. Held on Christmas Day, the gig was a benefit for striking firemen at which Johnny Rotten sliced cake and handed out presents to children.

On the year's shortest day, Green Day made their acquaintance with the Lancashire town of Wigan. On a night that saw the other bands on the bill at the Den club dress up as the Sex Pistols and Kiss, Green Day chose to celebrate the season by staging their own nativity play. Mike Dirnt, dressed in a Santa Claus outfit, narrated the scene. The band eschewed the three wise men in favor of one wise punk, a part played by Billie Joe. A friend of the band performed the duties of a midwife while delivering the baby Jesus, a role taken by Tre Cool. The production also featured a placenta made of soup and, for some reason, the Easter Bunny.

Two nights later, on the eve of Christmas Eve, Green Day headlined an evening at TJ's in the Welsh town of Newport, an event promoted as a "Cheap Sweaty Fun" gig. Support that evening came from the English group Knucklehead, whose hometown of Bath lay not far across the border in the southwest of England. Contenders they may never quite have been, but in terms of credentials the group were fully licensed. As an eighteen-year-old, the band's singer, John Montague, read about the Van Halle squat in a scene report in *Maximumrocknroll* and promptly moved to Amsterdam to live there. He simply knocked on the door and asked to stay for the summer. The building's outer wall featured a mural of Leatherface, the power-tool-equipped murderer from *The Texas Chainsaw Massacre*. Inside, free shelter was given to traveling Americans and Italians keen on avoiding national service. The Englishman became friendly with visitors from the United States who suggested that he visit them at their home in Oakland, an invitation that was accepted with haste. It was while in the Bay Area that John Montague saw "an absolutely incredible" band called Operation Ivy play at 924 Gilman Street.

In the dying days of 1991, the plan was for Green Day to spend Christmas with Sean Forbes, the frontman with the English punk humorists Wat Tyler. The only problem with this arrangement was that Green Day were keen on drinking and acting up while their host was partial to neither. Fortunately for the Americans, not to mention their intended host, the singer from Knucklehead was on-site with a counteroffer.

"I said to them, 'Come up to our house in Bath,'" John Montague remembers today. "We had this big old squat house, and on Christmas Eve they showed up and we fucked them up. We took them out around the town. I remember that Tre kept going on about how you couldn't get really good weed outside of California. He kept going on and on about it, so I took him to a friend of mine who gave him lots of Nepalese hot knives, after which he became a very, very ill boy. But we just spent the night tearing around Bath causing havoc, really."

Montague's memory of this festive period remains sufficiently alternatively minded that a question about what the squat had on Christmas Day is interpreted not as meaning dinner but, rather, stimulants.

"Oh, we didn't eat," he says, as if the very idea were as preposterous as sunbathing. "We were a bunch of twenty-year-olds living in a squat. Why would we want food? What we had was everything we could get our hands on. We had booze and we had a load of [magic] mushrooms and a lot of killer hash and we took it all and caused mayhem. It was a heavy one and it was a great one. We had electricity and power, so it was a proper party. Then we took them around the punk houses in Bath, and there used to be a lot of them, and we just got them wasted step by step. They were just decent people. I mean Tre didn't have an off switch, so occasionally he could have done with shutting up a bit from time to time. But really they were all great."

Barely two and a half years after finding room at the inn for three unwise kids guided by things other than a star, John Montague found himself at the Breminale festival in the German city of Bremen. Seeing that Green Day were on the bill that day, he hustled his way backstage in the hope of saying hello. Despite the band by now being well on their way to becoming famous, the Americans received their visitor and, following their set, headed out with him to decorate the town. As the evening blurred into double vision, Billie Joe lost at table football and paid the price of a wager by standing naked on the table and buying a round of drinks for everyone in the bar.

Three years after this, with more than twenty million album sales to their names, Mike Dirnt and Tre Cool were walking around a city in Italy when they came across a small doorway on a building covered with graffiti. They went inside and ordered two beers from the unlicensed bar. They drank and smoked a little hash. They watched impassively as some of the tenants beat up a fascist that had unwisely made his way inside. Then, with a smile and a nod, both men took their leave. The locals had recognized them but the pair knew from their time in Europe half a decade ago how to carry themselves correctly in such surroundings.

"During that first European tour was when we became Green Day," remembers Billie Joe Armstrong. "That's when we really became a band. It was in Europe that everything gelled. When we got back it was a whole different musical ballgame for us.

On our next go-round in the US and Canada we were playing to great crowds, and to bigger crowds. But after Europe we were ready for anything. Whatever could go wrong was going to be nothing next to what happened over there.

"It was great."

## CHAPTER FOUR

# I WAS A YOUNG BOY WHO HAD BIG PLANS

If any band in this book has been shortchanged of the respect owed to them, it is The Offspring. Many are the punks from this era who decry the music and achievements of a group that have been banging away for almost thirty-five years now. Despite being principal players in the cataclysmic change in punk rock's fortunes in the middle part of the 1990s, for some the group's rightful place lies beyond the city walls. This antipathy is about more than musical snobbery. In the fullness of time, Green Day, their neighbors to the north, escaped this fate. Billie Joe Armstrong himself once told the author that "The Offspring really don't get the credit they deserve." For while it took a number of years for many of California's second wave of punk groups to receive the critical acclaim owed them, for The Offspring the wait goes on.

"I remember seeing a list not that long ago of the best punk albums of the nineties," says Greg "K." Kriesel, the band's bass player and one of its three founding members. "It had Green Day and Rancid and Social Distortion and all the other bands on there, and we weren't even on the list. I see a lot of stuff like that. I remember the *Los Angeles Times* doing a thing in the late nineties about bands and their chances of getting inducted into the Rock and Roll Hall of Fame. They featured every band around at the time and what they estimated their chances were in terms of a percentage. And we weren't even on that list."

"We've never got a whole lot of critical acclaim, or critical notice, I don't think," says Noodles, the band's guitarist. "I don't know if we ever got nominated for a Grammy, even. I certainly know we've never won one."

As with every band featured in this book, The Offspring came together at the point at which forming a punk band was a daft idea. This was in 1984. Brian Keith "Dexter" Holland and Greg Kriesel were friends from their school's cross-country team. Kriesel remembers the pair listening to bands such as T.S.O.L. and Social Distortion, but stops short of describing himself and his friend as being punks. They didn't have the look and, in the case of Greg K., never would. But they did like the *otherness* of the groups and their sound. When it came to making their own music, it was more than the fact that a song by the Dickies was easier to learn than a track by Van Halen that led them to pursue punk.

Their first band was called Manic Subsidal, whatever that might mean, from which emerged The Offspring. Following a typical flurry of in-door-out-door early-day members, the lineup began to coalesce with the addition of guitarist Kevin Wasserman and drummer Ron Welty. Wasserman was given the nickname "Noodles" by the band's first producer, Thom Wilson, due to his tendency to play nonsense guitar doodles on recording tape whenever he failed to successfully finish a take. At first his invitation to step in with the band was casual and intended to last for no more than one or two concerts. But the guitarist knew a good thing when he heard it and hoped that his stay might be made permanent. He recognized that Dexter Holland's songs were much better than those written by anyone with whom he'd previously played.

"When Dexter asked me to join I said, 'Absolutely!'" he remembers. "But it was just punk rock. I loved the music, I loved the songs, but I didn't think it was really going to go anywhere. I didn't think it was going to be a career. Even to think that back then was ridiculous. If you'd said to anyone, 'I'm in a punk band and that's what I want to do for a living' they would have laughed in your face."

"First of all we simply wanted to learn our instruments and write songs," remembers Greg K. "Then when things got going and we started playing shows it was just a question of taking things as far as we could. At the time that would be something like Bad Religion, although I don't think we really believed that we could take it as far as they had. I guess we hoped that maybe we could play a show at the [Hollywood] Palladium or something. That was pretty much as far as you could aspire at the time as a punk rock band. You couldn't think about having a song on the radio or about being on MTV or selling millions of albums or anything like that. That would have been crazy."

In the years prior to 1994, Bad Religion represented the high-water mark to which all punk rock bands aspired. Today the group are the scene's tribal elders, but in the years that followed the release of *Suffer* they were its leaders in ways both commercial and creative. On the title track of 1989's *No Control*, Greg Graffin wrote and sang the words "there's no vestige of a beginning / no prospect of an end / when we all disintegrate it will all happen again" and in doing so delivered a stanza so devastatingly complete that other punk rock songwriters must have lost the will to live for at least a week. A year later, Brett Gurewitz began sewing into his band's fabric flashes of lyricism that at their best streaked like lightning across a darkening American sky. In the song "Walk Away" he writes of an elderly man who advises a youthful listener that "there comes a time for a man to walk away." The younger man notes that "fantastic the panic that shone in his eyes / [but] he shrugged when I asked him about it." The track is the final song from 1990's *Against the Grain*. On the day of its release the seventeen-song set shipped an at the time unheard of figure of a hundred thousand copies.

By this point Epitaph was on its way to becoming the Tamla Motown of punk rock. While the label's roster had not yet burgeoned to include most of the best of the Southern Californian groups, its status was fast becoming impregnable. Certainly, it was the label to which a young aspiring band would first send a demo tape. The Offspring did this as far back as 1988. But Brett Gurewitz was already approaching the point at which he could afford to be choosy. Politely, he told Dexter Holland that at this time he couldn't offer the band a home.

"I was very familiar with them already because they were a punk band in the LA scene," Gurewitz recalls. "They had sent me their demos, periodically. In fact, for their first album I declined to sign them. I thought the demos were good but not really good enough to make me want to take the plunge."

All the same, Brett Gurewitz did keep an ear on The Offspring. Spurned by Epitaph, in 1989 the quartet released their self-titled debut album on the small Nemesis label. Mr. Brett listened and liked what he heard well enough. He appreciated the fact that the record clearly owed a large debt to T.S.O.L., a band he loves. As the months turned into years, and as The Offspring prepared to record a second album, Dexter Holland continued to send demo tapes to Epitaph. The owner recognized that the group were improving and had developed a stronger sense of melody. He thought they'd taken a creative step forward, so he signed them. It's a story that doesn't sound much like love at first listen.

"At the time I signed them, I remember going to see them at a small club on Melrose called the Anti Club," he says. "It was a place that used to hold punk gigs. I think it held about two hundred people and that night there were ten kids there. That's the level they were at. They were a good opening band who would sometimes get good support slots, and they were a band who would get good crowds at parties. But as a headliner, at that time their draw was ten or fifteen people."

For Epitaph, this was small beer. As well as being home to Bad Religion, who along with Fugazi were one of only two bands of their type to sell more than a hundred thousand copies of their albums, the label boasted a roster that included NOFX, Dag Nasty, Pennywise, the underrated Down By Law and L7. By now the company was selling a million albums a year. Half of these were bought by listeners in the United States, the other half by fans in mainland Europe. For the most part, the audience in the United Kingdom would remain largely indifferent to the label's wares until 1994.

As a young business student was about to learn, Epitaph responded to this steady upturn in their fortunes by upgrading their operation not at all. In 1989, Jeff Abarta was just another college major on the hunt for an internship for which he was sure he wasn't qualified. Hearing that Bad Religion had their own record label, he bought one of the band's albums. He was pleased to see that the address printed on the back sleeve was in the city in which he lived, Los Angeles. At three o'clock one weekday afternoon he placed a call to Epitaph's office and hung on the line to a point somewhere in the distant future. Eventually a machine asked him to leave a message. To his surprise, his call was returned by Jay Bentley, who combined the role of bassist in Bad Religion with a job as the label's warehouseman. At the time, Epitaph was staffed by two people, Gurewitz and Bentley. Occasionally, NOFX's Fat Mike would pop over to lend a shoulder to the wheel. If Bad Religion happened to be on tour, the only sound emanating from the label's office was that of gently rolling tumbleweeds.

Brett Gurewitz knew that Epitaph needed help, but he wasn't sure what form this help should take. Like a nagging toothache, over the proceeding months Jeff Abarta called to offer his services with tiresome regularity. With a gravid sigh, the label's owner finally agreed to give the young hustler an interview. "We'll see what happens," he far from promised. In a strategy unlikely to earn him the title of Young Business Person of the Year, Abarta revealed that he'd willingly work for free. To Mr. Brett, these sounded like acceptable terms. Twenty-seven years on, Jeff Abarta still works at Epitaph, presumably now for money. In his rookie year he was given the job title "master of time and space." Today he is the label's product manager. In time he would be immortalized by NOFX in the song "Jeff Wears Birkenstocks." He also plays in a band with the untouchable name Punk Is Dead.

"My interview was in a house," Abarta remembers. "It was sort of behind the Palladium, right in the middle of Hollywood. And that house was also shared with Westbeach Recorders. They were literally recording the records in one room and then Brett was putting them out in the other room. By the time I actually started, Brett had found another space on Santa Monica [Boulevard] which was literally just a big warehouse space that had shelves and offices in the front and a big garage door in the entranceway. We got in and out of the building by lifting up the garage door, although we did eventually cut a walk-in door into it. We had a desk with a pile of mail in the corner. There was no copier. We did have a fax machine but we had to make a photocopy and then run it through the fax machine. There were no computers. There was a phone and there was a desk with paper and pens on it. And that's it. That should give you a sense of how bare bones it was back then."

Around this time, Westbeach Recorders moved to an address on Hollywood Boulevard where it would remain until its closure in 2010. As was the case with most bands on Epitaph, this was the studio at which The Offspring convened in the summer of 1992 to record *Ignition*, their second album. The notion that at the time of its making the record wasn't a big deal is supported by the fact that no one seems to remember much about it. "I want to say that it took a week or so, maybe a couple of weeks," is Greg K.'s uncertain estimation. "I guess we did most of [the album] at Westbeach," hazards Noodles, admitting that he tends to get his band's records from this period mixed up "because it was such a long time ago." Perhaps this haze has something to do with the fact that the band's world had not yet been lit by spotlights. It is as if the business of summoning memories of The Offspring prior to 1994 is akin to describing the moments that preceded the big bang. Even Brett Gurewitz seems to recall the band during this time as being part of a collective whole, rather than an entity unto themselves.

"In terms of sales, *Ignition* was coming along pretty strong," he says. "I think it had sold somewhere in the thirty or thirty-five thousand range. But I had a number of bands that were doing between twenty and fifty thousand. We had NOFX and Pennywise and The Offspring, and each of those groups was selling about thirty thousand records. At that time Bad Religion was the only band that was shipping more than a hundred thousand copies."

The eighteen months that followed saw little change. In 1993, NOFX found their groove and released *White Trash, Two Heebs And A Bean*. Brett's own band unveiled *Recipe for Hate*, an album which, along with its predecessor, *Generator*, helped the group escape the corner into which by 1990 they'd painted themselves. Despite a production that lacks richness and depth, not to mention volume, Bad Religion's seventh album features songs—"Skyscraper" and the instantly perennial "American Jesus," to name two—as good as any to which the group had then put their name. But beneath the hectic beats-per-minute tempo of the music released by Epitaph, the sound emanating from Santa Monica Boulevard was of a label ticking along. The growth was sustainable and the produce was locally sourced. But for the most part everything the label did went unnoticed by the wider music industry with which Epitaph shared a city.

"Because Epitaph was a punk label I used to say that anyone that sold fifty thousand albums had gone 'punk rock gold,'" says Gurewitz. "Fifty thousand was punk rock gold because back in the very old days the biggest punk records were *Damaged* by Black Flag and *Group Sex* by the Circle Jerks. Both of those had sold fifty thousand, so that was the gold standard . . . So as Epitaph started getting bigger in the late eighties and early nineties, we started a tradition where if you sold fifty thousand albums you got an ice cream cake. That was the tradition: sell fifty thousand, get an ice cream cake. That's what we started doing because we thought we'd never get an *actual* gold record."

On the early afternoon of Sunday 18, July 1993, Bad Religion performed a thirteen-song set at one of England's shortest-lived summer gatherings. Staged at the Long Marston Airfield near Stratford-upon-Avon, the Phoenix Festival endured for just two years, and for good reason. Its site was remote, its surrounding area bereft of infrastructure and its lineups lacked both quality and cohesion. On the festival's second night some in the audience watched *Duck Soup* at the outdoor cinema while others indulged in a refreshing spot of rioting. The many thousands of people who opted to sleep off the previous evening's exertions did not miss a Bad Religion performance for the ages. Before a sparse crowd who had little idea of what they were watching, Greg Graffin gamely pointed his way through songs such as "Generator" and "Along the Way," while a parrot-blue-haired Brett Gurewitz pulled well-chosen chords from a guitar that looked as if someone had vomited on it.

Under cement skies, in the artists' enclosure the band had a guest. A few years previously Mike Gitter had been a music journalist for magazines such as *Kerrang!* and *Rip*, for whom he had done valiant work securing a measure of attention for bands such as Bad Religion and Social Distortion. By 1993, the young New Englander had become director of artists and repertoire at Atlantic Records in New York. It was in this capacity that he visited England in the hope of enticing Bad Religion away from the label that had been established in their name. Three years earlier, in a review of *Against the Grain*, Gitter had written that the group "only have one song—but it is a good song." Greg Graffin remembered this review but did not allow it to interfere with the charm offensive led by a man now wearing a different hat. Given the tale of intrigue and consequence that was already beginning to unfold in the court of Bad Religion, Mike Gitter's decision to make an appearance at the birthplace of Shakespeare is fitting.

"I remember going to the Phoenix Festival and saying hello to the band," he recalls. "I did know them anyway, so it was great to reconnect. Like many American A&R people of the time, I'd come up through the world of American underground music. I also knew the hardcore scene. And I knew how good Bad Religion were. So we signed them to a deal. The first thing we put out was a reissue of *Recipe for Hate* [in the United States] that actually ended up doing pretty well for us."

It is not meant as an insult to Bad Religion to say that in terms of nonmainstream guitar music, in 1993 American major labels would sign *anything*. Two summers earlier, Nirvana's "Smells Like Teen Spirit" had given millions of teenagers their generation's equivalent of seeing Elvis Presley on *The Milton Berle Show*. This was the point at which the world's best known record labels began tossing cash in the direction of sometimes bewildered and often unsuitable artists. Bands who twenty-two months earlier would not have made it past a reception desk were suddenly coveted like cheerleaders for the Dallas Cowboys. In these patently berserk times, groups such as the unmelodious Tad were signed to a major label (twice, in fact) while elsewhere Interscope Records threw 1.3 million dollars in the direction of the untested Helmet, not at all concerned that their songwriter, Page Hamilton, counted John Coltrane as his biggest influence. Sometime later, with punk rock taking flight, Mercury even handed a recording contract to the suddenly and rather suspiciously reformed Circle Jerks. The band duly delivered an album that was atrocious even by their latter-day standards. *Oddities, Abnormalities And Curiosities* sold a pitiful twenty-five thousand copies.

In this context, Bad Religion's decision to nestle under the wing of Atlantic Records can be seen as merely one more betrothal in a mass Moonie wedding. But there were crucial differences. The band *didn't* play alternative music; they played punk rock in its purest form. Their songs were fast and featured lyrics that by mainstream standards were esoteric and sometimes inapproachable. By the time of their defection, Bad Religion's members were in their late twenties and early thirties. Since their reemergence with *Suffer,* they had operated largely as a part-time concern. This they were able to do because their guitarist owned the record label on which their albums were released. For as long as the band had been in existence, Bad Religion and Epitaph were indivisible. Despite this, the group contracted their services to the label that now courted them.

Without sentiment, they left home.

"Until we were approached by Atlantic Records, I do think that I believed that Bad Religion's relationship with Epitaph would last forever," says Brett Gurewitz. "It never occurred to me that we might try signing to a major. Part of the reason for this was that I just didn't have the imagination. That might be hard to believe because today if there was a band selling three thousand tickets for a show in Los Angeles it would be absolutely unheard of that major labels wouldn't be trying to sign them. But that was just how it was. Major labels were not interested in punk rock in the nineties. In the early nineties major labels could care less about punk rock. It didn't matter how popular a band was, and I can't really explain why. I just wasn't part of that world."

"When Bad Religion left the label I seriously considered leaving," says Jeff Abarta. "They were the reason I was there in the first place. There were other bands on the label that I loved, or that I'd learned to love, but when Bad Religion left I was heartbroken. The reason that I didn't leave, ultimately, is because I believed in what Brett was doing . . . I just knew that I was in a special place at a special company and deep down I knew that I didn't want to give that up. But the day [Bad Religion] signed to Atlantic was an awful day."

Mr. Brett recalls Mike Gitter calling his office and telling him that Atlantic Records wanted to issue the band's next five albums. The guitarist expressed surprise and said that he was flattered. He also promised that he would speak with the other members of the group and return with news. The most invidious problem he faced was an obvious conflict of interest. As one of the three founding members of Bad Religion, it would have been negligent, and perhaps even illegal, not to present without bias an offer that at the very least was deserving of consideration. It was an opportunity the likes of which had never before knocked on the band's door. But what had started more than a decade earlier as an informal alliance to which no one concerned paid much mind had by 1993 become a sinuous web. As owner of Epitaph Brett Gurewitz was in effect his band's employer. Were Bad Religion to leave, Epitaph would lose its prime asset and biggest source of revenue.

"I felt that the right thing to do was to eliminate any possibility of my conflict of interest having any influence on the band's decision," he says. "I thought I should say that it was an interesting idea and that I was leaning towards it, which is what I did. What I wanted the band to say was 'Don't be crazy, Brett, we would never leave Epitaph!' But they couldn't have known this and I didn't blame them for not being mind readers. But, yeah, I was secretly hoping that they'd say that they wanted to stick with Epitaph. The truth of the matter is—and I don't want to sound smug or judgmental here—but the truth is that it was beneficial to me whatever was decided. But had they stayed with Epitaph I think it would have been better, and I think it would have been better for the band as well."

"What we did was not a crime," says Greg Graffin. "It was an opportunity. Yet some people seem to think it was some kind of major label sellout offence. The truth is that from day one Bad Religion was always looking for someone to sponsor us. If we could have signed to a major label on the first record, we would have done. But no one was interested . . . When I heard that there were major labels interested in us I was pretty darn excited. It was exciting to be taking meetings to see what kind of offers were on the table and what they could do for us. It seemed like the right thing to do and it seemed like the right time to do it. In retrospect, history offers the best explanation; and that was the point when Bad Religion went from being provincial and to the point where we spread out to the suburbs of America and out to the rest of the world. From the distribution we got from them [Atlantic], we could now play all around the world."

Greg Graffin calls this "the democratization of punk rock." In recounting the decision to sign with a major label he confirms that Brett Gurewitz did not plead the case for Bad Religion staying with Epitaph, nor did he make a counteroffer to the contract presented by Atlantic Records. He also points out that as a member of the band the guitarist was also obliged to sign this contract if the deal was to be bound. But Graffin does admit that a lot of his thinking was based on assumption and intuition. During this time the group's songwriters were not communicating on a daily basis. By 1994, the singer had moved from Los Angeles to Ithaca in upstate New York in order to enroll at Cornell University. It was from these boondocks that he watched the mainstream emergence of punk rock. In 1990, he remembers that only one record shop in town sold underground music, albeit one that did a brisk trade. The record store at the mall stocked not a single punk album. In time, Bad Religion CDs were to be found racked a dozen deep. One day Greg Graffin saw himself singing as one of the band's videos played on a giant screen on the shop's back wall.

The song in question was "Stranger Than Fiction," the title track from the group's eighth album and their first released under contract to Atlantic Records. Released in the spring of 1994, the fifteen-song collection was the first Bad Religion album since *Suffer* not to have been made at Westbeach Recorders, as well as the first to utilize the services of an outside producer. This job was handed to Andy Wallace, the man who had mixed Nirvana's *Nevermind* and who by this point was so hot that it was advisable to wear boxing gloves when shaking his hand. Kurt Cobain had entrusted his band's second album to him because of his work mixing Slayer's eternal *Reign in Blood*. Bad Religion, on the other hand, were more impressed by the fact that their producer had played the piano solo on Madonna's "Into the Groove."

Recollections of the recording of what would become one of Bad Religion's most significant albums vary. Greg Graffin remembers the process as being harmonious and even carefree. He describes the band playing street hockey outside of Rumbo Recorders in Canoga Park. He remembers Gurewitz contributing fully to the songwriting process, although perhaps less so in terms of musical arrangements. Without it becoming obtrusive, he did notice that his bandmate was quietly but obviously "extremely encumbered." Conversely, Greg Hetson recalls there being "a lot of tension between Brett and Greg," as well as a number of "ridiculous arguments." He recounts one debate about the definition of the word "power" that became a circular row regarding what can and what cannot be described as "powerful."

"There were a few times when it got tense," he says.

"There was a lot of acrimony," says Gurewitz. "There was a lot of shit-talking and back-biting. But at the same time I don't want to paint a picture of a wholly negative experience because that period was extremely creative. And it was extremely gratifying, creatively. Greg and I went into the sessions with some of our best songs . . . It was a really wonderful experience to work with the great Andy Wallace, who we really respected, and to be recording some of our best material. It was a great feeling to be at the top of our game working with a producer and sort of doing things at a higher level."

*Stranger Than Fiction* met its waiting public in September of 1994 and would eventually secure for the band their first and only gold disc. Yet despite their improved circumstances, Bad Religion remained too strange and too clever to be wholly appreciated by listeners who were less than fully attentive. It's difficult to imagine a line more devilishly sarcastic than Greg Graffin's observation that "your life is historically meaningful / and spans a significant time" from the well-judged "Slumber." Elsewhere, a song pondering the sociological and political implications of a handshake—"there is restrained passion, mistrust and bigotry / and these have created the new foundations of society"—is going some even by the band's own standards. Elsewhere, *Stranger Than Fiction* is infused with a sense of abandon that is deliberately demented. "Can you imagine / for a second / doing anything / just 'cos you want to? Well, that's just what I do / so hooray for me / and fuck you" is the deceptively simplistic chorus of the otherwise complex "Hooray for Me," written by Brett Gurewitz.

Asked to nominate the best of his own songs, Gurewitz suggests the title be awarded to "Stranger Than Fiction." (The award should in fact go to "Beyond Electric Dreams," but this need not detain us here.) That the song does not tower over its neighbors on its parent album is evidence of the overall quality of the band's most widely admired release. Along with its intellectual sophistication and lyrical complexity, "Stranger Than Fiction" is also a blast. From the resonant opening salvo of "Mother, father, look at your little monster" from "Incomplete," Bad Religion achieve immediate elevation and manage to keep themselves airborne for the duration of the set.

It was somewhere between the end of the recording of *Stranger Than Fiction* and its release five months later that Brett Gurewitz decided that the time had come for him to leave the group. A year later, in an eatery on London's Piccadilly Circus, Jay Bentley spoke as unkindly of his former bandmate as the author has ever heard one musician speak of another. Certainly, an argument between the two was the catalyst that cleaved the guitarist away from the band, even if today Mr. Brett cannot remember what the fight was about. Greg Graffin recalls there being a fight but believes that in retrospect his friend's notice to quit "was based on a lot of factors."

"Me and Jay were not getting along at all," says Brett. "We both had a lot of ego. We were both young and dumb."

Graffin was at home in Ithaca when Gurewitz called. His parents were visiting at the time and he remembers the house being busy. Even when the weather between them was far from cloudless, the two men still spoke every couple of weeks. Because of this the singer thought little of seeing his phone's caller ID announcing the guitarist's name on the line from Los Angeles.

"Hey, Brett," said Greg.

"Hey, Greg. I quit the band," said Brett.

Graffin recalls that the news "definitely put a chink in my entertainment plans for the afternoon." Yet during the course of the conversation the caller said something that in the long run proved to be a source of comfort. He said, "Look, if Van Halen can get along without their lead singer and become more popular, I'm sure Bad Religion won't miss their guitar player." Graffin inferred from this that his friend "still cared about the direction of the band, but for some reason had decided to take some time for himself."

"I think you have to look at [my leaving] in the framework that we were guys who had been in a band for fifteen years and who were still young," says Gurewitz. "It's hard to stay in a marriage for fifteen years, let alone in a band with four other people; four insane maniacs playing punk rock and taking drugs and doing everything else that we were doing. It took its toll and we were just not getting along anymore . . . I have to say that I was mad with the guys. But I also thought I'd made a sensible decision. I thought, 'Okay, my band's been going for fifteen years [now]. They left my label and I didn't hold it against them. And despite [them leaving] I wrote the best record that I could and gave it to them. I played it the best I could. I wrote the best lyrics that I could. I wrote the best songs that I could. I made sure it was great. It was something that I was giving to my band to show them that I loved them. It was something that I wanted to do. I was thirty-two years old and I thought that that was a dignified time to stop touring as a punk rocker and to start running my label and helping eighteen-year-olds make their punk records. I thought [of Bad Religion], 'You guys go for it, man, right until the wheels fall off.' But for me it was time to grow up and be a man. So that's kind of what it felt like."

A month after the release of *Stranger Than Fiction*, on a weekend in October, Bad Religion and Brett Gurewitz were in Amsterdam. The band were there to play a concert at the lovely Paradiso hall in the center of the city, while their erstwhile guitarist was in town to celebrate the launch of Epitaph Records' European office, a branch that remains open to this day. On the last night of the weekend, a member of Bad Religion's road crew dressed to look like Mr. Brett appeared onstage at the Paridiso only to have his trousers fall down following a kick to the rear from Jay Bentley. Twenty-four hours earlier, at a press conference called to announce the start of Epitaph's European campaign, Gurewitz was asked by the author if he found it at all ironic that his old band had left his company at the point at which Epitaph was fast becoming the biggest independent record label in the world.

"I think if you look in the dictionary that'll be the definition of the word 'ironic,'" was his answer.

**W**ithout realizing it Brian Baker spent a full year and a half preparing to step into the space in Bad Religion vacated by Brett Gurewitz. In 1993, the guitarist received an advance cassette of *Recipe for Hate* from someone in the Epitaph office with whom he was friendly. Waving goodbye to the staff on Santa Monica Boulevard, the then twenty-eight-year-old guitarist slid the tape into the stereo of his 1956 Plymouth Barracuda. Although a beautiful car, Baker's ride was in a shocking condition with which the state of its stereo was consistent. Brian Baker was able to insert his new copy of *Recipe for Hate* into the tape deck, but was then forever unable to eject it. The stereo's radio didn't work, either. For eighteen months the only option available to the driver was to listen to Bad Religion's now no longer new thirteen-track album. Toward the end of 1994, Baker sold the car to a friend. The enduring cassette remained wedged into the dashboard. This transaction constitutes the vehicular equivalent of selling someone a haunted house.

At this time Brian Baker was a punk without portfolio. As a founding member of the Washington, DC, teenage sensations

Minor Threat, his credentials were impeccable. But as with anyone who accomplishes a thing of influence during life's first act,
the question of what to do as an encore was proving problem-
atic. The fact that punks tend not to play encores was hardly
reassuring.

By 1994, Baker was slumming it. A spell as a hard-rocker as the
guitarist in the not convincing Junkyard reaped a barren harvest.
The punk rock group for which he was at the time second-best
known, Dag Nasty, did record an album for Epitaph—*Four on the
Floor*, released in 1992—but to claim that he and Brett Gurewitz
were close would be an exaggeration. By now a resident of Los
Angeles, Brian Baker did count Greg Hetson as his friend. The
pair were social animals and would often find themselves at the
same gatherings. With many a true word spoken in jest, without
fail the Bad Religion guitarist would hear Brian Baker's smiling
sales pitch: "If Brett ever quits, please give me a call. I would love
to be in Bad Religion . . . If any accident were to befall him, or if
he decides to join another group, think of me."

In 1994, Brian Baker was working at a rehearsal studio.
Aside from this there was nothing going on. An offer from REM
requesting his presence at an audition for the job of second guitarist on the Georgians' forthcoming world tour came as a great
surprise. The band had grown from onetime vanguard of American college rock into one of the world's most popular acts. Following a successful audition, Baker was offered the gig, which
he duly accepted. With perfect comic timing, he then received
a call from Greg Hetson. At the time the guitarist was in England with Greg Graffin—the pair were on the stump promoting
*Stranger Than Fiction*. With wry humor, the two men happily
posed for photographs while wrapped in a Union Flag borrowed
from a pole atop a Central London hotel. Interviewing them that
day, the author was not let in on the secret that Bad Religion
were looking to recruit a guitarist.

"Obviously I was thrilled to get the call," says Baker. "Of course I said that I'd love to try out. And I wouldn't say that it was a big choice between playing in Bad Religion and playing with REM. Obviously the REM job was high profile and prestigious, but it was still as one of the supporting staff. I wasn't actually going to be a member of the band or anything. And while I didn't immediately become a fully fledged member of Bad Religion either, the understanding was there that after I'd performed with them on tour and passed the get-to-know-you period there was a chance that I would. That's a big element of being in a punk rock band: do we get along? In a way, that's more important than learning a couple of songs and playing them well with the band. I was incredibly flattered that I was chosen by REM for a job where they could have taken their pick of anyone, literally hundreds of musicians. But with Bad Religion it was a case of 'Well, let's give it a try. Let's see if it works out.' And that's why I made the choice to go with them."

By replacing Brett Gurewitz with Brian Baker in the autumn of 1994, Bad Religion lost a songwriter but gained a guitarist. Within the space of single rehearsal it was clear that this change of personnel had immediately put right a fundamental flaw of the group's music. The truth was that when it came to guitar solos, Bad Religion were below code to a point of frightful deficiency. In the days when they would merrily speed their way through songs such as "I Want to Conquer the World," this hardly mattered. Since then, the band had progressed in every aspect of their music save for this one area. An excoriating guitar solo from Wayne Kramer, once of the MC5, on *Stranger Than Fiction*'s opening song, "Incomplete," highlighted the possibilities afforded by a superior player. It also cast stark light on the shortcomings of Greg Hetson and Brett Gurewitz. With the addition of Brian Baker, Bad Religion were no longer required to hack their way through a song's middle-eight section while sensible listeners held their breath until the point at which Greg Graffin resumed singing. Suddenly the band's musical arrangements were emboldened by the arrival of one of punk rock's most fluent and tasteful lead guitarists.

With immediate effect, Brian Baker was once more elevated to the status of full-time touring musician. The author remembers how during this time the guitarist joked that he opted to join Bad Religion rather than serve REM because "I've been broke all of my life, so why change now?" In truth a man who earlier that year had humped gear in a rehearsal studio was now tearing down punk rock's Park Avenue. The audience for the band with whom he was soon to become a permanent member was bigger than that of any group with whom he had played in the past. As Bad Religion rolled off on the tour in support of *Stranger Than Fiction*, Baker found himself in Europe playing the largest clubs in town. It was not uncommon for the band to perform to crowds of two thousand people each night. Support came from a fast emerging Green Day.

Green Day had first toured with Bad Religion on the group's tour of the United States and Mexico in the autumn of 1993, on an excursion that served as a kind of coming-of-age coronation for the Berkeley trio. Their fast-expanding audience was younger than that of the headliners and featured a more equal balance of male and female fans. At each date these supporters arrived early and in some cases left before the closing act had begun their evening's work. Green Day were ferried from city to city by Tre Cool's father. Frank Wright II also had a sideline breeding and selling Bassett hound puppies that he showcased on a homemade videotape. This was good enough for Greg Hetson to pony up for his first dog. He named him Gaylord.

"Green Day are really great people," he says. "I remember watching them on that [US] tour and just knowing they were going to blow up. I didn't know *how much* they were going to blow up, but I could tell that something was happening."

The tour's final North American date was at the Warfield in San Francisco. Remarkably, this was only the second time the trio had performed in the City by the Bay. Despite this curious omission, two and a half thousand people arrived in time to witness the not quite homecoming forty-five-minute support slot. "Sellout!" cried one audience member. "This is about you, buddy," was Billie Joe Armstrong's response as the band unpacked "Chump." Brett Gurewitz recalls watching Green Day play songs in sound check. He recalls sitting with the band listening to the recordings of new tracks. "We had a good time," he says. "I'll never forget hearing all those great songs . . . Those really were good times. I had a couple of kids who were young at the time and they'd come out and visit us on the road a bit. It was a good tour. I mean, it was a great time for music."

Perhaps as part of his then ongoing quest to sign every punk rock band in California, Mr. Brett did of course make it clear that the East Bay trio would be a welcome addition to the Epitaph family. It is tempting to imagine such an offer as representing some kind of crossroads for both parties. In truth, the approach was casually dressed. "I loved Green Day so I guess I probably did try to sign them," Gurewitz says. "[But] I don't know whether or not they came close to accepting. It was all just as friends back then. I was touring with [Bad Religion] and running the label, so it really wasn't a big deal."

(For his part, in 2004 Billie Joe Armstrong told the author that for Green Day the question of choosing the label for which they would leave Lookout was key. "The issue of selling out was kind of different to us," he said. "In our eyes, going to a major wasn't selling out. Going to a bigger indie would have been selling out. If we'd have gone to Epitaph, which is a label that wanted us and a label I respect, I would have considered that more of a betrayal to Lookout than us going to a major.")

And, anyway, it wasn't as if life on Santa Monica Boulevard wasn't becoming hectic enough as it was. In the summer of 1994, Epitaph released two albums in under a month, both of which raised the batting average of American punk rock to a steroidal degree. On the summer solstice the label unveiled *Let's Go*, the second album from Rancid, whose personnel included Tim Armstrong and Matt Freeman. A number of the people interviewed for this book claim that this is the band to whom Brett Gurewitz's heart truly belongs. He denies this, saying that "I love all of my bands," but does opine that Tim Armstrong is "the Bob Dylan of punk rock." At the very least the band are tellers of tales in the classic American tradition. Their vignettes paint rich portraits of life in their country's less salubrious quarters—San Francisco's Tenderloin, for example, or the East Bay itself—with both lyricism and empathy. In 1994, they did this in remarkably short order. Produced by Gurewitz, *Let's Go* cranks through twenty-three songs in under three-quarters of an hour, with almost half of these taking their leave inside of two minutes. In keeping with their later assertion that "we're not fucking around," the group recorded their greatly loved second album in under a week, at a rate of four songs a day.

The existence of Rancid also served to highlight one of the key distinctions between punk rock from the East Bay and its equivalent in Southern California: class. America likes to pretend that it functions without a class system, and the country's dirty little secret is that it does no such thing. By the 1990s, punk bands from the Los Angeles area and Orange County tended to be both suburban and middle class. Often they were the beneficiaries of further education and college degrees. Five hours north along Interstate 5, the options were more limited. Billie Joe Armstrong once told the author that were it not for the living provided by punk he would probably have found employment as "a TV repairman or a pool cleaner." These are jobs held by some of his friends, he said, sounding not at all troubled by the prospect of either. Yet despite this rough hew, compared with Rancid, Green Day were guests of honor at a royal wedding. It is all the more remarkable, then, that *Let's Go* became the first Epitaph record to make an appearance on the *Billboard* Hot 200 album chart, albeit at a lowly number ninety-seven.

Four weeks later, Epitaph Records issued *Punk In Drublic*, the fifth album from NOFX. After years of creative dwarfism, the band were by now in the midst of the kind of growth spurt normally associated with the planting of magic beans. Once the authors of albums comprised entirely of bad songs, *Punk In Drublic* features not one. The record is witty, sharp, fast and perceptive. In singing an Oi!-style skinhead song that celebrates rather than denigrates Judaism, the band display a deft hand when it comes to subverting thuggish convention. On opening track "Linoleum," occasionally acknowledged by Fat Mike as the finest song to which he has put his name, they deliver a track so impossibly contagious that its absence of a chorus goes unnoticed. Elsewhere, the observation in "Punk Guy" that its subject has "got a face like Charlie Bronson / straight out of Green Bay, Wisconsin" is the equal of any couplet in the genre's history. "I don't think *Punk In Drublic* is one of our best records," says Fat Mike, ignoring the fact that it is. "I'd put it in fifth or sixth place."

By this point, NOFX had joined Bad Religion as one of the bands to which others aspired. Certainly, The Offspring's support slot on their European tour in the summer of 1993 would prove instructive. At the time, the Orange County quartet were playing their songs on equipment that was some way short of specifications. A man of intelligence, Dexter Holland deduced that one of the reasons NOFX sounded good was because their guitars weren't prone to drift out of tune at the opening of a door. The group returned home from Europe with fifteen hundred dollars in the band kitty; with this they bought a cabinet amplifier and head made by MESA/Boogie. "Suddenly we had real gear!" says Dexter Holland with something approaching wonder. With just a flick of a switch, suddenly they sounded like a much better band.

As The Offspring readied themselves to record their third album, its predecessor had struck "punk rock gold" and found its way into the homes of fifty thousand listeners. Despite this success, the band were queasy about discussing matters such as album sales. But on the occasions when their conversations did veer in this direction, they allowed themselves to think big. "It would be great if we could sell a hundred thousand records!" is Dexter Holland's memory of his band's idea of reaching for the sky.

For the sake of convenience, The Offspring originally planned to record their latest collection of songs at a studio in Orange County without it occurring to them that the reason why the region's best recording studios were all in Los Angeles was not a coincidence. Depending on whom one asks, the record's budget was set somewhere between twenty and thirty-five thousand dollars. While not quite the diet of a chicken, this figure was barely a quarter of the amount a major label would sink into the recording of an album by even their youngest and least tested bands. Down at The Offspring's side of the tracks, concessions to cost were such that the budget didn't even stretch to the price of a cheap hotel room for their producer, Thom Wilson. Instead, the game technician slept in his camper van.

As with *Ignition*, the band were well drilled. The majority of the fourteen songs they were set to record had been rehearsed time and again so as not to waste time and funds pondering endless decisions in a recording studio that ran on a constant diet of money. But despite a limited budget, The Offspring were not content to deal with shortcomings simply by sucking them up. Very quickly it became clear that the sessions in Orange County were resulting in a sound that was little more than mediocre. At the urging of Thom Wilson the band decided to start again. Epitaph supported this decision by block-booking a fortnight at Track Records in North Hollywood, the high-end complex at which many hit albums had been created and at which Bad Religion had recorded their first album. Noodles remembers the sessions at Track taking place in the night's smallest hours. Dexter Holland marvels at how the confluence of a number of seemingly minor decisions can combine to produce something life changing.

"Us getting good gear meant that the band sounded a lot better," he says. "If we hadn't made the decision to switch studios then the record wouldn't have sounded as good as it does. All of those kinds of things really added together. It was as if these crazy things had to line up in just the right place . . . It was just a strange turn of events to have everything fall into place. I'm very proud of the [music we recorded] and I'm very proud of the work we put into it. But I also see the luck that was part of it as well."

As with Greg Graffin, Dexter Holland combined his role as the singer in a punk rock group with being a student. The University of Southern California (USC) stood on the south side of Los Angeles. Each morning Dexter would drive through Watts and South Central, two neighborhoods that at the time at least had become shorthand for violence and urban disobedience. Just a year after LA had torn itself apart in riots, he would drive his "very shitty car" and see signs of gang activity. He witnessed evidence of the strange phenomenon that is a disadvantaged community turning against itself. It was a war between a team in blue, the Crips, and a team in red, the Bloods. As with all wars, it was a fight over territory and resources, in this case drugs. As everyone in Los Angeles already knew, in certain parts of the city life was cheap. Black life was cheapest of all.

Dexter Holland may have observed this only from behind the windows of a knackered car, but it was still a good deal closer than most white people would ever get to these parts of town. The songwriter in him was inspired. He wrote a track that featured a section that cried out for a hip-hop delivery. But the band didn't know any rappers, and the idea of hiring a voice-over artist struck them as being phony. Holland turned to a friend nicknamed "Blackball." "He's from the 'hood," says Holland of a man with whom he remains on close terms. "He doesn't know how to sing or rap or anything, but he is real." While the band worked on their new song, down the hall Snoop Dogg was also recording. Dexter Holland remembers being reluctant to knock on the door and say, "How are you? We're suburban guys from Orange County." Blackball, though, had no such reservations, which is why today he owns a picture of himself posing with a world-renowned rap artist. The Offspring also treated their guest to an In-N-Out burger, for some reason the fast food of choice for otherwise discerning Southern Californians. In return for this kindness, Blackball was asked to speak just one line into one of the studio's microphones. This job took no more than a handful of minutes. The line was repeated twice. It is the second take that would soon be recognized by listeners from Anaheim to Adelaide.

"You gotta keep 'em separated."

## CHAPTER FIVE

# LOSERS WINNING BIG ON THE LOTTERY

On the first anniversary of the release of *Kerplunk*, on January 17, 1993, Green Day appeared at the City Gardens club in Trenton, New Jersey. Inside, a "house full" crowd of a thousand people bounced like rag dolls in a tumble dryer. It was the band's largest show to date and, remarkably, the first time they had played with the aid of onstage monitors. As the performance progressed, a photographer captured a shot of someone in the pit holding up a glove puppet of the *Sesame Street* character Ernie. At the merchandise stand, supporters were exchanging thousands of dollars for cotton. The band's share of the night's gate receipts exceeded the figure the venue had guaranteed them four times over. Fans without tickets were left outside to contemplate the slush and cold of a Jersey winter. Those who postponed the prospect of warming their bones at home were rewarded when Green Day emerged from City Gardens' stage door. Their night's work done, the band took the air with people who had seen the concert as well as some who had not. A number of these were asking just one question: "Where can we buy a copy of *Kerplunk*?"

"It was frustrating," says Mike Dirnt. "We were touring the US and people couldn't get our records. I remember there being about twelve hundred people outside City Gardens. We'd just packed the place out. I could not believe it. But the main question I kept getting all night was 'Where can I get your record?' I kept being asked that again and again. 'Where can I get it?' And I was saying, 'You know, we've got to get our records out to people, man.' We were bottlenecked. We couldn't sell as many records as we were drawing people."

On its day of release, *Kerplunk*'s initial pressing of ten thousand copies sold out in eight hours. Despite orders being doubled and then trebled, Lawrence Livermore's provincial record label could not accommodate the clamor from those who wanted to purchase Lookout's newest LP. As Green Day gained traction, their record company did not; problems of supply and demand grew at the same rate as the band's popularity. A year on from its release, an album that had cost one thousand dollars to record—small beer, but still three hundred and fifty bucks more than its predecessor, *39/Smooth*—demand for *Kerplunk* had led to the record becoming scarce. At home in Berkeley, the time had arrived for the band to have a serious talk. The gist of this was "What do we do now?"

Just three years earlier, Green Day and Lookout Records were as well suited as fish and chips. The label was busking it, and so too were the band. Billie Joe Armstrong remembers a moment of epiphany after watching MTV in disbelief as the Primitives' pop gem, "Crash," came in second place in a video face-off against a band about whom he remembers nothing. In the space of three minutes his thoughts went from "This is going to be great! This is a great song! Finally we're going to get something good!" to "Fuck this channel, fuck the radio, I just can't take it any more." By this point punk rock had supplanted metal as his music of choice, and he realized that he wanted in on the act. "I remember feeling, like, 'I don't care if I become popular or famous. This is the kind of music that I love. This is the style I love, and this is what I want to play' . . . It was just ten times better than anything else," he says.

As luck would have it, Lookout Records always had room on its roster for bands who didn't care about becoming popular. In contrast to the owners of other record labels, Lawrence Livermore takes a contrary pride in not being a businessman. His label's office was a place of chaos. Teetering piles of CDs competed for space with a backlog of correspondence. A hand-drawn pie chart outlining the company's "profit motive" pointed out the label's delight in their own corporate disobedience. Twenty-five percent of revenues were earmarked for "Lawrence's dancing lessons," while sixteen percent were set aside for "Cheez Whiz." Anyone who had any "questions or comments [should] contact Lawrence Livermore (if he isn't practicing the cha-cha)."

Running to stand still, Livermore was not unduly concerned that Green Day had yet to reveal to him their plans for making a third album. He told himself that there was nothing unusual in this. Two years had elapsed between the release of *39/Smooth* and *Kerplunk*, he reasoned; and, anyway, the group had been busy playing everywhere from Wermelskirchen to Winnipeg, The absence of specificity regarding studio schedules could be explained, clearly, by a devotion to the road. Even when people began suggesting that Green Day's next album might emerge on a larger label—and, whisper this, *maybe even a major label*—the idea was dismissed without due consideration. But as weeks turned into months, Livermore's thoughts about his professional relationship with his label's most successful act grew cloudy with concern. This uncertainty was allayed not at all when a conversation with Tre Cool revealed that the band were thinking of signing with a management team. In point of fact, they had *already* signed with a management team. This revelation was correctly interpreted as a sign that the band were in the market for a move to a more established record label.

Lawrence Livermore convened a meeting with Green Day at the Au Coquelet eatery, known to most as "Café Hell," at which the three younger men appeared awkward and not at ease. They listened as their friend delivered his sales pitch. They were told that it was in the best interests of both parties that the band and their record company remain united. He advised them that major labels chew through bands like rats chew through power cables and that if they didn't hit at the first time of asking—or at a push, the second time of asking—then they would be dropped. This would be a morale-stealing setback from which most bands do not recover. But another album recorded for Lookout would sell twice as many copies as *Kerplunk*. This in turn would strengthen the group's hand should they decide to sign with a major label for their fourth LP. Respectfully but resolutely, Billie Joe Armstrong said, "No, we're ready to go for it now."

Less than a week later, at Lookout's office, Lawrence Livermore and Green Day met again. This time the group were accompanied by their new managers, Elliot Cahn and Jeff Saltzman from Cahn-Man management. At Café Hell the three musicians had agreed to the request that they sign a contract stipulating that Lookout retain the rights to the records already released on the label. Without the help of a lawyer, Livermore laid out his terms on two pages of A4 paper. On the proviso that the band were paid the correct royalty rate at the due date, Green Day's first and second albums would continue to be issued by Lookout. The contract's final clause read: "Lookout Records and Green Day agree to treat each other with respect and openness at all times, and recognize that while this agreement provides specific guidelines as to what is expected of each other, the truest contract is one based on trust and friendship." With this, the deal was sealed. Next to his signature, Billie Joe drew a doodle of an amplifier. In the intervening years, the band have honored this contract and have made no efforts to reclaim the music released on Lookout Records.

"I had very mixed emotions about [Green Day leaving]," says Lawrence Livermore. "My philosophy in running a record label was to be a genuine alternative. I wanted us to grow along with the bands, at least in principle . . . so they didn't need to leave. And to this day, I think that's not a completely unrealistic viewpoint. To some extent, Epitaph have proved that this can be done . . . I really did feel that for the first few years the label grew and the bands grew. But it was just a case that at some point they [Green Day] felt, or people around them felt, that they weren't growing fast enough. And that part is true. We couldn't have sold millions of records for them immediately. A few years down the line we could have, but when you're at the age that they were, a few years down the line feels like an eternity. I had the perspective of being almost twice their age so I kind of thought, 'Oh, it's no big deal if you become a millionaire next year, or in three years from now. You're going to be fine either way, and in the long term you'll be better off [remaining with Lookout] because being on an independent label means that you get to keep a lot more of the money and you have a lot more control over your destiny.' So they took a big chance. But even as I was [laying out the case for remaining with the label], in the back of my mind I thought that if we did a good enough job they'd want to stay indefinitely and they could continue to grow as a band and us as a label. But Billie said, 'No, I think we're ready to go now.' And unlike about ninety percent of the bands that make that decision, for them it worked out well. But I'm not sure that even now I'd say it was the correct thing for them to do."

Despite Green Day's eventual departure from Lookout in 1993, the band's name had been mentioned in conjunction with a major label once before. Original pressings of *Kerplunk* featured a mocked-up letter from IRS Records, the distribution of which went through EMI. Printed on letterhead, the letter read: "You may not know this but we've been watching you and we think you're one of the hottest punk bands out of the Bay Area since Dead Kennedys! [sic] . . . We will try and get in contact with your lawyer and possibly buy out the rest of your contract with Lookout." Predictably, IRS was not impressed by this jape. Whispers of a lawsuit were silenced only by the diplomatic skills of Lawrence Livermore.

For most young bands, the offer of a major label recording contract is almost always irresistible. But in terms of wreckage strewn all over the place, it is a treacherous road on which to embark. The promise of enormous success is as nothing compared with its portent of failure. In the field of punk rock, the success of the majors was markedly minor league. Along with the Ramones and X, publicly traded record labels had failed to further the causes of both Husker Du and the Replacements, this despite both bands being the recipients of critical adoration. Sweet Baby saw their album *It's a Girl* plummet from view as if it had been dropped down a mine shaft. Even Social Distortion, at that point the American punk rock band with the fewest major label hard luck stories, seemed to be viewed with bewilderment by Epic Records. One English music executive watching them play at the Garage in London remarked, "I can't believe we sunk half a million dollars into *this*."

But while signing to a major label was often the triumph of hope over other people's experience, the success of Nirvana did present genuine opportunities. Suddenly it didn't matter that at this time the labels with the deepest pockets were busy making the daftest decisions. It didn't matter that many American marketing departments understood the lay of the new land no better than the rules of cricket. It didn't matter because this was the point at which a band secure in its identity and equipped with the potential to appeal could emerge into the light. *Nevermind* had transformed the wider public's appetites in an instant. For one thing, the resulting earthquake heralded the death of many hairspray metal bands that had been chancing their arms for far too long. But in under three years these appetites would change once more, albeit in a more subtle way. By the time Nirvana's blood-stained throne stood empty, listeners were ready for an equally credible band, but one with a less oppressive touch. That Green Day were the right group for this role is obvious. But that they arrived at the casting call at precisely the right time is also true.

"*Nevermind* opened up a very small window for Green Day and we went straight through it," Armstrong told the author in 2016. "I think we were completely different from Nirvana. I don't think that we were riding anyone's coattails, for sure. But Nirvana's purity opened up the door for other bands that were pure."

Certainly, the group's circumstances were pure to the point of being ascetic. Green Day first became an urban rather than a suburban band when its three members shared a squat in West Oakland. This move would provide the inspiration for "Welcome to Paradise," a track first heard on *Kerplunk*. What has since become one of the group's most enduring songs was rescued from a pile of ideas that were refusing to blossom. This salvage operation was necessitated by the need to bolster *Kerplunk*'s otherwise anemic track listing. "It would have been a nightmare if I hadn't put it on there," says Billie Joe. The band's new living quarters saw the singer swap the drone of suburbia for the dangers of an inner city. "This sudden fear has left me trembling / 'cos now it seems that I am out here on my own / and I'm feeling so alone," he sings in the first verse of a song that is best viewed as a letter to his mother written in rhyme. Today he says that "Welcome to Paradise" "is about moving out of my [mom's] house and moving to West Oakland and what a shocking experience that was. Basically I went from a working-class suburb to the ghetto."

By 1993, the band had moved again, this time to Berkeley, an improvement in circumstances that would not trouble the editors of *House & Garden* magazine. Green Day now resided in a low-rent apartment built into the basement of a Victorian townhouse. Then, as now, Berkeley was a college town in which the demand for rental property was high. A common way of meeting this need was to build what are effectively concrete bunkers beneath the ground floors of otherwise desirable properties. Inside, drywall was used to compartmentalize the space into small rooms. Chez Green Day featured three small bedrooms, an even smaller kitchen and a bathroom so compact and bijou that it lacked the space in which to draw a picture of someone swinging a cat. The band's new home also featured a living room that doubled up as a rehearsal space. Viewers of MTV would later catch a glimpse into this lifestyle of the poor and obscure when Green Day chose it as the location for their debut music video. The four-minute clip accompanied a deft and subversively clever song inspired by a place in Washington State at which the band had played. The town's name was Longview.

In the autumn of 1992, Rob Cavallo, a twenty-nine-year-old producer and A&R man for Warner Bros. Records, was ensconced in Sound City Studios in Van Nuys recording the eponymous debut album by one of Los Angeles's most overlooked punk rock bands, the Muffs. Led by bassist and vocalist Kim Shattuck, the Muffs combined candy floss melodies with lyrics that were sharp and displeased. Impressed by this, Cavallo signed the band and secured two thousand dollars from his employers with which to record four tracks. Despite being "the lowest of the low" on the company's totem pole, his efforts met with the approval of Lenny Waronker, then the president of Warner Bros. Records. Waronker approved a budget of one hundred thousand dollars with which to record a full album

Like so many bands of their type from this time, the Muffs were short of everything except talent. In need of both legal representation and management, they engaged the services of Elliot Cahn and Jeff Saltzman. One night while mixing the Muffs, Saltzman placed a cassette on the desk at which Rob Cavallo was sitting. You've got to listen to this band, he was told. We're just starting to represent them and they've decided they want to get a major label deal. They're called Green Day.

"Okay," said the producer. Looking at the cassette he thought, "Oh Jesus, not another band."

Rob Cavallo remained at the mixing desk until one o' clock in the morning. Readying himself for the drive home, as an afterthought he slipped the tape he had been handed only an hour earlier into the pocket of his jacket and, presently, into his car's stereo. With most of the citizens of Los Angeles asleep, and with Cavallo ready to join them, it was with weariness that he pressed the play button. "I thought, 'I better listen to it,'" he remembers. "You just never know; you never know and you can't be lazy." Among other songs, the tape featured four-track demo versions of compositions titled "She" and "Basket Case." Despite the night by now being in its smallest hours, Cavallo was jolted awake. Just bars into the first song he thought, "Holy shit, I fucking love this! Who *are* these guys . . . This band is fucking amazing!" The next morning he phoned Jeff Saltzman and delivered his verdict. "Great!" said the manager. "Why not come up to Berkeley and meet the guys?" By this point, the low-flying employee of the world's most powerful record label had already made the decision that he wanted to sign Green Day *and* to produce their next album. Short on corporate leverage, instead Cavallo decided to strategize.

"Typically, in an A&R department some people will support you and some people won't," he says. "And you have to remember that at that time the Muffs' album hadn't even come out yet, and that on a major there was no punk anywhere except for the stuff that had been put out in the seventies and early eighties . . . There were people in the A&R department who said to me, 'Why do you want to sign a punk rock band? That stuff doesn't sell.' And my whole thing was to say to them, 'Well, I think there are a hundred thousand cool kids who remember what punk rock was and who, like myself, will like this.' So I was running around saying, 'Well, if you give me two hundred thousand dollars to sign this band, we're going to make four or five bucks a record and we're gonna generate a little bit of profit. I think we're gonna sell a hundred thousand albums.' I thought it was obvious that this band had something to say and that they were going to find an audience."

Major record companies hunt in packs; once a band is perceived to be emitting a "buzz" the music industry's bigger cats begin to prowl. While other punk rock groups of their age and scale were ignored, it was Green Day in whom the industry's high rollers suddenly believed. The trio had a number of suitors. By the time Rob Cavallo gained permission from Warner Bros. to raise his paddle in the auction for their signatures, meetings had already been held with representatives of Geffen and Columbia Records. Save for one crucial detail, Warner Bros. were merely a third corporate concern with cash on hip. But Rob Cavallo had a secret weapon: its name was Rob Cavallo.

Green Day were reassured by the fact that the two parties were of a similar age and shared similar musical points of view. Interest was piqued by Cavallo's work with the Muffs, a band of whom they were fond. On learning that their suitor had also signed the group, they asked, "And you did that on a major label?" "Yes." "Well, we really like that and we really respect that 'cos that's the first punk band, or pop-punk band, that a major label has done anything with." It began to dawn on Cavallo that Green Day were beginning to regard him as a man whose walk and talk were in sync. Frank Wright II had for years been telling his son's group that they should sign to Warner Bros. The fact that until now the idea was laughable did not concern him. The reason for his preference was simple: Warner Music Group was the home to ZZ Top, of whom he was a great fan.

During their courtship, Rob Cavallo and Green Day met a number of times. On a visit to their very humble home in Berkeley, the producer was beckoned into a living room with dirty white walls and a coffee table strewn with detritus. A bucket had been turned upside down in the hope that it might pass itself off as a chair. "Close enough," he thought, and sat down. In the spirit of *mi casa es su casa,* the band invited their guest to join them in getting high. On learning that Cavallo knew how to play songs by the Beatles, Billie Joe Armstrong handed him a guitar and asked that he play "Help!" As it turned out, the producer had been obsessed with the Fab Four since childhood and could play *every single one* of their songs. Despite the fog from smokable materials hanging heavy in the air, his mojo did not desert him. For the next half an hour Green Day tested their visitor by shouting out the names of songs credited to Lennon and McCartney, clearly impressed that he felt no need to ask for a pass. Cavallo then threw in a few old blues tunes free of charge. By this point the unsigned band were entertaining the thought that they were in the company of a man with whom they could perhaps do more than business.

Green Day's liking of Rob Cavallo might not have been in itself a good enough reason to sign with the label for which he worked. On top of a major label recording contract, the band also had another demand to make of Warner Bros.: they wanted a van in which to tour. Jittery that he was in danger of losing his quarry, Cavallo remembers thinking that it was imperative that he convince Lenny Waronker to agree to this. He later learned that his boss okayed this proposal because he was impressed that the band were willing to tour without the support of their record company. The previous year Green Day had played one hundred and twenty-two concerts all over the United States, as well as in Canada and Europe. He intuited, correctly, that the trio did not view a contract with Warner Bros. as equating to their post being delivered to Easy Street.

"Doing all that touring on their own dime is an incredible feat," says Cavallo. "It made me respect them so much. So the idea that they wanted just a little bit of comfort so they could continue to do that was great. It was great that a band would ask for that rather than saying, 'Okay, well, give us a [tour] bus so we can tour around in style. Oh, and we want first-class airplane tickets as well.' I thought Green Day was really smart and I related to that sensibility much more than I would to a hair [metal] band. So I went up to Lenny and told him the story and he said, 'Yeah, you know what, this is cool, let's give 'em the fucking van' . . . We gave them twenty grand for a van and that's how they ended up signing with us."

(Many people interviewed for this book mention Green Day's van without prompting. A converted mobile library in which the band were ferried around the country by Tre Cool's dad, who also handled the conversion, the "Bookmobile" has become an iconic feature of punk rock's fittings and furnishings. For years after its decommission, the vehicle was parked outside Frank and Linda Wright's home in Mendocino County. "It was sitting there waiting and ready to be fired up again in case it needed to be," remembers Lawrence Livermore.)

Green Day signed to the Warner Music Group's most prestigious subsidiary, Reprise Records, with an advance of two hundred and twenty-five thousand dollars. From this they spent twenty thousand dollars on their new set of wheels. They cut a check to cover their managers' percentage. They paid themselves eighty thousand dollars by way of a salary. A hundred thousand bucks was reserved for the recording of their next album, and the band cleared two months in the summer of 1993 in which to accomplish this. For Rob Cavallo it would be the first of eight of the band's studio albums on which he is credited as producer.

Green Day's upward mobility proved immediately controversial. But while for punk rock's moral guardians no crime was more heinous than signing to a major label, it would nonetheless be lazy to describe the source of this outrage as being wholly predictable. Today it is remarkable to recall the rhetorical violence that rained down on those who rescinded their independent status in such a way. In this collision sport, no band took more hits than Green Day. For many, the decision to align with Warner Bros. amounted to more than them leaving a club, or even a community; it was a renouncement of their citizenship of the People's Republic of Punk Rock. And while it is tempting to counter this militant viewpoint with the words "get a life," it is at the same time unreasonable to attribute every aspect of this upset simply to piety. Many were the people who honorably and sincerely believed that Green Day had done their community a profound disservice.

"It was definitely one of those things that I understood and where I respected people's sense of ownership of their bands and of their scene," says Mike Dirnt. "I understood that. But for us, we didn't *have* anything else. There were a lot of kids that had a lot of shit to fall back on who were really self-righteous, and I said, 'Well, you *can* be indignant when you've got a fucking trust fund.' I was sleeping in the back of my truck half the time, you know? To me selling out is compromising my musical intentions, because for me the most important things were those songs. We protected them with our lives back then, and we protected each other. That might sound stupid but I always thought of the word 'band' meaning that you band together and do something. Billie, Tre and I made a commitment to each other to see this thing through because we knew it was the most important thing we'd ever do in our lives."

"I never thought less of Green Day for signing with Warner Brothers in the slightest," says Brett Gurewitz. "I think all that stuff is silly. Green Day are an East Bay band and they didn't change their music at all when they signed with Warners. And as a label, Warners has a great legacy. They put out everything from Devo to Jimi Hendrix to REM to Tom Waits [through the Asylum subsidiary]. They were known as one of the best majors. Plus, anyway, the way I look at it is that a label is a label. But it was very fashionable back then for punks to be militant about this kind of thing, even though clearly none of them remember that the Sex Pistols were on a major label."

The mission statement for recording Green Day's new album was to capture the energy of the music without corruption or unnecessary embellishments. Both the band and their producer understood without being told that the first step in the direction of achieving this aim was to pay close attention to preparation. Work did not begin in a recording studio, but in the low-ceilinged practice space in which the group played music, ate food and watched television. Each day their producer would sit on his upturned bucket and listen as a new batch of songs were built, broken down and built up again until the musicians were as synchronized as Fred Astaire and Ginger Rogers. Green Day knew that the only way to bring their music to full maturity was to work as hard as they knew how.

"I remember talking to other bands back then and they would say, 'Yeah, we're going to go in the studio and start writing for our next record in about six weeks now,'" says Mike Dirnt. "And I'd be, like, 'You mean you don't practice for four, five or six days a week?' Because that's what we did, every single fucking day; we would work until we had things right, every single day. At band practice we would go over and over each song. We'd work on each section and then look at the parts of the songs that we felt weren't as good as the greatest part of the song and then make the whole of the song as great as that."

By the time Green Day entered Fantasy Studios in Berkeley in the dog days of the summer of 1993, they had their new songs locked down tighter than gold reserves. The band were neither underprepared nor overwhelmed. Billie Joe Armstrong laughs as he remembers that even at the time of *Kerplunk*, which its authors produced alone, the shock and awe of making a record had worn off. "It was weird," he says, "but by that point we were like eighteen-year-old veterans of the punk scene." Yet despite a respectable body of work to their name, by 1993 the band had spent barely a week in a recording studio. Suddenly they were working to a budget of a hundred thousand dollars, a figure *one hundred times* as much as they spent making *Kerplunk* (in the end, one hundred and five times; the band went over budget by five grand). Yet despite this, by the standards of most major label releases this was still the kind of change one finds down the back of the settee.

As well as money, Green Day had a producer who knew how best to spend it. By the time he made the band's acquaintance, Rob Cavallo had worked in various capacities with numerous acts, including Black Sabbath. With the means by which a band might find its ideal guitar sound fast becoming a science, the producer knew people who were experts in amplification. Seeking their advice, he lined up a number of amps through which Billie Joe would find his perfect tone. The winning rig was a 1971 Marshall Plexi. Today this is known as the "Dookie model" in honor of the title Green Day would bestow on their album.

After auditioning each of Fantasy Studio's three recording rooms, the band began work in earnest. At least by the often maddening standards required to make music to a professional standard, Green Day's newest collection of songs was delivered without alarming complications. But even music as fluid and intuitive as theirs is recorded with precision, attention to detail, tenacity and constant hard work. Green Day and Rob Cavallo utilized these qualities so effectively that it's tempting to view the results as being easy. In reality it took a good deal of effort to sound this effortless. After Green Day had recorded each of their fourteen new songs at Fantasy—fifteen if one includes Tre Cool's doodle "All By Myself"—their producer heard deficiencies in the cojoined compositions "Chump" and "Longview." He had allowed the pairing to be recorded at too few beats per minute, an oversight out of keeping with the caffeinated energy of the rest of the collection. As well as this, during sections that featured only drums and bass the ambient noise from the tape registered at too high a level. Rather than return to Fantasy Studios, the band and their producer decamped to the Music Grinder rooms in Los Angeles and cut the pieces again.

Green Day were wise enough to know that many a good record had been ruined by a bad mix. But while a number of big-name technicians gave *Dookie* a go, the band were dissatisfied with the results. Instead the gig was handed to the untested Jerry Finn, the album's engineer. Brett Gurewitz remembers the group listening to Finn's rough mixes on their tour with Bad Religion. Each day, a new compact disc would arrive by Federal Express to the venues in which they were playing. Back in California, the plan to mix *Dookie* at Fantasy Studios had been scotched after Rob Cavallo discovered that a bass-compressing ceiling prevented the music from attaining its ideal levels. With Frank Wright II honking the horn of the Bookmobile to let the band know that it was time to clamber aboard, the producer suggested that the mix should be done at Devonshire Studios in Los Angeles, the facility at which he had set the levels for the Muffs. Despite the expense of recording and mixing in three separate studios in two different cities, the album would prove to be a bargain. Despite its beginner's budget, *Dookie* waltzed onto the scene as if it and the major leagues were made for each other.

"I was in the mindset of doing things very inexpensively," says Cavallo. "That was the thing that would show that I had given value to both the band *and* the record company. I made sure that we worked six days a week, Monday through Saturday, so we could [block book] the studio. [Warner Bros.] were looking at the Muffs and Green Day and saying, 'Well, these are little punk bands so you should make these records for a hundred or a hundred and fifty thousand dollars . . .' I actually took no advance [payment] on *Dookie*. I took [percentage] points but I took no money. That's how conscious I was about the budget. I was, like, 'You don't even have to fucking pay me.' I had a salary from the label, a grand total of about twenty-eight thousand dollars a year, so you might say that I was living just above the poverty line. I had just enough money to have a car and an apartment. I was not complaining 'cos it was great; it was the salad days, as they say. But out of the two hundred and twenty-five thousand dollars [advance], I took nothing. Other record producers would take seventy thousand dollars out of a four-hundred-thousand-dollar budget. But, then again, it should be noted that I was unproven [as a producer] and that I was just starting out. *Dookie* was the second record I ever produced for a major label. And I've really got to hand it to the Green Day guys because them and the Muffs really gave me my start."

With *Dookie* nearing completion, Rob Cavallo was paid a visit at the Devonshire by Warner Bros. product manager Geoffrey Weiss. With the producer's head fizzing and his ears blown by the demands of countless competing details—how loud should the bass be? does this thing even sound any good, anyway?—he nonetheless played his colleague *Dookie*'s first half. "You did it!" he was told. "You fucking did it!" "Really?" asked Cavallo, a touch doubtfully. With eyes like cue balls, out in the studio's parking lot Weiss threw out a look that is rare in the music industry. It was a look that predicted the future in certain rather than hopeful terms. "This music is unbelievable," he said. "This album is going to be so fucking huge it's insane." Before driving away, Weiss promised that the next day he would go into Warner Bros. Records and tell everyone who cared to listen that he had just heard a multiplatinum album. Rob Cavallo duly delivered this verdict to Green Day. "Oh." the band said. "Well, we're glad that he liked it; we always liked that dude."

In the closing months of 1993, Weiss's swivel-eyed reaction to *Dookie* seemed like the response of a man with a fondness for long shots. Listened to today, the fluency of the album's songs seems preternatural, as if each one held a warrant permitting access to every teenage bedroom in North America and beyond. But as the record's release date approached, no one from Warner Bros. was counting on Green Day to be the band that determined the size of their Christmas bonus.

In this, their sight was short. From the moment Billie Joe Armstrong delivers the album's opening couplet—"I declare I don't care no more / I'm burning up and out and growing bored"—*Dookie* is airborne and gliding on currents of unending melody. With the help of Rob Cavallo, the band's music was now well represented in recorded form. A five-year apprenticeship had turned Green Day into a powerful and pliable musical union. Their irrepressible energy was utilized in the service of their songs rather than as a force behind which weak material might hide. Here there is no weak material.

"Well, no one here is getting out alive," Armstrong sings on "Having A Blast." He does this with such tasteful melody that the song's subject matter, a mentally unstable narrator armed with a grievance and a gun, arrives inside a Trojan horse. This is a scene of permanent destruction, a point made with amoral insouciance in the line "to me, it's nothing." In case there were any doubt about this, the words are repeated four times. Yet even while carrying this terrible weight, "Having A Blast" still sounds like a song written in celebration of summer.

Despite its coming popularity, *Dookie* is an album veiled in alienation and, sometimes, loneliness. Unusually for a punk rock record, it isn't particularly angry. Its tone is offhand and often knowing. "Do you have the time / to listen to me whine?"

asks "Basket Case" with a shrug. "I don't need no accuser / to slag me down because I know you're right" is the weary realization kicking its heels on "When I Come Around." "I locked the door to my own cell / and I lost the key" is the verdict of "Longview," a couplet sung by someone who realizes that the concept of freedom includes the freedom to take it for granted. The song also proposes the irresistible argument "my mother says to get a job / but she don't like the one she's got." Over time, Billie Joe Armstrong would express guilt about this in light of his own mother's work as a waitress, a position she held long after her son had the means to keep her in the style to which she had never been accustomed.

The space that *Dookie* would soon occupy in the public imagination has something to do with the realization that alternative music was becoming a drag. By now there were few smiles and little energy. Fans of Nirvana watched the soap opera the band had become with irresistible interest and lowering feelings. Of all the reactions to Kurt Cobain's final act exploding from the barrel of a gun, surprise was not one of them. In comparison to this, Billie Joe Armstrong's own dislocation seemed more universal; less livid and certainly less frightened. Many of the sentiments expressed on *Dookie* distilled the human condition down to just three words: so it goes.

In the weeks that followed its release on the first day of February 1994, *Dookie* did not quicken many pulses. Despite being the first Green Day album to chart, its pallid position at number a hundred and forty-one was no more than a ticket in the cheap seats. There were, though, reasons for this slow start. On its first week of release, Warner Bros. planned to ship between twenty and twenty-five thousand copies to the record shops of America. But a severe storm decommissioned enough delivery trucks that only twelve thousand units found their way to retailers. By the end of *Dookie*'s first seven days in the public domain, copies could not be bought with either money or love. This scarcity increased demand. It took Reprise three weeks to press and distribute a further forty thousand copies, each of which was bought by people who were already members of the band's core audience. Barely a month after its release, Green Day's big league debut saw a drop in sales that Rob Cavallo describes as "precipitous." While it remains true that Warner Bros.' investment in Green Day was modest, business is still business. A tally of fifty-two thousand copies of an album that appeared bereft of what the music industry calls "legs" is a failure.

Original pressings of *Dookie* featured on its back sleeve the brilliant photograph of an arm holding a glove puppet of Ernie from *Sesame Street* taken the year before at City Gardens. Following complaints from the program's producers, the Jim Henson Company, later editions would see the character absented by an airbrush. Also missing from the album's artwork and liner notes was any mention of a website. The reason for this was simple: in 1994 no one knew what a website was. If this makes *Dookie* sound like the product of a bygone, sepia-hued age, this is because it is. Further evidence that 1994 was a profoundly different time from today arrives in the fact that Green Day's record label were content to take a long-term view of short-term problems. In the nineties, marketing and promotional departments could afford to be patient. It would be another ten years before the music industry became consumed by panic.

"Longview," the first of *Dookie*'s five singles, at first performed poorly. But things that seem dead are rarely buried, and by the summer Green Day's first stand-alone track had begun to find traction. MTV had taken to airing the video that accompanied the song—these being the days when MTV actually played music videos—outside of the confines of slots intended for insomniacs. Directed by Mark Kohr, the clip was shot on a far from bank-busting budget at the band's Berkeley-based practice space and living quarters, parts of which had been upgraded by a red-and-blue paint job. Despite having never before played in front of a film crew, the band were naturally telegenic.

Since its launch in 1981, Music Television's default setting was to play so much crap that its shows ought to have been sponsored by the California Prune Festival. But in 1987, a torrent of requests for Guns N' Roses' "Welcome To The Jungle" threw the channel's switchboard into a meltdown and proved that when it came to its viewers' habit of tuning in to a largely awful channel there was a difference between complicity and contentment. By 1991, fissures were beginning to appear all over the broadcaster's indifferent wall of sound. Impossible to ignore, Metallica's "Enter Sandman" became the first full-blown metal song to be placed on daytime rotation. That same year came the firework display that was Nirvana. Pearl Jam, Soundgarden and Smashing Pumpkins were three other beneficiaries of the channel's newfound open-mindedness. By airing "Longview," MTV may have helped introduce a new musical wave into homes all over North America and Europe, but its decision to do so was not without precedent.

MTV's decision in 1981 to introduce itself to its viewers by airing the Buggles' "Video Killed The Radio Star" had proved to be less prophetic than the channel might have hoped. Thirteen years on, in 1994 getting a song on the radio remained a key part of a major record label's strategy when it came to breaking a new artist. Warner Bros.' head of alternative promotion during this time was Steve Tipp, a man who simply refused to concede defeat in his quest to get "Longview" noticed. The fact that *nine months* elapsed between its release and the unveiling of *Dookie*'s second single, "Welcome To Paradise," bears testament to this tenacity. In Los Angeles, victory in the battle to convince KROQ to play the song would prove a key moment in the wider war. Cleansed of its numerous profanities, not at all suddenly "Longview" began to appear on the playlist of America's most influential radio station.

"I'd drive around waiting for the song to come on," remembers Rob Cavallo. "I'd stop off at Tommy's Burgers to get a burger. I think I'd gotten a cell phone for the first time, one of those ones that goes in a car, 'cos I thought that I needed it. I used to call the radio station requesting that they play the song. I wouldn't do this more than once or twice a night, but I'd put on voices. So I'd speak in a scratchy voice and say, 'Hey, man, I heard this song called 'Longview' which is really cool. It's by a band called Green Day. Would you play Green Day for me?' All of these calls I'd make in a funny voice. Later I'd call up sounding like a fraternity guy. I'd say, 'Hey, would you play that song by Green Day? That song is fucking cool! Play it, yeah!' And then I'd hang up."

Months after its release, Green Day's slow burner became their first hit single. Like a tortoise beating a hare, by the summer of 1994 "Longview" had climbed to the summit of *Billboard*'s alternative rock songs chart. It had also reached the top twenty of the mainstream rock chart, and the top forty in *Billboard*'s list of radio songs. Internationally, the band's first single also featured on the charts in Australia and, crucially, the United Kingdom. Suddenly the ground war was on. On the first day of October, Warner Bros. finally released "Welcome To Paradise," the successor to "Longview." For the second time that year, Green Day made the charts. The band's fear of being one-hit wonders was dashed. For now at least, they were two-hit wonders.

The promotional clips that accompanied both "Longview" and "Welcome to Paradise" showcased the band well, albeit on less than lavish budgets. Whereas Green Day's first video was a compendium of claustrophobic close-up shots of a sneering, buck-toothed Billie Joe Armstrong, a spasmodic Mike Dirnt and a gurning Tre Cool, its successor captured the group in the more

Green Day's Billie Joe Armstrong gets political in Washington, DC. *Photo by Paul Harries*

A clean and serene Mike Ness of Social Distortion poses in Berlin. *Photo by Ashley Maile*

Bad Religion, prior to the departure of a purple-haired Brett Gurewitz.
*Photo by Paul Harries*

Bad Religion and their classic "no cross" logo. *Photo by Paul Harries*

Billie Joe poses with his good friend Ernie. *Photo by Lisa Johnson*

None more punk. Rancid in the era of . . . *And Out Come The Wolves*. *Photo by Paul Harries*

Green Day pose for world exclusive *Kerrang!* shots to promote a not-yet-finished *American Idiot. Photo by Paul Harries*

Green Day on the comeback trail on the Pop Disaster Tour in Chicago, 2002. *Photo by Paul Harries*

NOFX terrorize the Sunset Strip in 1995. *Photo by Lisa Johnson*

Fat Mike in the role of recruiting sergeant for very young punks. *Photo by Lisa Johnson*

The Offspring pose, unaware that worldwide fame is beating a path to their door. *Photo by Lisa Johnson*

Pennywise bring an element of chaos to the Warped Tour. *Photo by Lisa Johnson*

Punk in public. Bad Religion and NOFX share a stage.

924 Gilman Street, which is, along with CBGB, the most famous punk club in America.

Lawrence Livermore, the man who signed Operation Ivy and Green Day to his record label, Lookout.

Brett Gurewitz, songwriter and owner of Epitaph Records, onstage as a member of Bad Religion. *Photo by Kenneth Bachor*

familiar environment of a concert stage. The clip was filmed at one of the band's shows, onto which the studio version of the song was then overlaid. It is interesting to note that despite a burgeoning profile, the venue in question stands at the smaller end of the touring circuit. Green Day may have been only months away from securing their first *Rolling Stone* cover story, but the shock waves the band were causing were not yet striking with the same force in the same places at the same time.

But by now the wheels were in spin; suddenly singles were arriving like BART trains to the East Bay. Just a month after "Welcome To Paradise," Green Day's third stand-alone release, "Basket Case," made its public bow. On an album stuffed with ear-catching songs, this was *Dookie*'s catchiest. As with "Longview," the band chose Mark Kohr to direct the accompanying video. The filmmaker remembers being handed a budget of "definitely more than a hundred and twenty-five thousand dollars"—he guesses that the figure might even have been as high as two hundred grand—which while as nothing compared to the million bucks Guns N' Roses dropped on "November Rain" was still rich for Green Day's blood. The clip was shot at the Agnes Development Center, a former mental institution in Santa Clara County, California. Here the band performed as if they were sharing a wing with Jack Nicholson. Kohr relates that the three musicians required little by way of direction. When the cameras began to roll, they knew what to do, and when to do it. This is hardly surprising.

Both Billie Joe Armstrong and Tre Cool had been performing in one way or another long before anyone outside of their circle knew their names. As a young child, Armstrong would provide entertainment for senior citizens living in retirement homes, while Tre Cool attended Camp Winnarainbow, a children's circus and performing arts camp founded by the countercultural entertainer Wavy Gravy. Here he would dominate proceedings by flying by on a unicycle that he'd learned to ride only moments before. He would also invent characters defined by the hats he'd found in a trunk. By the time Mark Kohr shouted, "Action!" on the set of "Basket Case," both Billie and Tre had put in long shifts as centers of attention.

The look of the video was inspired by a terrible idea. In the 1980s, the cable channel Turner Classic Movies began showing "colorized" versions of famous black-and-white pictures. Each frame was hand painted so that viewers could see what Joan Crawford would look like with green teeth. This affront to aesthetic integrity had nothing to recommend it aside from the fact that it planted an idea in Mark Kohr's mind. It would be interesting, he thought, to deliberately subvert this technique in a music video that pushed this process to an even more glaringly colorful extreme. With three months in which to work, he shot the video in black and white on sixteen-millimeter film. The stock was then sent to India where a post-production unit colorized each frame in a way that shone like Times Square at midnight.

"I wanted the colors to contrast and I wanted them to be really dramatic," says Kohr. "I wanted the video to have this kind of coloring book quality, where the different colors are almost in blocks and are very stark. It may have been selfish on my part, or it might have been a little indulgent of me, but what I wanted was for people who saw it to come to a dead stop. I wanted it to look very dramatic. And I wanted it to be striking enough that if someone came across it when they were surfing through the channels, they'd stop flipping the remote and would watch it."

This they did. On the last day of 1994, when MTV counted down its chart of the top hundred videos of the year, "Basket Case" was ranked at number one. In capturing Green Day's fast-emerging onscreen charisma, the persuasive and peculiar clip was soon all but ubiquitous. Its success would help make its accompanying song the band's first bona fide smash-hit single. "Basket Case" appeared in the top twenty on charts in no fewer than nine countries, including the *Billboard* mainstream top forty. Once again, the band reached the top spot on the *Bill-board* alternative songs chart. In the United Kingdom the track reached the top ten. By doing so it sold more than four hundred thousand copies.

The purpose of a single is to serve as bait with which to entice listeners to buy its parent album. In this, "Basket Case" was like an irresistible combination of catnip and crack. By now the sales of *Dookie* were supersonic. At its highest point the record was selling as many as two hundred thousand copies *a week*. Despite having had a quiet first five months, by the end of 1994 Green Day's third LP had sold almost three and a half million copies in the United States alone, a tally that made it the fifth best-selling album of the year.

"It was the first time a punk band in America really became huge, so we were kind of the ultimate guinea pigs," says Billie Joe Armstrong. "And with Nirvana not around any more, it felt like we had no more kindred spirits. I do remember that we had a fear of failure and a fear of success at the same time. But I really didn't know what would happen [with *Dookie*]. I think I was somewhere in between two extremes. I was expecting the best *and* expecting the worst. The last thing that I wanted was to be anywhere in the middle. I didn't want to be in the middle of the road, and I didn't want to be mediocre. I thought, 'Well, if we're gonna do this let's make it as big as possible, or else let's go down in flames.' And there was fear when it came to both of these things. But this is what we signed up for. We wanted to do this for the rest of our lives and that's what we've done."

"I remember everything started moving at such a breakneck speed that a part of me felt that it almost wasn't real," remembers Mike Dirnt. "Everything was new and I guess I did enjoy that. I wish I'd stopped to appreciate it a little bit more, but at the time everything was moving so fast. Everything was new and everything was exciting. I also probably could have stopped smoking weed a little bit sooner than I did. But when you're young, that's the time to go out and make a mess. That's the time to figure shit out and to have fun and to explore and be creative. You can be serious about things later on. But when you're young, you should go for it."

Rob Cavallo's decision to forego a producer's fee for *Dookie* and opt instead for percentage points was by now reaping rich rewards. The more copies the album sold, the wealthier he became. "I'd never really had any money before," he says, "and then my wife and I realized that with the proceeds from *Dookie* we could now afford to buy a little house. Suddenly I was able to get a mortgage and become a homeowner, which at the time seemed crazy. And while we were looking for a little house, we realized that actually we could afford a house that was a little bit bigger and a little bit nicer." Cavallo realized that investing his money in a place in which to live was more sensible than spending it on the kind of cars that would turn heads on Rodeo Drive. This decision was remarkable for having been made by a young man employed in the music industry and living in the most image conscious city in America.

One investment he did make was in a computer. He signed up to America Online and registered an email address that featured his full name. Cavallo accessed this account every few weeks in order to read the handful of messages sent his way. The delivery of these would be announced by a pop-up box that read: "You've Got Mail!" As *Dookie* began to take flight, he remembers dialing up one day and seeing that an inbox that normally housed no more than twenty messages was suddenly filled with something like eight thousand emails. "There were thousands of them," he remembers, "certainly more than I could read. At first it kind of freaked me out." The thumping majority of these messages were from strangers compelled to write after listening to *Dookie*. Some people wanted to thank him for being a part of an album that had made them happy. Some wrote to say that the record was their favorite of the year. A remarkable number of correspondents wanted its reader to know that his collaboration with Green Day had acted as an antidote to thoughts of suicide. "It was an amazing experience because the stories were just so personal," he says.

**A** curious aspect of overwhelming success is that its recipients are sometimes the last to notice it. For bands, the slow process of receiving royalty payments means that it takes time to recognize the wealth created by their name. In terms of insulation, few bubbles are quite as bombproof as the one provided by being on tour. This was particularly true in the days before mobile phones and instant online communication. In 1994, the majority of people wishing to contact a band would do so by writing a letter to a fan club or a record company. As people across continents began to hum the band's songs, Green Day themselves were at first cocooned from the speed at which their world was changing.

In the summer of 1994, Rob Cavallo met the band at an airport on the American East Coast. *Dookie* had not yet slipped its leash, but it was obvious to the producer that the record was on its way to being sold in enormous quantities. The band had been in Europe, and then on tour in the United States and Canada. They had been appearing in clubs and playing daytime slots at festivals that had been booked for them months before. The producer sat with the three musicians in his rental car and observed "that while they kind of knew [what was happening] they didn't *really* know." He laid out the events that were unfolding in bald terms.

"I said, 'Okay, guys, I just want you to know that we did it,'" he says. "'You guys are a big band. You guys are stars now.' And when I told them this, their eyeballs were popping out of their fucking heads. But they were cool about it, too. They were, like, 'Really?' They weren't sure how to take it. They were being very humble and kind of circumspect about the whole thing. 'What do you mean? Are you sure?' I'm, like, 'You guys have fucking made it. You have solidified your place in the rock world already and we're estimating that you're going to sell at least five million records.' It was crazy. Anyway, finally they hooped and hollered a little bit, but really they were very cool about it all. They were, like, 'Cool, we made it.' And then we went out and had hotdogs or something."

Green Day were about to lay claim to the always fleeting title of the "biggest band in the world." Despite this, their sense of understatement was so convincing that even in the face of an all-conquering album, the group were able to maintain the sense that in ways that mattered they were still the underdogs. A little over two years earlier the heavyweight music press had gone into spasms hurling both praise and abuse at representatives of the "alternative generation." Inevitably, Nirvana were heralded, while others, most notably Pearl Jam—and how ludicrous that now seems—were lambasted. But by 1994, the press appeared to lack the energy to do much more than fondly ruffle Green Day's hair. It appeared that music journalists were tired after a thirty-month party at which they had made passes at half the room while noisily insulting the other half, and had come away from the experience hoping not to embarrass themselves in this way again, at least not for a while. *Rolling Stone* waited until *Dookie* had sold more than four million copies in the United States before paying it any mind. The group did grace the front cover of *Spin* magazine in the autumn of 1994—in what was, astoundingly, their first major press piece in the United States— but the accompanying article featured both Green Day *and* The Offspring, among others. Billie Joe Armstrong's knack of writing about apparently small things either went unnoticed by the Fourth Estate or else was judged too adolescent to warrant serious inquiry. For years afterward, Armstrong would describe Green Day as being "a fan's band" rather than one beloved of music critics. But while the national media was unconvinced that *Dookie* was an event of genuine significance, its listeners held no such doubts.

"I remember at the beginning we didn't get the respect you would normally associate with a band that had sold fifteen million albums," says Rob Cavallo. "I was, like, 'Don't *Rolling Stone* realize that this guy [Armstrong] is a fucking genius and that every lyric on *Dookie* is the truth?' They're the truth of every young man and every young woman's experience coming out of high school and embarking on life. A lot of them came out of school and were going to work at Walmart or to work in a retail job. I used to quote lyrics all the time and say, 'These are experiences that kids all around the country are going through.' I just thought the whole thing was great. We got respect for the sales but we didn't get as much respect for the music. But for me, that was okay. Warners patted me on the back. But the thing that I thought was interesting is that a lot of people [there] thought, 'Well, that's okay because this is just some little rock band, but let's see if they can do it again . . .' But I remember saying to my wife, and eventually to the band, that I think we did good. We didn't pollute. We're not killing dolphins. We're not adding to the fluorocarbons out there. If you're going to add to the worth of the universe, what we did was for the most part pretty good. As a piece of art we brought a lot of good to people. I couldn't have been prouder to have been a part of it."

## CHAPTER SIX

# DO YOU REMEMBER WHEN WE WERE YOUNG, ADVENTURE HAD NO END?

In February 1994, Brett Gurewitz was driving from Santa Monica Boulevard to his home in Studio City in his 1984 tan Volvo station wagon. In his car's stereo was a tape that featured the final mixes of The Offspring's third album, scheduled to emerge two months later under the title *Smash*. With the tape deck turned as loud as it would go, the driver listened to the music abounding inside the car with growing disbelief. "I couldn't believe how catchy the songs were, or how big they sounded," he says. Rather than pull into the driveway of his home, instead he circled the block "maybe twenty times" in order to listen to the music "over and over and over and over" again. When he did finally slow the vehicle to a stop, he walked through his front door and greeted his wife with the words "'Honey, everything's going to be different now.'"

If it was obvious to Brett Gurewitz that 1994 was to be both his and The Offspring's *annus mirabilis,* the same could not be said for the band themselves. But here their record label's owner was benefitting from hearing his charges' music as a listener rather than as a participant in the white heat and occasional panic of the recording studio. Inside Track Records, *Smash* had come together in fragments, some of which made more sense than others. Noodles was unimpressed with both the tempo and the structure of the song "Self Esteem" and was puzzled why it wasn't played in his band's highest gear. Elsewhere, he failed to understand the relevance of the spoken words "you gotta keep 'em separated" from the track "Come Out And Play," and was required to place his trust in Dexter Holland's assurances that in context the line would make sense *and* be effective. Despite careful preparations, Holland himself was reworking songs while in the studio. He spent hours writing new lyrics and then as many hours recording the lines. The words to the songs "It'll Be A Long Time" and the album's title track emerged from this process. Even on the band's final night in the studio, the work was proceeding in this way. The singer would emerge from the sessions bathed in the sunlight of a brand new day. By the time the album landed in the can, every red cent of *Smash*'s recording budget had been accounted for.

On Santa Monica Boulevard, Brett Gurewitz wasn't the only person at Epitaph whose ears were caught by The Offspring's latest collection of songs. Jeff Abarta, Epitaph's one-time master of time and space, remembers the album coming in and thinking, "Oh my God, what have we got here?" There are many people who work in the record industry who claim to love whichever bands they happen to work with. Abarta, however, doesn't seem like one of these people. "[*Smash* is] as punk as fuck," he says. "It's a super-high-energy album." Still, he'd had his hopes dashed before. On hearing the song "Dirty Magic" from Ignition, a track that Dexter Holland also nominates as having played a key part in The Offspring's development, he thought that this, too, was "fucking amazing." But his high hopes for the parent LP were, at least in his view, scotched "when the album didn't really pan out." Nonetheless, he "could already see good things coming from this band."

Brett Gurewitz remembers identifying "Come Out And Play" as being *Smash*'s obvious lead-off single. The song that Dexter Holland had written about his experiences while driving through Watts and Compton en route to USC clearly occupied the position of first among equals on the album's track listing. A punk rock stomp of fine vintage, the track also features qualities that set it apart from the chasing pack. The spoken-word contribution from Blackball is of course crucial. Just as fundamental is Noodles's memorable Middle Eastern–sounding guitar motif that is played before a word has been sung, and which reemerges throughout.

The tone set by the music is jaunty and even carefree, but the lyrics carried atop its major-key power chords are a well-judged take on a serious subject. "By the time you hear the siren / it's already too late," sings Holland. The fracas he describes isn't witnessed firsthand; only its aftermath is described. This is an astute and authoritative decision. The narrator isn't in the thick of this story, just as the lives lived and lost here are not his own. "One goes to the morgue and the other to jail / one guy's wasted and the other's a waste," he says. En route to an effervescent chorus the observation that "your never ending spree of death and violence and hate / is gonna tie your own rope, tie your own your tie your own . . ." floats as if it were nothing more than the froth that it is not. Here, again, the vantage point is sound; the perspective as that of an observer is crucial. Dexter Holland doesn't sound like a suburban kid slumming it, or like a middle-class narrator taking an angle to a story to which he has no right to lay claim.

Following its release on March 10, 1994, KROQ began playing "Come Out And Play" immediately. In the six years that had elapsed since the broadcaster placed Social Distortion's "Prison Bound" onto heavy rotation, to the great surprise of everyone and without any precedent at all, much had changed in the radio game. As ever, the etymology of this came with the release of "Smells Like Teen Spirit," as well as from the subsequent singles released from *Nevermind*. With this glass ceiling smashed open, others followed; very suddenly, it was common to hear Rage Against the Machine, Smashing Pumpkins and Soundgarden on KROQ's playlist. From this, stations elsewhere in America followed suit. But here, again, there were crucial differences. The Offspring aren't a band inspired by punk, or one that embodies a punk rock spirit—they *are* punk. More than this, they represented a community that until now the station had been content to largely ignore. In fact, Epitaph's success rate in getting its bands played on the 'ROQ had failed to spread beyond the parameters of just one show.

"Bad Religion were first played on *Rodney on the ROQ* in 1980, which is what gave us our first break in the true punk world," says Brett Gurewitz. Along with a girlfriend, Greg Graffin remembers being invited down "on a school night" to the KROQ studio to watch Rodney Bingenheimer's late-night broadcast and to "listen as he played all the newest music, which was really fun." The broadcaster liked to invite young girls down to the studio, "although there was nothing improper about it," says the singer. Gurewitz recalls that "after 1980, Bad Religion really became a staple of that show, as did many bands in the early punk scene, such as the Germs and the Adolescents and Black Flag. In the days before the internet, part of the culture back then was that we would all tape that show and have them on cassette to listen to throughout the week . . . I think it broadcast every night after midnight. So everybody would tape it. But it was absolutely unthinkable that punk rock would be broadcast on regular commercial radio, whether it be KROQ or anyone else."

It is Rodney Bingenheimer who is credited with being the disc jockey that first put The Offspring on the air. If this sounds like a remarkable claim, it isn't. As with the BBC's John Peel,

Bingenheimer was the man who gave a great number of bands their first exposure on radio waves, many of whom were barely heard from again. By 1994, however, *Rodney on the ROQ* had been relegated to a weekly three-hour slot broadcast at 3:00 A.M. on a Monday morning. A man with a rare status of autonomy over the music he played—"I was always anti-Eagles, anti-beards. Within a few months I was playing four solid hours of punk," he once said—had been sidelined by the radio station he more than anyone else had helped legitimize. He was finally fired in the summer of 2017.

If nothing else, by the time of the release of "Come Out And Play" KROQ's center of gravity had moved in Rodney Bingenheimer's direction. The track began popping up on Jed the Fish's *Catch of the Day* slot; following this, regular airings appeared on the *Furious 5 @ 9* slot. As with Rob Cavallo calling the station to ask that they play Green Day's "Longview," Noodles helped further the correct impression that the song was attracting a positive response from listeners by ringing up the broadcaster himself and requesting that it be played. Here he was doing little more than pouring teacups half filled with water into an already full infinity pool. Bassist Greg K. remembers that "it was cool to hear ourselves on the radio. It was, like, 'Hey, man, that's us! [The] *Furious 5 @ 9* was where they played the top-five go-getters at nine o'clock. And 'Come Out And Play' was number one for, like, a month straight. We'd listen to it every night and go, 'Hey, we're number one again!' So it was kind of exciting to hear that and to realize that things were starting to happen."

"We sent [the song] to KROQ and they literally called my office and said, 'We're putting this into power rotation,'" says Brett Gurewitz. "They called me personally and told me that, and the next thing you know you couldn't turn on the radio in LA without hearing the song. At that moment KROQ was the most influential radio station in the States, so other radio stations followed suit. And immediately the orders [for *Smash*] started accumulating to the point where I had so many orders that I couldn't possibly press enough copies to supply them."

By this point, things begin to move at such a pace that it's difficult to know in which order to present the information. Fortified by the attention "Come Out And Play" was receiving from KROQ, Mr. Brett sought the services of the radio plugger Mike Jacobs. It was Jacobs's job to speak to stations up and across the United States and further press the case that The Offspring's second-ever single—and their first for *eight years*—be placed on heavy rotation. In 1994, this practice was widely employed by the music industry's bigger fish, often at a significant cost. If not quite a dark art, the trade of the radio plugger does give lie to the notion that good music appears on a radio station's playlist simply by virtue of it being good music. The technique also shows why a broadcaster's schedules are weighted so heavily in favor of material released on major labels. But in the spring of 1994, Brett Gurewitz was a bantamweight who was suddenly punching at a super-middleweight level. What's more, he fancied a shot at the heavyweight title. With this in mind, he cut Mike Jacobs a check for sixty thousand dollars so that he might devise a campaign in the name of "Come Out And Play."

This figure was by far the largest Epitaph had spent on The Offspring, or indeed on any of their bands. It exceeded the tab for *Smash* itself by up to three times. Astoundingly, it exceeded the figure the band spent on the video clip for "Come Out And Play" by more than *ten times*. Shot at a friend's garage in the suburbs of Los Angeles and directed by Darren Lavett, the clip that accompanied what was fast becoming one of the most talked about songs of the season cost just five thousand dollars to make. Captured in an afternoon, the quartet performed in front of a film crew in a room designed to house a car. Space was at a premium, as was breathable air. In terms of inconvenient quarters, only Mr. Punch in a tent with his wife, their baby and a crocodile could beat it. To mitigate the pizza-oven temperatures, the band brought in a fan. When switched on, the device caused the Mylar (a pliable metallic material also used to make helium balloons) affixed to the garage's walls for the day to shimmer and blow to good effect. On a rare shot from outside the garage's sweltering interior, Dexter Holland sang to the camera with a steady gaze and an authoritative charisma that belied his inexperience at the business end of a camera. A lesson in how to give the appearance of having spent money without actually having done so, the big cat's share of the modest budget of the "Come Out And Play" clip was reserved for the beer and meat needed for the barbecue-cum-wrap party that took place at the end of the shoot.

"On the radio, with 'Come Out And Play' you could feel that things were happening," says Dexter Holland. "It was expanding geographically, but slowly. So it went from LA to the next big cities, which were Phoenix and Las Vegas, and it kind of expanded in that way for a couple of months. Then MTV got the video and played it on [the alternative show] *120 Minutes*, and slowly it got into rotation outside of that slot. And that's when it went. MTV was literally like the biggest radio station in America. It was national; it broadcast to the whole country. And when they started playing the video, that's when things started happening really fast."

Holland remembers sitting in the living room of his "tiny five-hundred-square-foot apartment" watching MTV. It was a Friday night and the channel was running down its chart of that week's most popular videos. On this particular evening, the show's presenter was Leslie Nielsen, the actor who played Frank Drebin in the *Naked Gun* series of comedy films. The singer remembers Nielsen announcing that The Offspring were number one as being "about as surreal as it could get."

"I don't think that we thought we could have a hit single," says Greg K. Here, once again, the band's limited expectations were superseded by seemingly limitless possibilities. "Punk rock bands didn't have hit singles. I remember telling my friends that "Self Esteem" was a song that I thought could become big. But I also remember in the studio our producer at the time [Thom Wilson] wanted to change it because he thought it was too boring and too long. But we fought to keep it as it was. Then when the record was done [Epitaph] called us and said that they're gonna try and get 'Come Out And Play' some radio plays. And we were, like, 'What are you talking about? Okay, go ahead—good luck with that.' And then before you know it, I heard it on the radio and it just took off. So I was, like, 'Okay, I guess you were right.' [But] 'Come Out And Play' just seemed a little too strange for the radio."

"We didn't think we'd get any radio play," says Noodles. "When we were recording 'Come Out And Play' and the other songs on *Smash*, *Dookie* hadn't even come out yet. And Green Day were already signed to a major label when they were recording that album. We were just on Epitaph, which was an independent."

On May 26, 1994, The Offspring performed a concert at the Whisky a Go Go club on the east end of the Sunset Strip. The booking was unusual, but not quite without precedent. Noodles remembers that the Whisky didn't traditionally host punk rock shows, but here his memory is not wholly reliable. For one, the most famous room in Los Angeles did provide the setting for X's impressive album *Live at the Whisky A Go-Go On The Fabulous Sunset Strip*, released in 1986. But it is true that by the end of the 1980s and the start of the 1990s, the club had turned its collar to the punk scene. These were the days of glam metal, where the "Strip" found itself infested by young men with sore noses and hair that constituted a fire hazard. As the bands in which they played died a pitiful death, and as the world's eyes turned to small-city Seattle, for the first time in almost fifty years Los Angeles was largely a ghost town when it came to headline-hogging guitar-based music. Blinking with surprise, it was The Offspring who stepped into this void. The days when their audience consisted of ten people gathered at the Anti-Club were now behind them.

"It was The Offspring that really filled the vacuum in LA music," says Lisa Johnson, America's foremost punk rock photographer and the first lady of the Californian scene. "Obviously there was Bad Religion, and Pennywise were bubbling under, but it was The Offspring that first broke through in a big way. The show at the Whisky was kind of like their album release party, and it was just crazy. I'll never forget it. The walls were sweating—it was just *so* crazy. It was like a sea of people crawling over each other. And it was so sweaty and hot in there. It was so hot that I thought I was going to get malaria, and that is not a joke. I remember going, 'Oh my God, like, *the walls are actually sweating.*' I thought I was going to contract some horrible disease."

It should be stressed that up until "Come Out And Play" began floating through the heavy air of Los Angeles, The Offspring were not much more than a part-time band. Dexter Holland was studying for a doctorate in molecular biology, a course he duly put on hold, much to the displeasure of his mother. At great speed, he was experiencing firsthand the evidence of changing circumstances. At home one morning in his tiny apartment in LA, he looked out of the window while dressed in his boxer shorts and, while eating a bowl of breakfast cereal, saw a tenant in the apartment opposite holding a cordless phone into which he was exclaiming, "Yeah, dude! I'm looking at him right now!"

Greg K. had handed in his notice from his job at a print shop the week before the release of *Smash*. The Offspring had returned from a tour with Pennywise one spring Sunday and, realizing he had to be at work the following day, decided he didn't much fancy it. His band's most optimistic member, he allowed himself to imagine that *Smash* might sell a hundred thousand copies, maybe more. Noodles recalls the bassist telling him that he hoped that as many *as a hundred and seventy thousand people* might buy the record. Anyway, he says, "I thought, 'I have enough money to live' —I still lived at my mom's house—'so we'll see how far this can go . . .' And everybody thought I was crazy. They were saying, 'You quit your job on the basis of *that!*' And I thought, 'Well, if it doesn't work out then I'll just go back and get another job.'" Certainly, Greg K. had been made aware of the possibility of making a solid living from punk rock. During the band's tour of Europe supporting NOFX the previous summer, the headliners had asked him and his bandmates to carry some of the money they'd earned from their trip through customs.

Yet even at the time when "Come Out And Play" was making the sound of a heavy object entering a deep body of water, Noodles remembers that "I don't think any of us thought that this was gonna be our career. We just thought, 'Maybe we can do it for a few years and have some fun before we have to go back and get real jobs.'" Even as late as June 1994, Noodles was still gainfully employed as a school janitor at the Earl Warren Elementary School in the shadow of Disneyland in Anaheim. "I promised my boss that I'd finish the school year and that I wouldn't leave to go on tour if the band was taking off," he says. "And so we had our video on heavy rotation on MTV and there I'd be, sweeping up leaves each morning. There was a bus stop right across the street from the school, and there'd be these high school kids walking through the school grounds watching me work and pointing at me. They'd say, 'Man, what the hell are you doing? I just saw you on MTV right before I left the house!'"

Like many American punk rock bands at the time, The Offspring went about their business without the help of a manager. But as the horse they were riding out on began to gallop, Dexter Holland sought to engage an experienced hand. As the former manager of the now quietly successful Social Distortion,

Jim Guerinot seemed suited to the job. Not only had he handled the affairs of one of punk rock's most dysfunctional bands—and had done so without recourse to the services provided by a psychiatric hospital—but in the intervening years he had learned the workings of the music industry from inside its gilded walls. Following a spell at the Goldenvoice agency promoting shows such as Bruce Springsteen and eighty thousand friends at the Los Angeles Coliseum, he landed a job as the general manager of A&M Records.

It was at the start of this tenure that Jim Guerinot first heard from Dexter Holland. The Offspring frontman placed a phone call to the high-flying executive in 1992, saying that his band had formed after some of its members had seen a local Social Distortion concert. As it happened, Guerinot remembered the night in question because it had ended with him and Social Distortion guitarist Dennis Danell running with an amplifier through lawn sprinklers while being chased by the police. The pair spoke on the phone for a few minutes before Holland was told that his request was being turned down simply because of the scale of his job at A&M and the lack of time this would leave for handling the affairs of The Offspring. The frontman asked if he would mind if he sent over music from time to time, just to stay in touch. Jim Guerinot replied that this would be fine.

What Dexter Holland didn't know was that by 1992, his quarry's knowledge of modern punk rock was as rusty as a shipwreck. Two years later, what he also didn't know was that despite having overseen the release of Soundgarden's multiplatinum *Superunknown* album, Jim Guerinot had grown "extremely disillusioned" with life at the top of the major label food chain. He'd seen the record company for which he worked go from an operation run by mavericks to a tentacle of the polymorphous and deeply corporate Polygram group. He wanted out, and in April 1994 finally he became the manager of The Offspring.

His belief that Southern Californian punk rock represented a niche genre beloved of a small group of people hidden in the shadows of Los Angeles and Orange County did pose a problem. Jim Guerinot was aware that Social Distortion and Bad Religion had escaped the atrophy that had stricken the scene in the latter half of the 1980s, but that was about all he knew. Embarked on a vertiginous learning curve, at a Pennywise concert he introduced himself to Ron Welty without having any idea that he was shaking hands with the man who played the drums for the band he now managed. He believed that "Self Esteem" should be *Smash*'s lead-off single, while happily admitting that "I've made a career out of picking the wrong first single." Aware that The Offspring were fast breaking fresh ground, he called in at the Epitaph office to speak with Brett Gurewitz. If he believed that this was merely a courtesy call while he made plans to shepherd his band into the arms of a wealthier corporate suitor, his mind was quickly changed.

"I went to see Brett and his crew down at Epitaph and I was just floored," Guerinot says. "You have to remember that in 1994, I was thirty-five years old. I was way past my sell-by date when it came to the market for this kind of music. But I saw the operation they had going on down there and I thought, 'When it comes to handling the demand for The Offspring—you can do it.' I said to Brett, 'Dude, you can do this!' I don't know how Brett himself will characterize this, but in my heart of hearts I do not believe that he thought that they could do it. But I sat there with him and I said, '[I've run] a major record label. I can get us through to MTV. There's nothing that I'm doing on behalf of Soundgarden, or Sheryl Crow, or Sting, or you name them, that you guys can't do. There's nothing that you can't access. You've got it all.' All they needed was enough product, because if you've got enough product, you've got lightning in a bottle with [The Offspring]. It's on KROQ, and people are reacting. It's gonna play on MTV, and they're gonna put it on [the slot] *Buzz Bin*. Once that happens, this thing is gonna blow. I told him, 'You don't need [the help of] a major label to do this . . .' Dexter and myself were strongly advocating that Epitaph remain autonomous. I didn't think that they needed to do a deal even for the international market. Again, I told him, 'You can do this on your own.' He may remember things this way or he may not, I don't know, but I believed one thousand percent in what Brett was doing. And I believed that he could do it on his own."

What was about to happen is one of the most extraordinary stories in the history of rock and roll. The fact that it isn't more widely remembered is, at best, a shame; at worst, it's a crime. With *Smash* gaining altitude, the music industry's biggest players began to test the waters of a pond they'd previously thought of as a puddle, if indeed they thought of it all. Brett Gurewitz himself was in the curious position of being both a major label recording artist and the owner of an independent record label. With the decision to divorce himself from both Bad Religion and Atlantic Records imminent, suddenly he was inundated with offers from parties who were interested in buying a piece of his business. "I've had offers from almost every major [label]," he says. "I've had offers from the Warners group, to the Universal group, to the Sony group. But at the time [1994] one of the offers was for fifty million dollars."

One five.

"Five zero."

. . .

"For half of my company."

Right. Enquiring minds . . .

"Well . . ." says Gurewitz, and then pauses for quite some time. "Well, surprisingly, I don't think that I was tempted. So I didn't go for it. I think it just didn't seem real, to be honest. Numbers that big almost had no meaning. But, also, I just couldn't picture myself doing it. So what I did instead—and I guess no good deed goes unpunished 'cos I didn't receive any gratitude for doing this—but what I did instead was try to hold on to my ethics and my DIY values and my punk rock values. So I took out a loan and I started pressing records like crazy."

When Brett Gurewitz says that he took out a loan, what he means is that he remortgaged his house. Jim Guerinot remembers that he offered to help the label owner fund Epitaph's increased expenditure, but that Mr. Brett "wanted to do it on his own." In putting up the home in which he, his wife and his children lived as collateral, he was able to take out a loan for "a couple of hundred thousand dollars." He says that "my house wasn't worth that much so there was only so much that I could borrow. But," he says, "it was enough to get me going."

By now The Offspring's music was being played on each of what Jim Guerinot calls the United States' "key twenty" radio stations. The band were also being played on Australia's leading rock station, Triple J, as well as on BBC Radio 1 in Britain. Orders for *Smash* were arriving on Santa Monica Boulevard at a biblical rate. This was no music industry sleight-of-hand, either; the demand was legitimate. Three years previously, *Billboard* and the Recording Industry Association of America had introduced the information and sales tracking system Nielsen Soundscan as the means of counting the sales of singles and albums. This meant that there was no longer any need for record shops to file hand-tallied sales reports. In turn, there was no longer any need for major labels to resort to minor league bribery—a new refrigerator for a store owner here; tickets for a ball game for the regional manager of a large chain there—in order to artificially boost their weekly figures. (By definition, this practice came at the expense of smaller independent labels.) Nielsen also introduced a digital fingerprint for radio play that called time on the black art of paying hard currency to wide characters who would then file phony radio reports.

"By then, everything was digitally recorded [monitored], so anything that was legitimate was going to show," says Jim Guerinot. "And The Offspring record was legitimate. You didn't need a major label anymore. It was happening, you know. So you're in the middle of multiple storms. You're in the middle of people trying to get to me, for me to get them meetings with the band, so they can sign the band. You're in the middle of people trying to get to Brett so they can do a deal with Epitaph to get the band. Everything is going crazy."

"We did it with such a small crew as well," says Jeff Abarta. "We had five or six distributors all over the country who were helping. In the office, we would man the phones ourselves. We would call record labels and do fax broadcasts—this obviously being the days before email—and we would mail out posters and promo CDs. We were making sure that the band was visible while they were away on tour. And we were ordering so many CDs that pallets of the things were literally stacked from the back wall to the garage door [of the Epitaph office]. There were also pallets stacked high *outside* of the building because the space inside was full. And we had to sit out there and wait with the pallets; this is Hollywood, where you've got to guard your shit. But we were waiting for other trucks to come by and pick up the pallets because we couldn't fit them all in. It's pretty crazy just how much space all those CDs take up."

This, though, was just the start. Brett Gurewitz told *Rolling Stone* in 2014 that Epitaph's warehouse-cum-office was filled "from floor to ceiling" with Offspring records, tapes and compact discs to the extent that "it looked like a Rubik's Cube of pallets." A second building was rented in downtown Los Angeles; this, too, was soon full to capacity. Gurewitz rented space in other buildings. As the summer of 1994 gave way to the autumn, *Smash* was selling in excess of one hundred thousand copies a week. The demand was such that a plan was executed for the album to be sent directly from the pressing plants to the central warehouses of the major record chains.

These scenes of breathless chaos at the Epitaph office were relayed to The Offspring secondhand. Long before his band had combined with Epitaph and its staff to become a David that was suddenly getting the better of a Goliath, Dexter Holland would visit Brett Gurewitz's company to lend a hand manning the phones and calling college radio stations and record shops. But with workers now putting in serious shifts on behalf of his own group, The Offspring themselves were on the road. Greg K. remembers, "We knew what was going on, but we were on tour for the better part of a year and a half. We'd do the States and then Europe, and then Japan and Australia, and then we'd be home for a couple of weeks at a time and then it was time to go back out. There was *a lot* of touring. But it just kept on growing. In the States we did a club tour. And then we went out and did bigger clubs and theaters. And then by the end we were playing arenas. It was a pretty busy time."

I n 1994, it was impossible to hear or read a sentence that featured the words Green Day without it being followed by the name The Offspring. This was the punk rock equivalent of the Beatles and the Stones; or the *American* punk rock equivalent of the Sex Pistols and The Clash. Noodles still chuckles at the memory of being on tour and finding on the magazine rack of a truck stop a publication titled *Green Day Versus The Offspring.* "It was mostly just pictures and speculation. I thought it was the funniest thing ever, but it really wasn't great journalism." (In this, the guitarist is correct. "Whether you love Green Day of [*sic*] don't give a 'dookie' about them, one thing's for certain—they have an interesting story to tell, and their moods change as often as their hair colors!" is just one of the many sentences unlikely to trouble the committee for the Pulitzer Prize.) The Offspring's independent status meant that the more militant members of the punk tribe tolerated their presence, and in some cases even welcomed it. If the band wished to play 924 Gilman Street, they could; although as one of the club's founding fathers told *Rolling Stone* in 1995, "Green Day hung out in the punk scene, but their music wasn't punk; The Offspring's music was punk, but they didn't hang out in the punk scene."

Elsewhere, the distinctions were less clear. At an appearance by Dexter Holland and Ron Welty at Live 105, a modern rock radio station in San Francisco, a not quite on the ball DJ introduced the pair as members of Green Day. By way of retaliation, Holland instructed listeners to send in the most vulgar faxes they could think of, for which the crudest won a pair of tickets for the band's show at the Filmore the following evening. He then read the winning entry out on the air. (Green Day themselves would also partake in this less than fiery rivalry. Onstage at the London Astoria in the autumn of 1994, Billie Joe Armstrong told a fan who joined the band onstage wearing an Offspring T-shirt that he must "take that fucking shirt off." He was handed a piece of Green Day apparel by way of compensation.) Come the night of the show at the Filmore, The Offspring also instructed members of their road crew to hand out free tickets to fans who might be looking to employ the services of touts lingering outside the venue's front doors.

Even more than Green Day, the reaction to The Offspring in the established music press was mixed. A review of the band's show at the Garage in the British magazine *Metal Hammer* dismissed the band's success in short order and concluded with the word "Next!" In the same year, a review by Angela Black in the often prickly and at the time potentially career-changing *New Musical Express* suggested that *Smash* was the work of a manufactured band rather than one with a decade of active service to its name. The band's UK publicist, Chrissie Yiannou, received a call from Jim Guerinot, who had at that very instant become the latest in a long line of American front-office staff to be affronted by the occasional ferocity of the British music press. Jim had a question for Chrissie: what are you gonna do about this? Uni-laterally, Epitaph also sent a letter of complaint to the publica-tion's London offices, a course of action with which the publicist was in less than full agreement.

"I remember reading the review and going, 'This is wrong,'" she remembers. "I thought, 'What she's written is wrong.' But I had no idea how to handle it. But I also thought, 'I know she's wrong, but can't she just write what she wants?' In the end, I think I wrote to her, by fax of course. Quite nicely, I said, 'Just to let you know, they're not [a manufactured band]. They've been around since this time. They've had three albums out.' And of course she never responded. No one responded. And because of that, I became a bit protective of them. They were starting to get really big and suddenly everybody wanted a piece of them. People would be phoning me wanting to talk to them. But I'd become a bit wary about giving free rein to people just for them to say anything they liked. I'd rather know that people know what they're talking about before I'd let them do anything [with the band]. And that's how I became. People would call up and they'd be, like, 'Well, can we interview them?' And I'd say, 'Are you familiar with them? Do you know who they are?' And if I felt that they had no clue, or if I just felt that they were out to get them, I wouldn't let them go there."

This culture of wariness, if not quite outright mistrust, was in keeping with how the band handled their public affairs during the punk rock tsunami of 1994. The ubiquity of both "Come Out And Play" and "Longview" helped cement the idea that The Off-spring and Green Day were finding good fortune in exactly the same way. There were of course many welcome similarities. Both groups identified themselves as being punk rock—and still do—and both had hoisted the genre's black flag up the mast and watched in amazement as millions of people saluted. But while Green Day became famous, the same can be said only of The Offspring's *music*. This was by design, not by accident, and was consistent even when it came to the clips that aired on MTV as often as advertisements for Domino's Pizza. "We deliberately shot our videos with fucked-up film and black light because we don't want to be seen too well," said Dexter Holland in 1995. "Once they see a close-up of your face plastered on a screen, it's over. There's no more mystery or fun to it."

"We don't want to be overexposed," Greg K. told *Rolling Stone*. "Not to knock Green Day, 'cause I like Green Day, but it's, like, every time you turn on MTV, you see Billie Joe's face."

By the middle part of 1994, "Come Out And Play" owned property in the mainstream so prominent that the USC marching band played the song on their brass instruments prior to home games of the Trojans American football team. But in the face of overwhelming success, The Offspring themselves were uncommonly secretive. In the United States and Europe, the band did very little press. Much more surprisingly, offers to appear on the *Late Show with David Letterman* and *Late Night with Conan O'Brien* were declined. Most startlingly of all, an invitation to play on the hugely influential *Saturday Night Live* was also rebuffed.

"I guess what you would call the really high-profile stuff just didn't feel natural to us," says Dexter Holland. "It was for a few reasons, one of which was because at that time we hadn't come from that world. We were very much more of an underground band at that point. It kind of didn't feel right for where we were in our progression as a band to do that. Also, we were thinking about how at the time there were a lot of crazy things happening with bands like Nirvana. There was all this stuff where people were literally dying because of what was going on. And so we thought, 'You know, maybe it's not a good idea to all of a sudden turn up the heat to a million and a half and hog the entire spotlight. Maybe it's not a good idea, mentally, to do that.' So that was a real concern for us, the fact that we still wanted to have normal lives. Also, as crazy as it may sound, one of the reasons that we didn't do *Saturday Night Live* is that we didn't think we were going to sound very good. Four months earlier, you know, we'd been playing garage parties, and now we're supposed to play a live national TV show. I don't think we were ready for that. We were still basically touring in a van when all this stuff started happening. So we thought, 'Not only does this feel a little bit weird, but it might suck, too. So as politely as we could, we turned it down. I don't think that anyone had ever turned *SNL* down, so I don't think they were very happy about that. But it wasn't our intention to insult them. It was just right for where we were at the time."

"We wanted to do things differently," says Jim Guerinot. "When we got asked to play "Self Esteem" live [on TV], we passed. When we got asked to be on the cover of *Band* magazine, we passed. We passed on everything for the longest time because the band did not want to play by those rules. They really wanted to play in a much more underground Epitaph fashion. Eventually they *did* do *Spin* magazine, but even then we all considered that to be a mistake. We wished we hadn't done it . . . but, really, we hadn't done anything and Green Day were doing everything. In terms of marketing, at that point what Green Day was doing was indistinguishable from the Red Hot Chili Peppers. We didn't want to do that. And, by the way, I don't disagree with Green Day, because they've done great by it and that's what they were. We would eventually do that [stuff] but we felt at that point in our career, our life, that we wanted to separate ourselves from them a lot. But both of us were still selling unbelievable amounts of records."

Faced with countless requests from people wanting to trade a moment's exposure for a pound of flesh, The Offspring simply circled their wagons. Whereas Green Day would at first be bewildered by their own success, and then, for a time at least, alienated by it, their neighbors to the south carried on as if not much had changed. It's difficult to nominate a band who, upon finding their first taste of major league success, broke more of the golden rules from the music industry playbook than The Offspring did. Being on Epitaph certainly helped. No one got greedy and neither the band nor their label made stupid or reckless decisions, although there'd be plenty of time for that. Brett Gurewitz, anyway, was being knocked many times sideways by the galloping improvement in the fortunes of both parties; more than this, the company's ethos, such as it was, was to let its artists get away with murder. The Orange County band were also fortified by the fact that by 1994 they were at the older end of the young man market. Each had other things in their lives. Ron Welty and Noodles were both fathers. Greg K. once described punk rock as being "something I started listening to because it was around, and I got used to it." For Dexter Holland, a life in academia awaited if a future with The Offspring did not. Even though punk did eventually pay its way many times over, he still found the time to coauthor a paper packed with punchy and clearly comprehensible sentences such as "an important post-transcriptional regulatory step in gene expansion is that the 59 ends of mRNAs can base-pair with the complementary sequences in the 39 untranslated regions (UTRs) or their target mRNAs and suppress translational capacities of those mRNAs."

"It was exciting to be a part of something that kept growing, although parts of it were tiring," says Greg K. "It was great that something we'd been doing for ten years had finally come to this. And I think we were old enough it to enjoy it more, too. When bands are in their early twenties, that kind of success can overwhelm them. But I think we were old enough—I was twenty-nine when *Smash* came out—to feel more grounded and better able to appreciate what was going on."

"That year was fun, and some of those days I'd describe as salad days," says Noodles. "But there's so many times that I can look back on and say, 'That was really fun.' The bad days were really fun, too. Sleeping on NOFX's tour bus in Europe the first time we were over there was so much fun. As things were taking off for us, we weren't really sure what it really meant. It was like the earth was shaking beneath us a little bit, and us not being sure if the foundations were steady. It was fun and it was exciting, but I don't think they were the best days the band has ever had. It threw us for a little bit of a loop. I think it's been much more fun before then and since. But I'm not complaining 'cos those times were fun and exciting. But I'm just glad that we lived through it."

On December 7, 1994, The Offspring broke their boycott of live television. The occasion was the *Billboard Music Awards Show* held at the Universal Amphitheatre in Los Angeles. Comprised of a self-congratulating gathering of artists worth their weight in platinum, the event was hosted by actress Heather Locklear and comedian Dennis Miller. No space was found in the winner's circle for the Little Punk Rock Band from Orange County That Could, and Did. That month, Epitaph Records had issued "Self Esteem" as the second single from *Smash*. Released a mere *nine months* after its predecessor, the song would go on to become the band's biggest-selling stand-alone release to date. That this was the most expedient track to play live on television was a proposition without a brain. The Offspring, though, refused, and agreed to appear onstage only if they were given free rein to do as they pleased. If the organizers of the *Billboard Music Awards Show* were aghast at this news, they held their tongues. More than this, they allowed the band to play the fast-paced and foul-mouthed "Bad Habit," one of *Smash*'s deeper cuts, in its place.

Jim Guerinot describes the performance as constituting "a fucking mess." Here, he's clearly onto something. Dressed in a loose-fitting purple suit and modeling long green cornrows, Dexter Holland looks like the Joker after a heavy night with the Scarecrow at Arkham Asylum. Greg K. has dyed his hair blue, which he wears well. In his oversized T-shirt, baggy shorts and backward baseball cap, Noodles's getup is that of a five-year-old. As the musicians clatter through the music, the sound is thin. The frontman struggles to reach the song's numerous high notes. They play in front of a backline that would fit comfortably on the small stage of the Whisky A Go Go. But for all its sonic deficiencies, as played here "Bad Habit" surges with an energy that in the context of network television is nothing short of confrontational. Now shorn of his jacket, Dexter Holland stands at the lip of the stage and sings, "I feel like I'm God / you stupid dumb shit goddamn motherfucker." There is a five-second delay between the words heard by the audience at the Universal Amphitheatre and those heard by millions of television viewers. This is probably just long enough for someone at the network to lose their job. The Offspring had warned the show's organizers that they might do something "eccentric" during their allotted four minutes—the band even toyed with the idea of playing "Too Drunk To Fuck" by Dead Kennedys—and here they were, as good as their word. As those watching at home wondered why the sound on their television seemed suddenly to be on the fritz, Dexter Holland stage dives into the audience. He is a wearing a T-shirt that reads: "Corporate Rock Kills Bands Dead."

Somewhere in the Bay Area, Fat Mike was watching the broadcast with Tre Cool. The NOFX frontman was "so happy when Green Day got big," but admits, "that when it came to The Offspring, I was a little bit jealous." The drummer had returned home from his own band's tour just two days earlier and was now decompressing with the help of a bong and some good company. Watching through a pea-souper of pot smoke, Tre, a man who only forty-eight hours earlier had played on a bill that also featured Jon Bon Jovi, said, "The Offspring—what a bunch of sellouts!" Fat Mike looked at his friend and said, "You know they're on Epitaph, right? They are on a punk label. Aren't you guys on Warners or something?" Tre Cool filled his lungs from the bong. "I really couldn't believe that he called the band sellouts," says Fat Mike. "Neither The Offspring *or* Green Day are sellouts. Neither one of those bands knew that they were going to get big like that. They didn't write music to be big. It just kind of happened that millions of people discovered that punk rock is awesome."

Come the final reckoning, *Smash* spent one hundred and one weeks on the *Billboard* Hot 200 album chart. It peaked at number four. By the end of 1994, it had sold just shy of four million copies in the United States and was the country's ninth best-selling album of the year. In the fullness of time, it would sell six million copies in the United States, and eleven million copies throughout the world. It is the best-selling independent rock album of all time.

"Brett risked it all," says Jeff Abarta. "He remortgaged his house so he could do it on his own. He did not want to bow to major label pressure and sell out. And he was getting astronomical offers. I just can't imagine being on the phone and being offered those kinds of sums . . . And I remember that no one thought we could do it. And so the payoff for Brett in proving that he could do it would be much bigger than any of those offers. It equates to a lifetime of credibility. And he was able to pull it off. He got the right loans, he got the right distributors and he got the right team around him. And I am very proud to be a part of that team."

"When I think back to what happened back then, pride is a big factor," says Brett Gurewitz. "I'm very proud of two things.

One is the decision to stay independent. And the second thing is the effect of us staying independent, the positive effect it had on the independent music community. It really raised the sea level for the indie music business in general. For example, suddenly there's an indie label that's selling five million records a year. In the rock genre, right. And independent stores around the world are able to buy these records from distributors for the same price that they can buy records from a major label. Let me explain what that means. Prior to that, independent record shops had to buy their records from what are called 'one-stops' because major labels would not sell to them because it was too much work to sell in copies of one or two. So major labels would sell to one-stops, which were distributors that would cater only to independent stores. The one-stops would raise the price by a couple or three dollars and would sell the albums on to the independent stores. So in other words, the independent stores—basically the punk stores that were interested in catering to people who are interested in finding out about new artists—those stores were at a disadvantage compared to major chain stores.

"As punkers, our allegiance was to the indie stores 'cos that's where we'd buy fanzines and that's where we'd find out about new music. That's where we congregated. That's where we'd buy copies of import albums from Japan or England. Suddenly these stores were flourishing because they could buy The Offspring's *Smash* and Bad Religion's *Against The Grain* and *About Time* by Pennywise, and they're selling tons of these things. These were huge records. They were flying out the door. And they were able to have parity with the chains on these records only. So it helped the distributors. It helped indie retail. It helped fanzines and magazines. It basically raised the sea level within the whole community. There are distributors in Europe and Australia that cite that time as the period when their companies grew and they were given the opportunity to establish themselves. So it kind of had a very powerful 'knock on' effect, as they say.

"And those are my people, so I'm really proud that my decision sort of caused that."

## CHAPTER SEVEN

# HEY, HEY, COME OUT AND PLAY

It's rarely a good thing when a band finds itself on the news. Late in the evening of September 9, 1994, MCVB TV news in Boston aired an item about a Green Day concert at the Hatch Shell, a crescent-moon-shaped stage at the Charles River Esplanade in the city's Back Bay region. The report informed its viewers that "Boston's esplanade is out of control tonight as thousands of young music fans go wild." A police spokesman told the station that "for a while Boston Avenue was shut [on] Longfellow Bridge and Mass Av [Massachusetts Avenue]." Earlier in the day, local channels had broadcast reports of the band's date with their city for the benefit of viewers who had recently awoken from a coma or who for other reasons were unfamiliar with their music. "Their sound is basically pretty upbeat," began one. "They're known for being very frenetic and energetic. The band is made up of three people. Tre, the drummer, has green hair; Billie Joe Armstrong is the lead singer; and Mike Dirnt, who plays bass." There then followed a clip of Tre

Cool, with blond hair, destroying his drum kit. "The hallmark of this group is that they like to act up onstage and are given to sort of crude antics such as spitting and throwing things around." "Thousands of students have descended on Boston [to see] the show from hot new punk sensations Green Day," announced another reporter.

The Welcome Back Weekend was an event staged by the city's leading alternative rock radio station, WFNX. The concert was free and organizers anticipated that somewhere in the region of twenty thousand people planned to make their way downtown to see a band who at the time of their booking were not yet generating the kind of heat one finds in a smelting plant. But as stage time approached, a crowd wildly in excess of this number had arrived on-site. Broadcasters announced that the figure was thirty thousand people; this then rose to thirty-five thousand, then fifty, then sixty, then sixty-nine, then seventy. Bidding finally stopped at one hundred thousand concertgoers. If WFNX's on-site representatives were feeling pinpricks of cold sweat at the prospect of learning the hard way that a crowd can only be controlled with its own consent, they weren't yet showing it. Tai Irwin, a station DJ known as the "Morning Guy," told his listeners that "this is fun. This is a crowd that's out to have a good time tonight no matter what. And we're gonna do it, we're gonna have a great time. We're gonna bring rock back to the esplanade in a big way. We're gonna behave ourselves and we're gonna have a wonderful time. Nobody's gonna get hurt. That's what this crowd is about tonight."

On closer reading, the molasses-voiced broadcaster's hyperbole betrays traces of nervousness. The promise that "nobody's gonna get hurt" sounds as if the Welcome Back Weekend is pitching the idea that concertgoers might not end their night in hospital as some kind of unique selling point. That "we're gonna behave ourselves" seems like something a supporter of England's national football team might have to say, as if expecting thanks for *not* wreaking havoc in a foreign city during a World Cup.

The event's organizers were at first beside themselves that their event was clearly a significant draw; later they would twitch nervously at the potential for turmoil. Things that had initially seemed like good ideas were rapidly becoming less so. Snapple, at the time the country's favorite densely sugared soft drink of choice, had sponsored the event at a cost of one hundred and fifty thousand dollars. This meant that after being refreshed with a drink of iced tea or pink lemonade, tens of thousands of people had in their hands an empty glass bottle. A WFNX employee said how the station "started broadcasting live and [the band] was going to be playing. We see kids and people streaming [in] and we think, 'Wow there's a lot of people coming to the event.' And they just didn't stop."

By the time Green Day arrived onstage the situation was becoming unmanageable. The open-access space in front of the Hatch Shell featured three barriers staggered at intervals so as to calm the crowd. As Billie Joe Armstrong tore into the opening chords of "Welcome To Paradise," only the barrier at the front of the stage remained standing. From the start the music was greeted by a slam pit that appeared to comprise half of the audience. Suddenly, Snapple bottles were arcing through air like the missiles they had now become. The fact that some members of the audience were crowd surfing while holding metal rubbish bins probably didn't help anyone who wanted to dispose of their glass receptacle in a responsible way. Security personnel attempted to handle the crush developing at the front of the stage by lifting fans over the barriers. For any punk band that proposed that society should be organized according the principles of anarchy—of which Green Day were not one—this was it in its basest form. As Johnny Rotten once put it: "Get pissed; destroy."

Despite an image that many older or more ardent punks believed to be far too cute, a generally pleasing aspect of Green

Day's character was that they couldn't always be relied upon to play nice. Realizing that the Welcome Back Weekend was essentially a corporate event, the band encouraged the crowd to remove a giant balloon that bore the WFNX logo. Incongruously, a number of flowerbeds had been planted in front of the Hatch Shell's stage; some reports state that both the crowd *and* Billie Joe Armstrong destroyed these. Before long, some members of the audience had decided that they'd enjoyed all the fun there was to be had front of house and chose instead to join the band onstage. Not long after this, Billie Joe Armstrong and Mike Dirnt took their leave. With his eyes down, Tre Cool continued to hammer away on his drum kit. When he did finally lift his head, he was confronted with the sight of a semicircle of people twitching like the tail of a rattlesnake.

Green Day's set had comprised seven songs and lasted for only twenty-four minutes. Watching the evening collapse, a WFNX employee said, "We're dead. We're so dead." By now a ruffled Tai Irwin was onstage, surely regretting the words he had broadcast just hours earlier. "Listen, you fucking assholes, we need you to get [off the stage]," he shouted. "Just remember, all the people on our staff and all the police officers are your neighbors. This is Boston! This is our esplanade! Take care of it!"

"I did try to quell the crowd, and I meant what I was saying, but it was the stupidest thing in the world," Irwin said later. "I'm sitting there feverishly going, 'This is our esplanade, don't screw it up. We want to keep doing concerts here, and, you know what, we don't want anyone to get hurt . . .' But no one heard a word I said."

With the crowd's exit strategy becoming a diaspora, some audience members grouped into factions keen to prevent the evening's manic energy from flagging. A police radio call was placed requesting that all officers attend the scene unfolding at the Hatch Shell. Boston Police Department officers already on-site became the targets of people armed with rocks. A number of concertgoers liked the idea of seeing what a squad car would look like with its tires in the air. Others rocked buses in an attempt to tip them over. By the time order was restored, fifty people were under arrest. Amid the debris in front of the stage there lay a calculus textbook and a prosthetic limb.

"Man, the Boston riot," says Mike Dirnt, as if still awed by the memory of the event. "I remember prison inmates who were allowed out for the day because of good behavior were used as security, along with police officers [to supervise them]. I also remember there being a bicycle rack for a barricade. I think they just figured it was going to be a leisurely day outside and they didn't realize—and *we* didn't realize, either—what it was going to be like. I think they figured that there'd be a few thousand people meandering around the park. But actually seventy thousand people showed up and all of a sudden things are out of control. We went on and did our normal show and the crowd were going ballistic and the whole place just went nuts. The funny thing is, the police freaked out but the inmates were totally cool. The inmates were helping people and probably thinking, 'This ain't a riot—I've seen a *prison riot!*' But the police were freaking out and hitting people with billy clubs. It was crazy. We had to do [court] depositions for a couple of years after that one. At the time, we were in as much shock as everyone else. We were basically locked up underneath [the stage] for a couple of hours while all the shit was going down. I remember finally getting back to my hotel room and people were calling me going, 'You're on the news in California! What the fuck happened?'"

(Perhaps the person most alarmed at the sight of the chaos wreaked in the band's name was Billie Joe Armstrong's mum, who called her son to express her unhappiness at what she'd seen.)

The following day, on September 10, the *Boston Herald* reported that "requests for the crowd—estimated by State Police at 65,000—to disperse failed to move a hardcore group of about 5,000 people, who taunted police and began throwing bottles at officers and concert staff. At 9:30 P.M., a line of approximately 100 state troopers and Boston police officers formed a human wedge and drove the crowd out of the Esplanade and into the Back Bay. Calm was restored by 10 P.M. . . . . roughly 50 [people] treated for minor injuries—from sprains to drug overdoses—suffered during the concert and the hour-long fracas between police and the crowd, police and medical personnel said."

Barely seven months before the donnybrook of September 9, Green Day concerts were staged in venues such as the Paradise Lounge in San Francisco and the Cactus Club in San Jose. Come the end of the summer, their third album was on its way to becoming a diamond-platinum concern—the award given to an LP that has sold ten million copies in the United States—while its music was on the radio more often than the traffic reports. In 1994, the band played a hundred and seventy-five shows in rapidly changing circumstances. They went from a group whose existence was unknown to the mainstream music press, to the season's hottest act. They appeared on network television programs such as the *Late Show with David Letterman*, *The Jon Stewart Show* and *Late Night with Conan O'Brien*. They released three singles, all of which were hits. They shot four videos, including the clip that accompanied "When I Come Around," released on the last day of January 1995, which reached the number-two spot on the *Billboard* mainstream rock chart and sold more than half a million copies in the United States alone. The following month, the trio were in the running for four Grammy Awards, from which they took home the prize for best alternative music performance for *Dookie*. By this point, the band's world was a place of constant change. The only exception to this rule were Green Day themselves.

"I couldn't have predicted that [*Dookie*] would sell twenty million copies, or whatever it was, but I do think that [level of] success would have destroyed a lesser band," says Lawrence Livermore. "By lesser band, I don't mean less talented, I mean less cohesive; Nirvana being a good example. They were a very talented band, but they basically went through almost exactly the same thing. Green Day came out of almost nowhere, sold millions and millions of records and became the center of everyone's attention . . . Suddenly they couldn't get a moment's peace. Also, beyond the standard stuff of being that age—what do I want to do with my life? do I want to settle down and marry someone, or play the field?—all those issues are hard enough for any twenty-year-old, let alone someone who's basically just set out to write some music and be liked."

"Things were kind of weird," says Billie Joe Armstrong. "We were an independent-thinking band and I think we had the scars and bruises to prove it. But there were some people who thought we came out of nowhere. And we were, like, 'Fuck you, we've been doing this for five years and we have two albums and two EPs out [before *Dookie*]. We definitely felt that we had some authenticity, or some independent cred, or whatever. The hard part was having a record like *Dookie* that just explodes and then the question is, 'How do we inform people that we've been around for a while?' Because we'd play a song like 'One Of My Lies' [from *Kerplunk*] in our set and there'd be a whole bunch of people that had never heard it before. It was like they were hearing a brand new song. And that can be good but it can also be frustrating 'cos it's, like, we were used to playing our older songs on tour and having people singing along to them."

One of the more striking aspects of Green Day's performances in 1994, particularly at events as enormous as the Welcome Back Weekend and Woodstock '94, is just how *punk* the band are. There is something coiled and combustible here, a snotty quality and an air of brattish insolence that curls its lip at anything resembling authority. They play with a kinetic energy that carries with it the possibility of becoming unhinged. The musicians twitch as if a current is surging through them. If this were a house, it would catch fire.

The following year, Green Day were presented with an award at the Kerrang! Awards, an annual ceremony staged by the weekly English rock magazine. Wattie Buchan, mainstay with the unreconstructed, and rubbish, Edinburgh punk group the Exploited, presented the gong to the band. Unconvinced of the Americans' authenticity, the Scotsman longed for their name not to emerge from the list of nominees with whom they had been bracketed. Photographed with Green Day afterward, Buchan looks displeased. At the after-party he was confronted by Billie Joe Armstrong who told him, "When you die, I'm going to be standing over your grave, laughing at you." The pair had to be separated by onlookers. Fortified by a tenure at 924 Gilman Street, two independently released albums and a debut European tour in circumstances at which even the Exploited might have balked, Armstrong was right to bristle at the idea that he and his band were nothing more than arrivistes of doubtful provenance.

The first leg of the North American tour in support of Green Day's third album rolled onto the road two weeks after the release of *Dookie*. Opening night took place at the Cattle Club in Sacramento on February 15, followed by a further forty-three dates. Support slots were shared by fellow East Bay punks Tilt and the occasionally brilliant Dead Milkmen, from Philadelphia. Despite Green Day twice performing live on US network television in less than a month during this stretch, the tour largely visited only the smaller clubs of major and not so major American and Canadian cities. This would be the case for the band's first five months on the road. A portent of the world that Green Day were about to enter came at an in-store appearance at the Costa Mesa branch of the Virgin Megastore chain. According to

Billie Joe Armstrong, the atmosphere inside the shop was "super cheesy," and that no one in attendance seemed quite sure how to behave. But the band's adeptness at extracting silver linings from oppressive clouds was already pronounced. With some ease, the event was transformed from an awkward first date to an unbridled one-night stand. By the end of the set, fans, and perhaps some shoppers, too, were throwing themselves off the band's sound monitors.

The tour's first European leg began with an appearance at the Garage in London on April 27, and would remain on the continent for more than two months. During this run, the band played three headline concerts in England's capital city. The third of these was an appearance at the medium-sized Astoria 2 club in the dependably hectic neighborhood of Soho, at which the author saw Green Day play live for the first time. In a venue abounding with energy, cries of "Sellout!" could be heard from people gathered at the rear. A committed Anglophile with family in London, Lawrence Livermore was in town that night and decided to head down to the subterranean club to say hello to the band. Despite their professional relationship having ended the year before, the two parties had remained friends. But he found the clamor of well-wishers and camera crews who were by now being drawn toward Green Day's flame to be tiresome and he decided to walk home to the house in which he was staying, in Bayswater. En route, a tour bus pulled up alongside him out of which leaned Tre Cool. His former bandmate ordered him to cancel his plans for an early night and instead grab himself a brush and a can of red paint and be ready to party (this being the time the word "party" was transforming itself from a noun into a verb). They ended up in a bar in the northwest neighborhood of Maida Vale and were later joined by one of the group's managers who was waving around a copy of *Billboard* magazine. Inside, Reprise Records had taken out a full-page ad. Announcing that Green Day's first major label release had sold half a million copies in the United States, the ad said, simply, "Dookie Is Gold."

Despite being resistant to most American punk rock, British audiences were beginning to hum Green Day's songs in the shower. In 1994, the band made their first appearance on what was at the time the BBC's flagship music program, *Top of the Pops.* Broadcast each Thursday evening, the half-hour show combined onstage appearances with promotional videos from a selection of artists resident in that week's top-forty singles chart. If nothing else, *"TOTP,"* as it was sometimes known, can surely claim to be the only music program in the world to have broadcast performances by both Mötorhead and the Wombles. But the BBC's insistence that artists sing live while miming the music itself—a rule that was later revoked—meant that an invitation to appear on the show was occasionally declined, most notably by The Clash. While Green Day did consent to appear on *Top of the Pops,* the decision to do so was taken not without qualms. As the music of "Welcome To Paradise" was pumped from the studio's speakers, Billie Joe Armstrong sang live while wearing a T-shirt on which were scrawled the handwritten words "Who Am I Fooling Anyway?" Before singing the song's opening line, he can be heard to shout, "Turn it up!"

By the summer of 1994, Green Day's Converse-clad feet were no longer touching the ground. Following their European visit, the trio returned to the United States and, just three days after landing at San Francisco International Airport, began the tour's second North American leg. This time the opening slot was given to a band who have to date yet to be credited as one of punk rock's more revolutionary forces. Formed in San Francisco in 1991, Pansy Division are a group of gay men the sexual orientation of whom is mentioned only because it forms the subject matter of virtually every one of their songs. The band were founded by vocalist, guitarist and principal songwriter Jon Ginoli, who after a stint in Los Angeles moved to the City by the Bay because he "wanted to be in a place where there were a lot more of us." He grew up in the small Illinois town of Peoria, three hours southwest of Chicago, a place where "I had one example of what it was to be an adult, which was to be a heterosexual who has a family." Despite knowing he was gay from the age of twelve, it took a further eight years before he felt comfortable enough to come out. But Ginoli was quick to recoup lost time. Pansy Division's debut album, *Undressed,* released on Lookout Records in 1993, gloried not in same-sex relationships but in same-sex *sex*. "In high school he'd spend hundreds of hours / fantasizing about boys in the showers / Billy was hung, Rick was thick / Daniel had a most upstanding dick" are just two of the rhyming couplets from the unambiguously titled "The Cocksucker Club."

"One of the reasons we formed is because by the time the early nineties rolled around you could sing about almost anything in a song except *that*," says Ginoli. "I wanted to sing about being gay because at that time it seemed like there was kind of this default setting where if you didn't sing about it people would assume you were automatically heterosexual. I knew there were gay musicians because I'd met a few of them and I knew other people who had slept with them. And I wondered why none of them had come out. So I thought, 'Okay, well, if no one is going to have the nerve to sing about this because they're worried about their careers, or because they're just reticent, then I'll sing about it.' I knew that we'd have the whole field to ourselves so I decided to be as bold, as out and as uncensored as possible. One reason I decided to do it when I did was because at the time there were political ramifications in our country . . . This was the time of the AIDS crisis, of course, and you had all the conservative politicians like Jesse Helms in the US Senate who were trying to keep money from going to research and assistance to people who were in need and who would likely die without it. So we thought that instead of playing nice and saying, 'Just give us something, please,' we thought, 'Well, we'll just go full barrel and do something that feels like liberation.' It was a time when simply saying you were gay, that you were openly gay and out, was a political statement. There were plenty of politicians who were ready to attack you for that."

It is striking to recall the degree to which casual and even explicit homophobia prevailed in the 1980s and the first half of the decade that followed. But while no one should have been shocked that some representatives on Capitol Hill believed AIDS to be a "gay plague"—an idea that was sometimes explained by it being unleashed by God as a punishment for "sinful and un-natural lifestyles"—the tendency of this kind of thinking to be echoed in creative industries is more of a surprise. The Beastie Boys toyed with the idea of calling their debut album *License to Ill,* released in 1987, *Don't Be a Faggot* (asked by the author how he felt about the decision not to do so, Adam Horowitz—"Ad Rock"—replied, *"Very* relieved"). In 1988, Axl Rose of Guns N' Roses caused an uproar that was soon conveniently forgotten with the song "One in a Million." In the track's second verse he sang that "immigrants and faggots / they make no sense to me . . . / [they] start some mini Iran / or spread some fucking disease." It is instructive to recall that the song's racial element caused far greater offense than did the sentiments regarding sexuality. A year later, on "Meet the G That Killed Me" the universally lauded Public Enemy caused nowhere near as much upset as they ought to have done with the lyric "man to man / I don't know if they can / from what I know / the parts don't fit." Two years after this, Sebastian Bach, the Canadian-born frontman with New Jersey's dude-metal band Skid Row, felt it appropri-ate to appear onstage wearing a T-shirt which proclaimed that "AIDS Kills Fags Dead." Bach later apologized for this, but still couldn't help himself from adding that "what no one mentions is in 2000, when I was in [a production of] *Jekyll & Hyde,* and at an auction for Broadway Cares I donated twelve thousand dollars of my own money to fight AIDS." (One exception to this rule was the song "Freight Train" by San Francisco's Sister Double Happiness, which Ginoli credits as being the first to be written about AIDS.)

"It pains me that Axl Rose got to live and Kurt Cobain died," says Ginoli. "The more open-minded sensitive guy was eventually done in. Axl Rose comes from where I come from, the middle of the country—he's from Indiana—and he has that hateful midwestern attitude that I was ready to run from. You can find [these people] anywhere in the country, to be honest, but here's a guy who sang a song about how he hated immigrants and faggots . . . so I thought, 'Why couldn't Axl Rose die?'"

(Asked at this time by *Rolling Stone* to defend himself against charges of homophobia, Rose fared poorly. "On the way to the Troubadour [club] in 'Boystown' on Santa Monica Boulevard, I'll yell out of my car, 'Why don't you guys like pussy?' 'Cos I'm confused. I don't understand it . . . I'm not against them doing what they want to do as long as they're not hurting anybody else and they're not forcing it on me. I don't need them to be in my face or, excuse the pun, up my ass about it.")

For a scene that is disproportionately white, male and heterosexual, the bands who formed the second wave of Californian punk can be proud of their record of disavowing homophobia, sexism and racism. Each of its artists found ways to express their sense of opposition without attacking the genetics and preferences with which someone was born. Even without reference to the often questionable standards of the time, the community's progressivism has aged *very* well. No allowance is asked of the listeners of *Dookie, Smash, Stranger Than Fiction, Punk In Drublic, Let's Go* or any of the albums from the groups that recorded them. In the days before mobile phones, when Pansy Division headed out on their first US tour, the band's bass player, Chris Freeman, was asked by his boyfriend that he place a call back to San Francisco each day to let him know that he had not been harmed. And while Jon Ginoli believes there were some in the Bay Area punk community who were uncomfortable with the idea of homosexuality, he is quick to add that he doesn't recall any incidents of cut-and-dried homophobia.

"In fact, there were some people in the punk community who were, like, 'Oh, I've been waiting for someone like you to come along!' he says. He adds that "what we've learned from being on tour is that when we were playing in other cities or maybe opening for bigger bands, no matter where you go in the US there are [punks] who are going to be supportive of the kind of ideas you espouse. And they do come out of the woodwork for you. But although we were popular for a while in the mid-nineties, we never got big enough where the average citizen would have heard much about us. So therefore we were insulated from the kinds of attacks that might have come had we been more visible targets."

The first leg of Green Day's North American tour with Pansy Division began on July 8 at the MaCewan Hall in Calgary. The opening band were paid two hundred and fifty dollars a night for the tour's first leg; when the two acts reconvened on Halloween for a five-week run of larger venues, payment rose to five hundred bucks. "That might not sound like much now, but it was a lot then," says Jon Ginoli, adding that "it was much more than we were earning on our own." During the summer stretch, the headliners were booked into clubs that rarely held more than a thousand people. At these venues it was not uncommon to see as many people again bereft of tickets on the street outside. Rather charmingly, the musicians were still traveling in the Bookmobile. Jon Ginoli remembers being struck by the dichotomy of its passengers inside their modest ride watching the as yet unreleased video for "Basket Case" and predicting how well the clip was bound to be received by the American public. Outside, Green Day's long-standing habit of chatting with fans by the stage door after each show was given up for good after only a handful of dates. By this point it was obvious that the sheer number of people hoping to meet the band posed a danger to all.

Despite living in cities just miles apart, Green Day and Pansy Division had never met. Even the omnipresence of Lawrence Livermore had failed to bring them together. During sound check at the MaCewan Hall, Billie Joe Armstrong told Jon Ginoli that he hoped his band would mess with the heads of the more traditionally minded members of the headliners' emerging audience. He said that he hoped this would be a tour for the ages and about which people would lie about having attended for years to come. Today one wonders if the lies told by a number of people who *did* attend the tour would center on their own behavior.

Following an appearance at a bowling alley in Omaha, Pansy Division had to be protected from the attentions of homophobes by a cordon of young supporters who saw them safely to their van. At the Cobo Hall in Detroit the band were subjected to such abuse that after their set they collected *forty dollars* in coins thrown by the audience, along with lighters and, for some reason, shoes. In Fairfax, Jon Ginoli was obliged to listen for fifteen minutes to a promoter who told him that he believed Pansy Division's lyrics were unsuitable for Green Day's young audience, and that if he had his way the band wouldn't have been allowed to play. The promoter *had* in fact tried to get his own way, and had told the headliners that while they themselves were welcome to appear at the George Mason University Patriot Center, their support band were not. Their reply to this was that the tour was a package deal—the choice was both groups, or neither. This would not be the only time Green Day would tell a promoter who wanted to censor Pansy Division to pick on someone their own size.

In other cities, the response to the first band of the evening was more encouraging, with Jon Ginoli remembering a date at the Nassau Veterans Memorial Coliseum on Long Island that went particularly well. While on the tour the headliners also allowed their opening act to sell copies of *39/Smooth* and *Kerplunk* at their merchandise stand in the hope that Pansy Division might sell more of their own records and T-shirts. On the caravan's second leg, space was made in Green Day's equipment trucks for some of the support band's equipment so as to free up room in their own modest van.

"When Green Day asked us to go on tour, I had never even seen them," says Jon Ginoli. "I had tried to see them twice in San Francisco, but for some reason they kept canceling. I was, like, 'Okay, I'm never going to get to see them.' But we were very surprised that we were asked to open for them. They asked us because we were on Lookout, which they'd come from, and they wanted to demonstrate their roots. But they also wanted to make a statement. When we met them they turned out to be really nice people who were helpful to us in so many ways. The fact that their crowd had a very mixed reaction to us *was* a challenge, though. The thing about us is we're a band singing about gay sex and gay love. We are not filtered. We are not aiming to be presented to an audience of teenagers who were listening to mainstream rock. So when the chance came up, we thought, 'We're just going to have to keep doing what we're doing. Some people are going to get embarrassed and angry, and some people are going to ask their parents questions—and that's good.' By being there we are part of the mainstream conversation . . . So I thought, 'Good. We are a good band for being a part of that.' And Green Day of course wanted to make a statement about their tolerance and their values and their friends, basically. And in that they were successful.

"If Green Day hadn't come along, I think my band would have continued to grow in popularity," he says. "But we would never have had the spike that we had that year. That spike sustained us for many years because so many people who wouldn't have got to hear us or see us did get to hear us and see us, and that carried us on. We were aspiring to the five hundred dollars a show that Green Day were paying us [on Pansy Division's second leg of the tour] because we thought that would probably have meant that we could make a living off our band. As it turned out that was a little tight, but we still did it. Green Day helped us so that we were able to do nothing but play music for five years. We managed to make a small living out of just making music, and they were a big part of that."

One day after headlining the thousand-capacity Stone Pony club in Asbury Park, New Jersey, on August 3 Green Day crossed the Hudson River and played a venue twenty-two times its size. When the band were invited to join the latter half of that summer's Lollapalooza festival, their profile was a good fit for the opening slot of the larger of the tour's two stages. They would play early in the afternoon, not long after the venue's doors had opened, and were allotted thirty-five minutes of stage time.

In 1994, Lollapalooza was in its fourth year. The two-month traveling festival was part founded by Perry Farrell, the frontman of LA's druggy onetime underground rock pioneers Jane's Addiction as an antidote to the standard burger-and-suds nature of other open-air events on the American rock calendar. If not quite the first US festival that traveled the country—Van Halen's Monsters of Rock tour of 1988 holds copyright on this claim—Lollapalooza was the most eclectic and the most carefully curated. It also featured a greater number of bands than the five acts that had comprised the Monsters of Rock enterprise. Over the course of the festival's first three summers, the traveling show featured groups such as Red Hot Chili Peppers, Nine Inch Nails, Rage Against the Machine, Primus, Tool and Soundgarden. Away from the two musical stages, ticketholders could watch performers in the Jim Rose Circus Side Show hang breeze blocks from their nipples, gaze at framed artwork, play virtual reality games, listen to poetry and, even, smash televisions. Stalls advocating for numerous political and environmental causes were also on-site. For all of this, fans were charged an average of just over thirty dollars. The fact that this was seen by some as being a high price is one of the starker examples of just how much the live music business has since learned about gouging cash from its customers.

For anyone wishing to send a letter of thanks, Perry Farrell can be credited as the person that coined the term "alternative nation." He believed the description perfectly defined Lollapalooza's ideological identity. Others were less sure. In an interview in 1993, the music producer Steve Albini described the event as "the worst example of corporate encroachment into what is supposed to be the underground. It is just a large-scale marketing of bands that pretend to be alternative but are in reality just another facet of the mass cultural exploitation scheme . . . What it really is [is] the most popular bands on MTV that are not heavy metal." That year, Albini had produced Nirvana's third album, the defiant and defensive *In Utero,* which challenged the notion that commercial success would be welcomed by any band that received it. In the first week of April 1994, Lollapalooza's organizers announced that Kurt Cobain's band would no longer appear as headliners on the coming summer's tour. Twenty-four hours later, Cobain was dead.

With Chicago's oddly derided Smashing Pumpkins now occupying the main stage's closing slot, on numerous dates the band's frontman and songwriter, Billy Corgan, would shorten their set so as to allow Hole frontwoman Courtney Love, Cobain's widow, to address the crowd. Love would speak about bereavement and perform a small selection of acoustic songs. Those who believed that Green Day represented a sanitized version of Nirvana might be surprised to learn that Love and Billie Joe Armstrong are close. "I'm proud to call her my friend," he told the author in 2016.

By the time the Californians joined the tour on August 5, they had far outgrown the slot that Lollapalooza's organizers had reserved for them. Green Day were at this point the fastest-selling band on the bill; come the year's end, *Dookie* would out-sell every album by the other bands on the tour. That summer, Lollapalooza offered ticketholders who had yet to see the group the chance to right a wrong. It was an opportunity that tens of thousands of people did not want to miss, and the sight of fans sprinting from the turnstiles toward the main stage was com-monplace. The venues visited by Lollapalooza were often am-phitheaters and pavilions, each of which looked like they were ordered from the same catalogue and some of which were as far as thirty miles out of town. With space for between twenty and thirty thousand people, the design of these open-air "sheds" saw those who had bought the most expensive tickets seated toward the front of the stage while those whose means stretched only to the cheap seats were placed on rising grass verges at the back on which there were no seats at all. Traditionally, Lollapalooza's opening band would draw a crowd of a thousand people, but in 1994 this figure increased at least tenfold. Many ticketholders did not have reserved seats. Green Day's solution to the pros-pect of playing to dozens of empty rows in front of them and a sea of faces a distance away was to offer an upgrade to thou-sands of people: the band invited everyone at the back to make themselves at home in the front.

"They walked onstage and they said, 'This is ridiculous, come on down,' and they urged the crowd to rush the stage," says Kevin Lyman. Lyman was Lollapalooza's artist liaison man, a job for which he "was kind of overpaid so that I could teach the monks that traveled with the Beastie Boys to play basket-ball," among other things. "And the crowd did rush the stage and consequently a lot of people got hurt. After their set I got the band and we took them to the medical tent and I said, 'You're now responsible for everything that happens at this venue to-day.' I've done this with other bands, too. If the crowd rushes the stage because of the power of your music then all the li-ability falls on the venue for not having enough security. But when you tell the crowd to rush the stage, you're responsible for pretty much everything that happens to them for the rest of the day. I think I realized then that this wasn't some little club band anymore, and that they held a power over the crowd. But people were coming in [to the venue] when they'd already started play-ing, even though we were getting them in as fast as we could."

When it came to understanding the often reckless energy of punk, Kevin Lyman was far from a new kid in town. Back in Los Angeles, as a promoter at the Goldenvoice agency he had helped in the staging of up to three hundred concerts a year, including shows by Bad Religion and their sonic kissing cousins Pennywise. Lyman had been part of the Lollapalooza caravan from the start. His job as production manager in 1991 was also his first tour worthy of the name. He learned the fundamental lesson that touring is long and grueling work, similar to the US Marines but with added deafness. After three days he collapsed from heat exhaustion only to have the older crew members chuckle fondly at him. But his colleagues' predictions that he wouldn't last a week underestimated his resolve. Lyman proved himself to be a hard worker and come the following summer his role as stage manager had been expanded to include co-production management duties. His approach to Lollapalooza's logistics was simple: he equated the quick turnover times and multiple acts as being nothing other than a club show on a much larger scale.

But Green Day represented a real problem. Lollapalooza was not only the first time the band had performed regularly in large outdoor venues; it was also their first tour on which the shows were staged in anything other than a club or, at most, a theater. Even on the road with Bad Religion—remarkably, the only tour on which the band has ever played as a support act—the largest room in which they played was the Hollywood Palladium, which has space for fewer than four thousand people. On Lollapalooza Green Day were in an environment with which they were yet to become familiar, let alone comfortable. Suddenly they were faced with avid audiences the size of which they'd never had to contend with before. It wasn't that the band's unruly energies didn't translate to the amphitheaters and pavilions in which they were now playing—it's that they translated all too well.

"There was only one show where the band encouraged the audience to rush the stage," says Kevin Lyman. "But on the next couple of shows we did, things didn't settle down. And then we did more shows, and still they didn't settle down. Every time, the kids would charge the stage. I had to tell the venues that 'you have the power [to control this].' I had to deal with each venue because it was the venue that could control the audience. We had to ramp up security. We had to give advance warning to every venue about what the situation could be like. A lot of times when an opening act plays, you know, security isn't as tight as it ought to be. We had to make sure we were fully ready, as if it was going to be a full house. While we were doing this, me and the band built up some sort of respect for each other."

This, though, would take time. By August 1994, save for a week here and there Green Day had been on the road for seven months. What had begun as a campaign in support of a modest album had taken on a life that no one had the power to control, least of all the band themselves. A month earlier, Billie Joe Armstrong married Adrienne Nesser, whom he had met in Minneapolis in 1990. Adrienne moved to the East Bay in the spring of 1994 at a time when her fiancé was hardly ever there. The day after their wedding, the newlyweds learned that they were going to be parents. Each of these life-changing events took place under extraordinary circumstances. Neither Armstrong nor his bandmates would have the chance to fully reflect on their remarkable year until the end of the tour, in December. In the meantime the ride that could not be stopped and from which they could not get off was beginning to make them dizzy.

"We toured a lot before *Dookie*, but after *Dookie* we toured a shit ton and we started to see both sides of things," says Mike Dirnt. "It was a carefree existence up until then, and [then it becomes] a bit of a job, too. And not only do we have a job, but we're also dealing with the repercussions of signing to a major. You're dealing with starting new families. You're dealing with alcoholism on the road. It's like one foot's at the party and the other foot is in the grave, while the rest of you is trying to figure out how to make a plan for the future."

"I remember that [one day] they ended up trashing their dressing room," says Kevin Lyman. "That's just not cool in my book. There are people who have to clean up after you. I've always tried to teach bands about respect, and that we're lucky to do what we do. So at the next show, I didn't give them a dressing room. I just told them, 'You don't get a dressing room today.' I put their food out in the parking lot. This caused a big uproar with other managers. I remember [Nirvana and Beastie Boys manager] John Silva being really mad and saying, 'If this was my band you wouldn't do that.' And I said, 'I would do it to any band.'"

Three months later, as the tour of 1994 wound to end, Green Day were still at it. Following an appearance at the Newport Music Hall in Columbus, the Ohioan publication the *Lantern* quoted a backstage source who knocked on the band's dressing room only to discover that "they'd trashed the place. I went . . . to see what was going on and they threw a full beer can right through the door. It barely missed my head." By now Green Day were getting good at acting up. At the Aragon Ballroom in Chicago, Billie Joe Armstrong held up a copy of *Spin* magazine on which his band were on the cover and set it on fire. He told the crowd, "This is a crock of shit, and if you believe it, you are too," presumably while having his cake and eating it. In Toronto, the frontman let loose a string of weapons-grade expletives that he then dedicated to the parents in the room. *Toronto Arts* magazine were sufficiently appalled by this as to write that "Green Day epitomize, and promote, the rampant adolescent attitude of today that is ruthlessly hateful, purblindly self-centered and bafflingly self-righteous."

The tour in support of *Dookie* ended with an appearance at Madison Square Garden in New York City on December 5. The event was staged by the radio station Z-100, a mainstream broadcaster based over the Hudson in the city of Newark, New Jersey. When Green Day accepted the invitation to perform at the station's Christmas concert they believed that the bill would comprise just themselves and Pansy Division. With the Garden sold out on the strength of the headliners' name alone, Z-100 then proceeded to add other acts to the roster. By the first week of December, the lineup also featured Hole, Weezer, Melissa Etheridge, Jon Bon Jovi, Sheryl Crow, Toad the Wet Sprocket and Indigo Girls, all added without the knowledge of the band that topped the bill. The band at the bottom of the bill was Pansy Division. Even this modest status was guaranteed only after Green Day threatened to withdraw their services after the broadcaster had told the San Franciscans that their presence that night was not welcome. As if to add insult to irony, the concert was a fundraiser at which each artist donated their appearance fee to charities fighting AIDS. (Pansy Division were eventually allotted ten minutes of stage time, into which they packed four songs. "The response was really good," says Jon Ginoli. "Plus, I get to say that I played Madison Square Garden, which is not a bad bragging right.")

Green Day were also unpleasantly surprised to learn that the show was billed as the Z-100 Acoustic Christmas. Given that the band had never before performed a live acoustic set, the odds of them doing so at the world's most famous arena were not short. The news that the night would end with music played on electric guitars reached the radio station in a manner nonnegotiable.

If Green Day needed reminding that their status at the end of the year contrasted starkly with their standing at its start, a place on the same bill as Jon Bon Jovi was hard to beat. The contrasts in how each artist went about their business ran deeper than the mere stylistic differences between poodle rock and punk; the two camps also had profoundly different perspectives regarding the power that rock stardom affords. Whereas Green Day threatened to walk away from any concert from which their support band was threatened with eviction, Bon Jovi was more interested in mutual back-scratching. In 1989, New Jersey's second-favorite son offered to take an emerging Skid Row on tour on the understanding that they sign a publishing deal with his and guitarist Richie Sambora's Underground Music Company. This arrangement meant that the pair took a large percentage of the younger band's royalties. At Madison Square Garden, Jon Ginoli remembers "JBJ" commandeering more than one dressing room and leaving other artists to share smaller rooms. As his stage time approached, the order came that the corridors leading to the stage be cleared of people. Watching from dressing room doors held ajar, the other performers sniggered at the sight of Bon Jovi punching the air like Rocky Balboa. His set was the only one of the evening that significantly overran, an indulgence that contributed to the event breaking its curfew by several hours.

The headliners had decided that the Acoustic Christmas wasn't something they wished to be a part of just minutes after entering the venue. They reluctantly changed their minds only after being persuaded to do so by one of their managers. As it was, Green Day walked onto the stage at Madison Square Garden at a quarter to one in the morning. With the night

approaching its slimmest hours, they were faced with an audience that had given Jon Bon Jovi a fulsome reception but who
were now knackered. The contrast between the untrammeled
energy of the Lollapalooza caravan, Woodstock '94 and the
Welcome Back Weekend was striking. Suddenly the tour was
in peril of ending on an indifferent note. Latterly, Mike Dirnt
would tell the author that "there isn't an audience in the world
that Billie Joe can't hold in the palm of his hand," and at Madison Square Garden, this talent was already in evidence. At the
end of a twelve-song set that saw the band's best-known songs
packed into its first half, Armstrong jolted the audience awake
by playing the night's final track naked. "Green Day needed to
be on top form to jolt the tired audience," wrote the *New York
Post.* "At close to 2 A.M. the band finished their set and headed
backstage before their encore. Fans would be in for a surprise
when Billie returned to the stage wearing nothing but his guitar
for a performance of 'She.' His impulsive need to be noticed
turned a musical endurance test into what will be one of the
most talked about concerts of the year."

"Nineteen ninety-four was a really exciting time," says Mike
Dirnt. "And it was an influential time, too. If you listen to the radio today, you'll still hear all the music that we and other bands
who came through at that time were making. So obviously as a
punk rock movement and a musical movement, we flew a flag.
We put a flag in the earth and it's still standing tall. I loved being
a part of it and I'm very proud of it. Because we did care about
the scene we came from. We did have doubts about the decision we'd taken [to sign with Warner Bros.]. But I take pride in
what we've created and what we've been able to influence over
the years. That's the thing that's been carried forward. Back
then, people wanted to kick my ass. I was running around with
bright-colored hair and I'd have jocks shout, 'Hey, fag!' at me
because I was different from them. Nowadays things are way

more open, you know; the captain of the football team might have a nose ring or have green hair. And I can deal with that. It might be a little irritating, but at the end of the day I'd rather deal with that than all of the turmoil of a segregated and hateful society."

## CHAPTER EIGHT

# SPLINTER

When Tim Armstrong's often troubled life reached its nadir, the young musician could be seen around Berkeley up to all sorts of no good. One day, his brother Jeff found him stumbling along Telegraph Avenue in a state of acute inebriation. Armstrong was placed in the passenger seat of a car and driven to a hospital at which it was learned that the younger brother was presenting a potentially fatal blood-alcohol reading of 3.9. "Your brother is trying to kill himself" was one doctor's diagnosis. In the years following the dissolution of Operation Ivy, Armstrong was hospitalized a further three times due to complications with alcohol and drugs. Told by his mother that he was no longer welcome to sleep in her home, he would go missing for nights on end. Matt Freeman stood by his friend during these trying times by driving him to and from detoxification clinics and giving him money for food. But after learning that his dollars were being used to buy alcohol, he insisted on standing lunch and dinner for his friend only if he was there to break bread with him. Soon enough, things had become so dire that Matt Freeman imposed the ultimate sanction: for the first time in seventeen years he stopped playing music with his friend. Get your shit together, he was told, and we'll pick up where we left off.

By now Armstrong was spending his nights sleeping in a Salvation Army hostel. In exchange for bed and board, by day he would patrol the streets of the wealthy Blackhawk suburb asking for donations and cast-offs for those, like him, in need. This period in his life is captured beautifully in the song "Salvation." "Every day we drive into Blackhawk and we pick up the offerings / microwave, refrigerator, for the suffering." If this all sounds redemptive for everyone concerned, it isn't quite. "I'm a rat out on a mission / I'm in your front yard under suspicion" is the rattle in the tail.

The song is taken from *Let's Go*, the second album from Rancid, the first band of note formed by Armstrong and Freeman following the fracture of Operation Ivy. To distinguish themselves from their now legendary former selves, Armstrong and Freeman decided that Rancid would play punk rock sans the ska. They recruited drummer Brett Reed and recorded a self-titled EP for Lookout and their first LP, also self-titled, for Epitaph. Between their first album and *Let's Go* the band decided to expand its ranks to include a second guitarist. Billie Joe Armstrong played a show with Rancid at Gilman Street in this capacity, but talk of this being anything other than a one-night stand was purely wishful. "[Billie] had other things going on," Tim Armstrong told Lawrence Livermore in 2009. "[He had] another band he was doing pretty well with."

While resting his head at the Salvation Army's pleasure, Tim Armstrong managed to stop drinking. The band in which he now played was also free from intoxicants. (The only time this rule was broken was when Armstrong relapsed in 1996. Matt Freeman drove to Los Angeles to be with his friend, while Mike Ness literally picked him up from the ground—"I was eating dirt," he told Lawrence Livermore—and put him to bed.) When a potential fourth wheel rolled into shot, he was asked whether or not he drank. Lars Frederiksen replied that perhaps he enjoyed the odd beer or two, an estimation that was promptly shown to be a wild underrepresentation of his appetites. After he embarrassed his new bandmates on a night out by pulling out his penis and peeing on the street in full view of a crowd of people—a bad habit compounded when a young female stranger was asked to return the appendage from whence it came—Frederiksen almost lost his new job on the same day that he found it. Freeman wanted shut of him, but Armstrong pleaded his case. By way of a compromise, the guitarist was presented with a rule book featuring just one rule: one strike and you're out.

Even by Rancid's standards, Lars Frederiksen is rough trade. Raised by his single mother in Campbell, California, as a young man he ran wild in the streets. He broke into houses and came away with framed photographs of families that he would look at afterward, just to imagine what a normal life might be like. With a gentle laugh, in 2003 Tim Armstrong told this author that "Lars's crew was a little bit wilder than ours." Frederiksen would later describe his early days in song. "Hell's Angels ran my neighborhood / it was always understood / I was running errands for the Angels / I was a little fucking hood" is one of the verses of the relentless "Spirit of '87." So redoubtable were the young delinquent's circumstances that a job playing guitar for England's second-generation UK Subs must have seemed like a scholarship to a finishing school.

Sober they may have been, but Rancid's world was still one of fraternal chaos. The photographer Lisa Johnson recalls heading to Oakland to shoot the band in and around their communal living quarters in Oakland at which they and other local punk groups stayed. She remembers Rancid's car-crash pad as being a "punk rock utopia," the toilet in which was "just awful. I would say that it rivals the CBGB's toilet, which is legendarily disgusting. I held my pee in the whole time I was in there." But, she says, "it was definitely a real punk house, and they were definitely a real punk band, and it was cool."

As unstable as their setup may have looked, Rancid had one thing going for them: talent, and bags of it. When Tim Armstrong first called Brett Gurewitz to ask whether he would sign the band he and Matt Freeman were planning on putting together he was living in the Salvation Army hostel. Despite this, the record label owner agreed to do so sound unheard.

"He said, 'I was wondering if we could be on Epitaph?'" remembers Gurewitz. "And I just said, 'Yeah, man. I just want to let you know that I'm a huge fan of your writing . . .' and I let him know that I believed in him and that the moment he got his head together enough to get his band going they had a home on Epitaph. I didn't have to hear music. I didn't have to hear a single note. I would be delighted to sign the band he formed with Matt. And that's the way it was. The way that Tim Armstrong can write—and he was young and at the peak of his creative powers—I didn't have any doubt in my mind that he didn't have anything but amazing music in him."

It took a short while for this potential to be realized. The band's first album for Epitaph was as much about maneuvering themselves out from the shadow cast by Operation Ivy as it was about the music itself. But on *Let's Go* they took flight. Recorded over just six days at Fantasy Studios in Berkeley, the facility at which Green Day recorded *Dookie,* the album was produced and mixed by Brett Gurewitz. The material even survived a last-minute panic when Mr. Brett realized that the mixes that sounded blockbusting on the stereo of his rented car sounded dreadful on every other system available to buy. Over two days at Westbeach Recorders, the tracks were remixed. "It was lucky that I knew the mixing desk there so well," recalls Gurewitz with a laugh still tinged with relief.

It is testament to the music released on Epitaph in 1994 that *Smash* dominates only in a commercial sense. Despite Fat Mike's misgivings, NOFX's *Punk In Drublic* album has also aced the test of time, while Down by Law's overlooked *Punkrock-academyfightsong* merits mention, too. While Rancid themselves fit without a squeeze into the company's stable of remarkable talent, there *are* crucial differences between them and others on the label. For one thing, the Bay Area quartet are the only band on the Epitaph roster whose members looked incapable of doing anything other than making music together. The company's other acts had an abundance of qualities and punk rock necessities such as oppositionalism, energy, bite and insight— but Rancid had rough edges that the others did not. In a musical sense, they were unaligned with the punk rock style of Southern California. Lawrence Livermore rather dismissively describes his neighbors to the south as constituting "baggy shorts punk," and in the sense that some members of The Offspring, NOFX and Bad Religion did indeed wear baggy shorts he has a point. But the members of Rancid were no more likely to appear on-stage dressed in skate shorts than they were to pose for photographs wearing ice skates. Their music featured longing and loneliness. It shone with the idea that the threats posed by even the meanest streets could be held at bay by the unity of a family of outsiders. It was certain in the belief that music held powers of redemption and absolution. "When the music hits I feel no pain at all," sings Tim Armstrong on "Radio," a song cowritten by Billie Joe Armstrong. He adds that "when I got the music, I've got a place to go."

Their audience *loved* them. Any room in which Rancid played at this time was filled with an intensity that sometimes bordered on the unmanageable. The author witnessed an appearance at the subterranean Underworld club in London's Camden Town in 1995 that ranks as one of the most unhinged punk shows in the city's history. As the band onstage sang of a journey taken from Campbell to Berkeley on the number 43 bus, the lines "I say, 'Why even bother?' as I pick up the bottle / Hey Mr. bus driver please let these people on"—that "please" is a particularly nice touch—four hundred people packed like anchovies in a room without air imagined themselves aboard the vehicle inside which "Desmond Decker" was playing. At the end of the set such was the clamor for more that the band reluctantly obliged. "This isn't an encore, though," insisted Tim Armstrong.

But in the months that followed the release of *Let's Go,* Brett Gurewitz was in danger of losing the first Epitaph group other than his own to a major label. The band that Jim Guerinot describes as being "in a lot of ways, Brett's soulmates," were now being courted by Maverick Records, a company founded by, among others, Madonna and the Time Warner corporation. It appears today that the label's entreaties to the band were not much more than flirtations, but even so the Material Girl seemed sufficiently smitten with her quarry that she sent them risqué photographs of herself. The most serious offer for the band's services came from Epic Records, part of the Sony Group. The company's A&R man, Michael Goldstone, had signed Rage Against the Machine to the label and was now offering the Bay Area quartet one and a half million dollars for their signatures, plus a publishing deal worth half a million more. In an interview with *Rolling Stone* in 1995, Matt Freeman complained that "we got made to feel like we were fucking evil for even talking to these people." But Rancid were doing a lot more than batting their eyelashes in the direction of Epic Records. Rather, the group had gone up to the label's hotel room, dimmed the lights, ordered champagne and lobster and placed a "Do Not Disturb" sign on the hallway side of the room's front door. So certain was Michael Goldstone that he'd captured his prize that he dyed his hair blue in anticipation of the photographs that would be taken at the ceremony announcing the band joining his label.

Accounts of what happened next vary, but the outcome is the same. Jim Guerinot remembers meeting Tim Armstrong and Lars Frederiksen at an Offspring show at the Filmore in San Francisco in December of 1994 at which the pair seemed troubled and uncertain. Three days earlier, Epitaph Records had thrown a Christmas party to which they hadn't been invited because it was understood that they had accepted the deal offered by Michael Goldstone and Epic Records. The band thought this, too, but were by now experiencing a nagging sense of buyer's remorse.

"Tim and Lars come to the show and you can tell that they're conflicted," says Jim Guerinot. "They both have this hangdog expression. And I'm close with these guys 'cos they toured with us [The Offspring] and I got real close with them. I really love them a lot 'cos they're really sweet guys. And they just said, 'We feel awful. We feel like we have to do this [sign with Epic Records] but we don't feel good.' I just said, 'Then why are you doing it? Why are you doing it? You don't have to do it.' Tim was upset and he said, 'I need to get with Matt [Freeman]. Can I get with Matt and come down and see you?' And I said, 'Sure . . . I'll be back in Los Angeles, here are my details, I'll be back in a couple of days—come down.' So Tim and Matt come down and see me and they say, 'What if we don't sign with Epic? If we don't, will you manage us?' And I said, 'Sure.' They asked me how I would handle the situation and I said, 'This is what we do.'"

Jim Guerinot placed a call to Brett Gurewitz and laid out the terms for Rancid remaining on Epitaph. He tells the author the precise details of the deal in an off-the-record briefing, but suffice it to say they are astounding. He began the conversation with the words "If I told you you could have Rancid back, what would you do?" The answer was almost anything. "So I said, 'Here's what we're going to do,'" remembers Guerinot. "I say to him, 'This isn't a negotiation. Here's what you need to do, and if you do it, you've got the band back.'" I put down the phone and said to Tim and Matt, 'He's going to do the deal.'" And they're, like, 'Are you fucking kidding?' And that was that."

"It was reported in the press that Rancid were, like, one day away from signing to Sony, so I called the guys and asked if I could fly up and, you know, have a coffee with them," says Brett Gurewitz. "Tim and Matt agreed. So I went up there and said to Tim, 'Hey, man, listen. I know that major labels have an allure and I know there are a lot of people encouraging you [to sign with Epic]. Every kid who dreams of playing in a rock and roll band has heroes that are on major labels. I understand how that feels, okay. At the same time, we're punk kids and we came up in a DIY community and I know that's a big part of who you are. I just want to let you know that whatever you decide, we're still gonna be friends forever and I'm still gonna love you and we're gonna be family. But I just wanted to let you know that whatever you said to Sony, whatever you said to the A&R guy, whatever you said to your manager, whatever you said to your business manager, none of that matters. You don't have to sign with Sony. You can change your mind right now. If it doesn't feel right, you can change your mind. You are your own person. You can just decide not to do it, and I'm just letting you know that right now. You just got to decide it for yourself.' And that's what I did; that's what I said. And they called me back and said, 'Hey, Brett, we're staying on Epitaph.' And that's where they've been ever since."

On hearing the news that Rancid had decided to stay on Epitaph, Brett Gurewitz flew the label's staff to the Bay Area to celebrate. Lars Frederiksen would later tell *Rebel Noise* how "kids come up to us all the time and say, 'We're in a band and we're never going to sign to some major label. We're going to stay independent like you guys. You guys proved you don't need to sign [to] some major label and all that bullshit [to be successful].' That's the most gratifying thing anyone can say to me or any of us." Of course Frederiksen's words conveniently overlook just how close Rancid came to allying themselves to "all that bullshit," just as they overlook how in 2003 the group released the *Indestructible* album in partnership with Warner Bros. (all traces of the company's affiliation were kept off the back sleeve and inlay). But the fact remains that in 1994 Rancid took the decision to remain independent as a group that came from little yet had plenty to lose.

It was reported at the time that to celebrate the band remaining with Epitaph, Brett Gurewitz had a section of the artwork from *Let's Go* tattooed on his arm. Not true, he says. "I already had a Rancid tattoo."

As with grunge and its attendant offshoots just a few seasons earlier, 1994 was the year that major labels began circling above the punk rock flock like birds of prey. If the gold rush wasn't of quite the same intensity as that which followed the release of *Nevermind*, this was only because few things were. Clearly, the regard in which music corporations were held by the punk fraternity was more complicated than it had been for the grunge generation. It might well have been that many of the bands signed following the eruption of Mount Nirvana were so obviously unsuited to a seat at the high table that the only way they could respond to their new status was to laugh at it. But to the punks this stuff was no joking matter. Even those who did sign with companies listed on the Dow Jones Industrial Average did so fully aware that their reputations were now at risk. Every group interviewed for this book who attained major label status speaks with some measure of defensiveness about having done so.

By many accounts, it is NOFX who harbored the most profound reservations regarding the whole new hardball game suddenly thrust upon them. As if by instinct, Fat Mike was able to sniff the air and sense the problems this wanted and unwanted attention might bring. He realized that a scene founded in nonconformity might become its opposite in the glare of blue-chip scrutiny. "When did punk rock become so safe / when did the scene become a joke? The kids who used to live for beer and speed / now want their fries and Coke," he later sang on "The Separation Of Church And Skate," written as the dust began to settle. In this, he is right. Save for few exceptions, the legacy of Green Day and The Offspring has been poor. Similar anger was also directed at a corporate structure that actively encourages toothless mediocrity. "The dinosaurs will surely die and I do believe no one will cry / I'm just fucking glad I'm gonna be there to watch it fall," he sings on "Dinosaurs Will Die."

In 1994, Fat Mike took a phone call from his lawyer who told him, "Fatty, you're getting calls from the majors, do you want to take a meeting?'" His answer was "No, not really." Against his better judgment, he was persuaded to take one meeting "just to see what they were offering." What they were offering, it turned out, was an assault on their target's self-esteem. Given his time again Fat Mike would have walked out inside of ten minutes after telling his suitors what they could do with their oily passive aggression. But "Fatty" is actually a much more sensitive person than the more robust aspects of his public image would have one believe. So, instead, he sat there in the offices of Hollywood Records—one of the smallest majors, at that—and listened to the company's unusual method for seducing a potential partner.

"They made me feel really bad about myself," he says. "Because I said, 'Okay, tell me why I should go to a major.' And the guy said, 'Well, we've got more money, and more this, and more that, and we'll spend it on you.' And I said, 'Well, Epitaph just did *Smash* and Rancid [. . . *And Out Come The Wolves*], both of which went platinum—what can you do that's better than that?' And it was, like, 'Yeah, we've got better distribution around the world,' and blah blah blah, but really he didn't have an answer. So I said, 'Actually, we're pretty happy where we are.' And then they changed their approach and started saying, 'Oh, well, if you're happy playing third fiddle to The Offspring and Rancid for your whole career, then you should stay where you are.' At the time I didn't say, 'Fuck you, you jerk!' I didn't say anything.

But then two or three hours later when I was in my hotel room, I thought, 'Really? You're going to try and fool me into signing with you by making me feel bad about myself?' And I never took another meeting after that."

There are few punk rock pastimes more amusing than imagining how a major label might deal with NOFX. How would the person who signed the band explain to his or her label's marketing department that the cover artwork for the album *Heavy Petting Zoo* was a painting of a man pleasuring a sheep? Or how would the sales team explain to the buyers at Walmart that the group's latest EP was called *Never Trust A Hippy* and featured on its front sleeve a picture of Jesus? And how would a chief executive officer explain to the board of directors that the band were releasing a single about George W. Bush called "Idiot Son Of An Asshole?" For a band that spends so much of its time waving gleefully from beyond the sight lines of the Overton window, the idea of any corporation being capable of managing NOFX is a delight.

As the Year That Punk Broke rolled on, with pleasing contrariness NOFX turned inward. Tired of answering questions about Green Day and The Offspring, the band stopped doing press and didn't start again for more than a decade. Irritated that MTV wouldn't play the videos for the songs "Bob" and "Stickin' In My Eye"—both from *White Trash, Two Heebs And A Bean*—even on *120 Minutes,* the band did not let the slight pass. When in 1994 the channel wanted to air the clip that accompanies the song "Leave It Alone," the group refused. They also refused to allow KROQ to play the track, a stance they would repeat with "Dinosaurs Will Die" six years later. As ever, Epitaph supported these decisions. "Fat Mike said no and I sided with him," says Gurewitz. "I always side with my artists, no matter what." Eventually *Punk In Drublic* went gold, but it took eight years. There is something delicious in a band being so awkward that they are in effect stealing food from their *own* table. But as Fat Mike says,

"I didn't want MTV to play the video. I didn't want to be a part of the punk rock wave. When The Offspring got big, I said to my band, 'We're not going to be that band. I'm not going to write songs like that and I don't want to be that band. I want to have a long career. And if I think we have enough fans where if we stick with what we're doing and just get better and better at it, then we *will* have a long career.' And that worked.

"But, you know, The Offspring are still around and they have a decent career. But Dexter once told me—and I think The Offspring should get more respect than they do—but he said, 'Mike, I have some envy [of NOFX] because everyone respects your band and no one respects my band.' . . . But the thing is, The Offspring did it on Epitaph, too."

With Rancid's final-seconds decision to stay independent confirmed, it seemed as if no one on Epitaph was merely passing through. Life on and around the label also seems like an enormous amount of fun. Jim Lindberg, the vocalist with Hermosa Beach's evergreen Pennywise, remembers his band being so drunk at an ice cream cake party thrown in his band's honor that guitarist Fletcher Dragge was ordered down from a tree that he'd climbed by the police and then chased through the streets. Ever the friend, en route home Dragge attempted to facilitate Lindberg's need to vomit by waving a dead possum in his face.

Pennywise are Epitaph lifers. Formed in 1988 in Hermosa Beach, like many others in this book its members didn't become professional punks because they were unsuited to anything else in life except, perhaps, prison. Jim Lindberg was an English major at UCLA who during semester break interned at an advertising agency. While there he would cause consternation among his colleagues by arriving in the morning sporting a suit and a tie and a broken nose, this latter fashion accessory having been acquired at punk shows at clubs such as Raji's in Hollywood. His girlfriend and his parents were horrified that he planned to decline a job in the professions in favor of a life playing a style of music that most people assumed to be dead (including many who practiced it). But as was the case with Fat Mike, he heard Bad Religion's *Suffer* and realized that the scene's pilot light continued to flicker. He realized that lyrics that dealt with complex themes could be carried on songs the propulsion of which sounded as if it had been engineered at the Boeing plant in neighboring Orange County. Impressed, in time he saw Bad Religion selling more than a hundred thousand albums on a record label run by a man with chameleon hair. As Pennywise prepared to release their self-titled debut LP in the autumn of 1991, its members saw not a means to an end, but an end in itself.

"I couldn't believe it when Epitaph said they would put out our music," remembers Lindberg. "I was, like, 'Wait, you mean, I'm *going to get money* for doing this?' I remember going down to the Epitaph office after the album had come out. Dexter [Holland] was down there helping out. And Fat Mike had popped round, too. Our album [*Pennywise*] had sold twelve thousand copies, or something like that, and Mike was saying, 'That's really good. You did well.' And I honestly had no idea. I was, like, is that good? Is a hundred copies good? Is a thousand copies good?' I just didn't know . . . But there was a fierce battle going on between bands who signed to major labels and those that stayed independent. But where we were from, in Hermosa Beach, things were just very grassroots. You got in a van and you played shows and you did things at a local level. To us, the whole Hollywood machine was just soul sucking. We just didn't want to have anything to do with that. I remember our booking agent was telling us that there were [major] labels that wanted to talk to us about maybe signing with them, but we knew it wasn't right for us. We were quite militant about that. I even think that at a certain point we probably took it too far, because obviously there were some bands, like Green Day, who did sign to a big label and it worked out fine for them."

"I remember Maverick wanted to talk to us, I remember Sony wanted to talk to us . . . whatever," says Fat Mike. "But we were selling records on Epitaph. I just said to Brett, 'Give us a great royalty rate and we're good.' We saw huge advances from Epitaph and great royalties, so if you're selling records, why would you go to a major? Bad Religion did because they were, like, 'Let's see if we can take it to the next level.' And I just thought, 'Well, Epitaph can take you to the next level.'"

Reflected on today, Epitaph Records at this time sounds like the punk rock equivalent of the Laurel Canyon community of Los Angeles in the 1970s. But rather than Neil Young, Joni Mitchell or David Crosby writing songs on piano and acoustic guitars, there was an office from which Brett Gurewitz sent faxes, Dexter Holland hogged the phone pitching music to college radio stations and into which Fat Mike would pop bearing refreshments. In the warehouse, Jay Bentley knew how to drive a forklift truck and moved pallets of albums like a character in a Nintendo video game. The company was not just a musical hotbed, either—it was also a training ground for people who wanted to start labels of their own. In 1991, Fat Mike founded Fat Wreck Chords (pronounced "fat records") on which he issued albums by bands such as No Use for a Name, Bracket, Propaghandi and the exquisitely named Guns 'n' Wankers. Three years later, Dexter Holland established Nitro Records. The label reissued the first album from The Offspring, as well as original material from such acts as Exene Cervenka and the Original Sinners, T.S.O.L. and the Vandals. Three years later, Tim Armstrong went into partnership with Brett Gurewitz and set up Hellcat Records, through which music by the Distillers, Dropkick Murphys and Joe Strummer & The Mescaleros was released. Another Hellcat band were the unstoppably provocative Leftover Crack, a group who once authored an EP titled *Baby Jesus Sliced Up in the Manger*. In 2001, in the wake of the Columbine High

School shootings, the New York band wanted the title of their debut album to be *Shoot the Kids at the School*, with artwork that depicted a gun pointed at a playground. The pressing plant used by the label balked at this, but Hellcat Records, and Brett Gurewitz, did not.

Inevitably, there was a measure of friction and dissension in the ranks. Interviewed for this book, Fat Mike is stinging from an interview with Gurewitz he read two days earlier in which Mr. Brett is quoted as saying that he doesn't want Epitaph to be a nostalgia label that continually churns out ska punk, a description that "Fatty" takes to be aimed at Fat Wreck Chords. He is quick to point out that Gurewitz is "an incredible songwriter and poet," but he stops short of describing him as a friend. "I'd say we were friendly rivals" is his definition. He says that "what Brett has done with Epitaph is pretty incredible [and] I have a lot of respect for what he's achieved." But he says, "Brett is different from most people. He's a businessman. He's highly intelligent and a little socially awkward. But to him, it's just a game. It's business.

"When I started Fat Wreck Chords he called me and said that I'd stabbed him in the back after all he'd done for me," he says. "And I told him, 'We're [NOFX] not leaving your label, Brett, I'm just starting up my own.' You know, punk rock is supposed to be supportive. I loaned Propagandhi fifty grand to start their label [G7 Welcoming Committee]. When Side One Dummy started out, I helped them. I gave them all my numbers. I showed them how to do it . . . But Brett said I stabbed him in the back. And we stayed on Epitaph for many, many years afterwards [until 2000]. What he said really, really hurt my feelings. I was, like, 'Why don't you want me to do this too?'" For his part, Brett Gurewitz says that "this doesn't sound like something that I would say." But if his memory is malleable, he proposes that perhaps his is not the only one. "Fat Mike is one of the few people I know that has taken more drugs than I have," he says.

Not without justification, by 1994 Epitaph Records had become noisily pleased with themselves. A full-page ad was taken out in the trade paper *Billboard* in which the company's staff were seen raising their middle fingers to the camera. "That was our gesture to the industry and to everyone who said that we couldn't do it," says Jeff Abarta. "But it was, like, 'Yeah, we did do it, so here's the bird.'"

By now drugs, too, were starting to leak into the company's bloodstream. With his preference for "smoking a lot of pot and dropping acid and taking a lot of mushrooms"—not to mention liking the Grateful Dead—Abarta was out of step with the culture of harder drugs that was beginning to take hold. "I was much more interested in music and art," he says. "I sort of turned a blind eye to a lot of the craziness. I knew that stuff was going on, but I didn't want to be a part of it. I just wanted to do a good job." In 1997, recalling this period Dexter Holland would tell the author that "Brett was acting more like a rock star than we were."

"It was very exciting and it was very empowering," says Gurewitz of this tumultuous year. "But it was also a challenge in terms of keeping my feet on the ground. It made it difficult to *keep* my feet on the ground and to remain humble. Because I was young. I was, like, thirty-two years old. I'm fond of saying that ego is not my amigo, and that's the lesson I learned from that experience—that it's important to stay humble and keep your feet on the ground. I went through a period where I was huffing my own exhaust a little bit."

One of the more sizeable problems facing Mr. Brett was the law of unintended consequences. Following the departure of Bad Religion, there was for the briefest time some kind of commercial parity between Epitaph's family of bands. But with *Smash* having become just that, Gurewitz felt the need to reassure the rest of the groups on his label that their status was not suddenly that of second-class citizens. So an ice cream party for Pennywise was now suddenly imbued with a meaning greater than simply a gathering for a band that had sold one hundred thousand albums. The fact that in short order a hundred thousand units was not as impressive as it had been just a year before made things tricky. "I didn't want [the other] bands to think that I only cared about The Offspring," says Gurewitz. "But let's say you have four children, and one of them wins some incredible giant honor and is suddenly the center of attention around the world. Of course you'd be thrilled. But you'd also want to do something special for your other little kids so they don't feel like you don't love them."

"I'm not gonna lie. I think for some of the bands there was jealousy," says Jim Lindberg. "When Brett started giving a lot of his time to Rancid at the time that The Offspring was blowing up, there was probably some hurt feelings there. Everyone wants Brett's attention. Brett is an amazing producer in the studio, and we all want him to be involved in *our* band. Everyone's kind of fighting over Brett's attention. I think there was definitely a period there where, you know, people in The Offspring were going, 'Well, gee, we just sold all these records—maybe he's now going too far not to favor us.' There can be that feeling out there where when you're trying to be very fair, the golden child is gonna go, 'Well, I don't expect preferential treatment, but I do expect *some* treatment.' There was a little bit of that there."

Jim Lindberg remembers being on tour with The Offspring at the beginning of 1994. It was the thick of winter, and Pennywise were offered berths in the converted school bus in which the support act traveled in order to escape the frigid confines of their van. En route to the next date, Lindberg was offered the chance to hear *Smash*. Obligingly, he listened to the album on a Walkman. At the end of the thirteenth track he "just had the feeling that the album was going to be enormous. I could tell that there was something going on that was so catchy and so perfect for radio. I just knew that KROQ or another local station was going to leap on a couple of those songs and that it had the potential to become a giant album. Obviously I didn't know how big it would become, but I knew that something was gonna happen." At sound check the following afternoon, Jim Lindberg told Fletcher Dragge of his discovery and his prognosis for it. "He was a bit dismissive," remembers the singer. "He was, like, 'Yeah, tell 'em to get back to me when they've sold a hundred thousand albums.'"

Later that year, the Pennywise singer identifies an evening at a restaurant in Los Angeles attended by members of Pennywise and The Offspring, as well as another Epitaph band, the Joykillers, where things "were just starting to feel a little bit weird." Lindberg is at a loss to say exactly what this was, other than a taste in the air of unevenness and bite. "And it was weird," he says, "because all the bands were friends. We went to each other's weddings and we had a good time together." Gurewitz, who picked up the tab for that night's food, says that "there is always competition between bands, and I include myself in that, because we're only human and that's natural." But with the founder of Bad Religion no longer a member of the group he had formed in 1980, Mr. Brett's only job was to manage his record label, and thus, to some degree, the careers of the groups whose music it released. Like a grandmaster playing chess with a dozen people in one sitting, Gurewitz had only the hours in each day with which to strike some semblance of balance. He learned that a view from the top of the world and a hiding to nothing were not mutually exclusive concepts. Here, again, many people interviewed for this book identify Rancid as being the owner's one true love, the group for whom he would forsake all others should the need arise. The fact that this need would never arise was not enough to quiet factions within the label that were by now beginning to splinter.

"To Brett's credit, he tried really, really hard to be fair," says Jim Lindberg. "But it was difficult. The Offspring were being courted with all these really big money deals from these giant international conglomerates, and he has to figure out what's the best way to deal with everything that's going on. *Smash* is going nuclear, but Brett was also really excited about all the great music that was coming out on Epitaph at the time. And when he heard what Rancid were doing, he might have thought, 'Wow, maybe this could be as big as The Offspring, too.' So he decides to work with Rancid. And probably some of The Offspring guys are going, 'Whoa, you're spending all your time with Rancid now, while our album is selling millions of copies!?' Anyone in a band will tell you that it's very much like being in a marriage. There's always going to be jealousies. And so it probably felt like your husband or wife is suddenly spending more time with your best friend, or with someone else, than they are with you. You're gonna get jealous no matter who it is, even if you like the people. But on the whole, I think Brett did a good job managing the situation. But I won't lie, it was a difficult time."

I f Brett Gurewitz was spending a lot of time with Rancid, and he was, it was not without just cause. Leaving aside the matter of whether or not this was the group to whom his heart belonged, this *was* the band with whom he was most closely involved. There may have been a reason for this. By the time NOFX and The Offspring joined Epitaph, both were autonomous units that had gone some way to mastering their craft under the guidance of outside producers and separate record labels. Gurewitz rebuffed The Offspring at the first time of asking, while, initially, Fat Mike rebuffed Epitaph. In time both groups would become synonymous with the label, and in many ways still are, but though their alliances were forged in relative infancy, they were not spawned at birth. A closer parallel would be Pennywise. But despite an entire back catalogue of albums released by Epitaph, Brett Gurewitz's services as a producer were utilized just once, and then in partnership with Jerry Finn, on 1995's *About Time* set. Mr. Brett himself describes the record as having been "produced by Jerry Finn."

But Rancid were effectively signed to Epitaph before the band were formed. On making *Let's Go,* Mr. Brett and the group aligned to record a punk rock album that was recognized as being a classic from the moment it was released. Gurewitz had then bitten his nails to the cuticles as his friends stepped away from their patron and fraternized with one of the world's most powerful corporations. Here, he was cast in the role of a geek on prom night in a rented tuxedo and his mom's car. Across town, Sony was a starting quarterback with a wallet filled with credit cards and a limousine with a fully stocked mini bar. Sony had muscle. Brett Gurewitz had a tattoo on his arm.

On the credits for Rancid's third album, . . . *And Out Come The Wolves*, it is Jerry Finn's name that is listed as producer. But even before the reel-to-reel began rolling at Fantasy Studios, Brett Gurewitz had heard the music in its most embryonic form. Now living in Los Angeles, Tim Armstrong would arrive at Mr. Brett's home and play on an acoustic guitar the songs on which he was working. Even with this sparse treatment, the music stood tall. Outside in the wider world, punk rock was kicking up a storm; inside, the stars were aligning. "For sure, yeah, it felt that way," says Gurewitz. "I mean, it was happening for every band on the label at that time. The sound and the movement were just getting huge, and I felt that Rancid were next. And as the songs started being revealed, one after another, I felt it more and more. I knew that this was gonna be a milestone record, not just for them and for the label, but for the genre itself."

Unusually for an album recorded for Epitaph, the sessions for . . . *And Out Come The Wolves* overran. With only the music finished—"most of the music, anyway," says Mr. Brett—Jerry Finn had to honor a prior engagement with Rob Cavallo to mix Jawbreaker's *24 Hour Revenge Therapy* album. Left high and dry, Brett Gurewitz stepped into the breach.

Sessions for the record moved from Fantasy Studios in Berkeley to Electric Lady Studios on West Eighth Street in New York's Greenwich Village. Suddenly Tim Armstrong and Matt Freeman were a long way indeed from the days of frustration trying to record an album as Operation Ivy inside an empty 924 Gilman Street. Now the recording booth in which they sang lyrics and added the occasional hand claps had also captured the music of the Rolling Stones, Led Zeppelin and, fittingly, The Clash. The facility itself had been built by Jimi Hendrix just months before his death in 1970. If Rancid were in any doubt that they were now hopping with the bohemian jet-set, nearby the author and poet Jim Carroll was taping an interview for a radio program. The band enlisted the author of *The Basketball Diaries* and *The Book of Nods* to compose a short spoken-word section for the song "Junkie Man." Carroll's contribution may have lacked either sense or any particularly arresting images—the writer's prose always outshone his poetry—but amid the confusion of lines such as "my hand went blind / you were in the veins clairvoyant / my hand went blind / I make love to my trance sister / my trance sister," the New York writer did pen the phrase that gave the album its name.

"I'm incredibly proud of . . . *And Out Come The Wolves*," says Brett Gurewitz. "I'm very proud that it came out on Epitaph and that I played a part in the making of it. I think it's really stood the test of time and I don't think there's a bad song on there. It really does capture lightning in a bottle, and the band really were hitting the heights of what they are capable of doing."

Many are the people who will nominate . . . *And Out Come The Wolves* as being the finest punk rock album of the 1990s. It is a startlingly fine record, and one remarkable for its paucity of weaker material. The band's ability to retain their hectic, ragamuffin quality on a production that is loud and lightly polished is impressive. There is a duality at work in the songs themselves, too. The album is fundamentally punk in its sound but also accessible in a way that went on to pester the mainstream. That this is managed without contrivance is testament to the quality of the compositions. "Daly City Train" is an impossibly infectious and propulsive punk pop song that takes its cues from the 2 Tone clubs of Coventry and the sweat and clamor of Gilman Street. The track could be about *anything* and still retain its magnificence, but Tim Armstrong's fluent and evocative lyrics paint permanent pictures of fleeting moments. "He's shooting dope in the men's room / at the station Daly City Train," he sings. He asks, "Have you ever seen an angel / well, I know I have / you see, they stay for a while and then fly away." On the similarly thumping "Olympia WA," the singer recalls roaming the streets of New York City in the small hours. Stranded, the narrator surveys the scene of an unfamiliar Manhattan. "All I know it's four o' clock, and she ain't never showed up / and I watch a thousand people go home from work" the listener is told.

"Olympia WA" begins with Tim Armstrong and Lars Frederiksen "hangin' out . . . down on 6th Street." The song comes from a trip the band took to Gotham in the first week of December 1994. With Epic Records and their now blue-haired A&R man in hot pursuit, the group took late-night dinner with Green Day and Pansy Division at Planet Hollywood in Times Square. The Berkeley-based three piece were by now just two nights away from finishing the tour in support of *Dookie*, while Rancid were about to be made a breathtaking offer by Brett Gurewitz that would make them independently wealthy. Both bands were proof positive of what could be achieved with a nose filled with snot and a headful of melodies.

But this coronation was not without complications. Earlier that evening, Green Day had appeared on national television and debuted a song that suggested that this land of milk and honey was oversweet and starting to curdle. Broadcast from NBC Studios, viewers in the United States were treated to a song of a hue not heard on *Dookie* or any of the two albums that pre-ceded it. Its verse contained the lines "well, I don't know what I've got / and that's all that I've got / and I'm picking scabs off my face." The music was harsh, reductive and in no way cute. The song's title was "Geek Stink Breath."

## CHAPTER NINE

# SPONTANEOUS COMBUSTION, PANIC ATTACK

One afternoon in 1995, Billie Joe Armstrong was walking down Haight Street in San Francisco. Minding his own affairs, he was accosted by a character "who looked like a really early eighties English postcard punk." The young man had an oppositional attitude. "I remember I almost got into a fight with him," says Billie Joe. "He was shouting 'Sellout!' at me. I was, like, 'What the fuck do *you* know about me, or my band?'"

The clues that people who knew Green Day, or who knew of them, were changing were all around them. Tre Cool remembers that "other people had more difficulty adjusting to our success than I did. I think a lot of the friends that I had before suddenly had attitudes about 'Oh well, you don't have a problem in the world because your band's on TV and you're successful.' A lot of the friends that we had in bands would say, 'Well, it should have been some other band who became successful, not you guys.'"

There were those who thought that it was success, and success only, that separated Green Day from the chasing pack. It was of course much more than this; the separation existed long before Warner Bros. came calling. It existed in things such as Billie Joe Armstrong's adamant belief that he didn't want to become the kind of artist who drives around the neighborhood in a car that has a bumper sticker that reads: "Real Musicians Have Day Jobs." By the time their engines began to rev during the early part of their career, Green Day could never be accused of a poverty of ambition. "There were so many bands who looked at us and thought, 'Well, their songs only have three chords,'" says Tre Cool. "And they thought, 'Well, our songs have three chords, too, so we can be as big as they are.' It was as if the only explanation for [our success] was the number of chords in our songs."

On the tour in support of *Dookie*, Green Day had been away from the Bay Area for ten months. In this time, everything in their world changed. As the tour drew to a close in the holiday period of 1994, Roseanne Barr, then the country's most famous television personality, introduced the band on *Saturday Night Live* while wearing a *Kerplunk* T-shirt. They were by then so famous that no one on the show seemed to mind that they played the unheard "Geek Stink Breath" rather than the international earworn "Basket Case" as they had promised. ("Oh, we used to do that all the time," says the drummer. No big deal. "We'd show up at a TV show saying we were gonna play one song and then play a different one.") Upon returning home, Tre Cool found himself "in a state of denial [about Green Day's success] for about a year. I tried not to think about it. I just tried to carry on the way I always had. I never bought fancy things or anything like that. I just thought, 'I'm the same guy, right?' Obviously I had no more financial stresses, and I got that, but at the same time I wasn't buying myself gold chains and diamond grills or anything." Eschewing mounds of bling, instead Tre Cool bought himself an International Harvester Scout four-wheel drive off-road vehicle in which he would visit his mom and dad up in Mendocino County and rattle around the open spaces and mountain roads of Northern California. "It was a lot of fun," he says. "But then the next thing you know, it's time to go out on tour again."

It was Billie Joe Armstrong who suffered the acutest effects of altitude sickness. "I felt like I was being run out of town," he says. "I was, like, 'Fuck this, I'm staying!' I was angry and bitter about the way things kind of ended up. It's strange because with that level of success you'd imagine it'd be some kind of story like 'hometown hero boy,' or 'hometown hero does good.' But there was none of that at all. Suddenly people were calling me a rock star. It's weird because that was the worst insult that I'd ever heard. If someone called me a rock star, that was worse than being called a sellout. It was, like, 'Oh, the fucking *rock star* is here.' It was just so alienating. I just wanted to be a normal punk like everybody else."

Billie Joe Armstrong is on record as describing this period as being "a real ugly time." Drugs began to take hold in the Bay Area scene, and Armstrong watched as friends were held in thrall to amphetamines. Soon they would graduate to heroin. What began as a party had become a lifestyle; an experiment, even, to see how far one could gamble with one's own mortality. He remembers seeing friends who now looked like skeletons, or "walking dead people." He told Lawrence Livermore that "I have to say that I indulged in that scene myself at one time, but something scary was happening . . . And, you know, I had re-sponsibilities . . . I couldn't afford to turn into that.

"I think I was addicted to partying a little bit," he added. "But the older I got, the more I realized that I couldn't handle drugs. Because what people get addicted to is not only the high, but the low. They're into the low. But I can barely handle it when I'm coming down from coffee . . . It was a rough time for me.

But I'm lucky enough to be one of the people who learned from that experience and moved on, where some other people just got addicted and more addicted and more addicted until it killed them."

For Green Day, these were bleak days which proved that it can be as much of a shock to receive more than one expects as it is to receive less. "I'll tell you the truth—I had a lot more fun a couple of years ago," Mike Dirnt told *Rolling Stone*. Billie Joe's taste in music was hardening into angrier and faster forms. He watched as *Maximumrocknroll* turned on his band, an editorial volte-face that soon affected the line taken by magazines such as *Spin* and *Rolling Stone*. The frontman made no attempt to hide the fact that these things bothered him. Quickly he became worried about what other people thought of him. The backlash against Green Day was severe and unrelenting, and in hindsight Armstrong believes that he ought to have taken more time to reflect on what was happening and to spend more time with his wife, Adrienne, and their son, Joey, who was not yet one year old. He was acutely aware that he was no longer a part of the crowd. Even close friends seemed to be acting strangely. They would phone him up and say, "Hey, I don't want to bother you, but . . ." and this caveat would cause him to feel self-conscious about the mainstream acceptance of his band. He and Adrienne were forced to move house after their address was revealed on the *Live 105* show on KITS radio. He felt that people weren't backward in coming forward to tell him that he was doing the wrong thing. What felt to him like realizing his potential as a musician seemed to others like an affront to artistic justice.

"I think I was just lost," he told Lawrence Livermore. "I couldn't find the strength to convince myself that what I was doing was a good thing. I was in a band that was huge because it was supposed to be huge, because our songs were that good. [But] I couldn't ever feel that I was doing the right thing, because it felt like I was making so many people angry. That's where I became so confused, and it got really stupid. I would never want to live that part of my life over again. Ever."

"I know that there were a lot of people who were happy [for Green Day]," says Lawrence Livermore. "But they tended to be nowhere near as vocal as the detractors for fear of risking alienation from the rest of the community. Or else it might have been that they might not have been as central a part of the community in the first place."

"It's weird because it was as if people were looking at Green Day with shit-colored glasses," says Armstrong. "And it didn't seem to have anything to do with the music. We knew that we'd made the best record that we'd ever made up until that point. There were new people who were listening to it and connecting with it. We had new fans, and they were young kids. But then there was the other side of it—there were people who were the detractors. They kind of had it in for us even before they'd heard a note that we'd played. It's weird when people look at things in that context. I only listen to the music. If it's a good record and it's got the kind of production that I like, then I'll dig it, you know. Maybe that's because I'm a musician. I'm a player. I'm not one to sit around and scrutinize what other people do.

"But [at the time] I was sort of confused. Whether it was where I came from, which is Rodeo, a total refinery town, or whether it was Berkeley and Oakland, where I'd learned this whole new way of looking at life. There was politics and music there, and artists and weirdos that I had something in common with. But with the success, it felt like I didn't have either of those places anymore. I felt really out of place. We had success and we had money, and I was just trying to figure out what it all meant. It was weird."

Since forming as Sweet Children in 1987, Green Day had performed at 924 Gilman Street no fewer than *forty-seven* times. But as their Converse-clad feet touched down at San Francisco International Airport at the beginning of December 1994, the band had already been exiled from the club for more than a year. The charge sheet read that they had signed with a major label, and for as long as this status was maintained their presence on the stage was no longer welcome.

It seems certain that in the eye of the storm of Hurricane Dookie, this expulsion was a somewhat abstract notion. But as Green Day stopped to refuel in their old neighborhoods, the void was more keenly felt. Gilman Street was the centrifugal force of the Bay Area scene; for the four years following the demise of Operation Ivy, Green Day were by far its most popular band. But now, according to many, the revolution had been compromised. Billie Joe Armstrong, Mike Dirnt and Tre Cool were February Mensheviks to Gilman's October Bolsheviks. It is of course worth noting that even without the club's exclusionary door policy, it would have been impossible for Green Day to have appeared at 924 Gilman Street under anything other than a pseudonymous band name, and in circumstances of top-level clearance secrecy. But all the same, the fatwa had been issued. Green Day had been eighty-sixed.

"The place was volatile," says Tre Cool, "and in fact it still is. It's a constant struggle to keep the doors open. But I could see that our crowd had changed and it was no longer a Gilman crowd. We were already getting riots at our shows. The last thing we wanted was for thousands of people to crush onto the streets of Berkeley outside the doors of Gilman."

But.

"Of course, when someone says you can't have a cookie, you try and get a cookie. But it didn't really bother me in that sense. What bothered me was the way that some journalists tried to make it into a thing. They tried to take jabs and almost attack us and our character in a way. They would attack our history, because it might make it a good story for a magazine that would want to write something like that. So that was a little annoying. But I didn't have anything against Gilman. It was just having our history and our legacy attacked by people who had no business even typing the word 'Gilman' on a typewriter that was hurtful."

Billie Joe Armstrong viewed his band's expulsion with less sanguinity. For him, 924 Gilman Street was the place at which he went to college. It was his alma mater, and to have his name scrubbed from the roll of honor was bitter medicine indeed. The twenty-three-year-old had no recourse against the turmoil and dislocation washing over him other than through the medium at which he excelled. "I never really hid the fact that it bothered me [and] I think I reacted to it," he told Lawrence Livermore. "And it came across in the music." Following a brief rest, the trio were soon at work proving the maxim that the band that plays together stays together. Green Day may no longer have shared digs of a kind that could cause a rise in the share price of Rent-okil, but as their world tumbled around them the band at the eye of the storm were determined that the show must, and would, go on. "I remember at the time we felt that there was a real urgency to what we were doing," says Mike Dirnt. "There was a real urgency to stake our claim and say, 'No, we belong here.' It was really important to us to make sure people knew that we weren't just a flash in the pan."

This possibility posed a significant danger. The vertiginous altitude at which Green Day were now cruising meant that a cough from their engines could quickly make them victims of the laws of gravity. It's possible that at this time the band were trying to prove to *themselves*, too, that they were more than a flash in the pan. At this point they resembled an airborne car-toon character who knows he will plummet to earth the very moment he stops running. What is remarkable about this time is just how much the band were able to absorb while remaining a machine of perpetual motion. Without altering the dynamics of their sound, it was with ease that the musicians were able to find a higher gear and, if needed, a higher gear still. This sharper sound was accompanied by a lyrical anger hitherto unexplored.

It was neither theatrical nor hysterical and came with background notes of contempt and, even, disgust. In the course of little over a year Green Day had lost their baby teeth.

No song better embodies these qualities than "86." Named after 924 Gilman Street's ultimate sanction, the two-minutes-and-forty-seven-seconds-long track is a master class of defiant resignation. Whether or not the setting for the song is Gilman itself is not quite clear. But what is beyond doubt is the hurt and rancor with which Billie Joe Armstrong sings of the things that are not so much lost, as stolen. Unusually, "86" is written in the second person, as if the singer himself is listening, but never responding, to a lecture. "What brings you around? / Did you lose something the last time you were here?" he asks. "You'll never find it now / it's buried deep with your identity." Elsewhere, he is told to "exit out the back / and never show your head around again" and to "stand aside and let the next one pass / don't let the door kick you in the ass." As if the target of this weary admonishment were in any doubt, he is told that "there's no return from 86." Just to be clear, he's reminded of this a further eleven times; and, again, just to make sure, he's told three times to not "even try" to negotiate a change to these terms.

By now Green Day's ambivalence to fame was becoming confused. The band issued a virtual press blackout, but made exceptions for high-rolling publications such as *Spin* and *Rolling Stone*. They kept their ticket prices under twenty dollars—"We don't think we're worth $22.50," Tre Cool told *Rolling Stone*—but played venues the size of the Coliseum in Oakland. ("When they go to a major, you're never fucking seeing them at Gilman Street again," remarked Fat Mike. "You're going to see them in Oakland Coliseum. And I've seen Green Day at Oakland Coliseum, and it's no fucking fun.") The group also ditched their management team and decided to try and handle their own affairs, a move Tre Cool describes as being "a really bad idea." But he says, "It was good because it taught us how much work goes into stuff that we don't even think about, and that, actually, we don't really want to do. But it did give us a good perspective as to what goes on in the business side, alongside the music side."

The band were even willing to postpone a concert at the Convention Center in Niagara Falls in order to appear on the *Late Show with David Letterman*. As questionable as this practice may have been, at least they made it count. "The first time they were on the program they scared the hell out of me," said the best host in the history of American television, "but since they've gone on to sell millions of albums." Even before the name Green Day has escaped from Letterman's lips, Tre Cool is rolling out the opening beats to "86," a song that was never released as a single. Wearing a suit jacket and a spotted tie, Billie Joe Armstrong plays his guitar, Blue, slung so low that the lower half of its body is down near his knees. His eyes are round like golf balls. His head twitches. To his left, Mike Dirnt underpins his friend's forensic open-palm chords with a complex bass line that gives the song more body than it has any right to claim. The fact that he does this while spending some of his time in midair only adds to the magnificence of the performance.

The sound is of electricity on the loose and looking for trouble. The sight is of a band beginning to sour.

Rob Cavallo says that during this time he wouldn't have described Billie Joe Armstrong as being "necessarily unhappy." But he does believe that 1995 "was a period of adjustment. I think if anything it was a case of be careful what you wish for. There's a lot of kids out there that say, 'Well, I want to be rich and famous.' But when they get to be rich and famous, what happens is that they realize that their life has changed a lot more than they thought it would. Life has become much more complicated. Everything you do, even going down to the local coffee shop, is not as simple as it used to be. And I think they were just adjusting to that. I think they were trying to reconcile themselves with that idea. And, yes, they had some guilt about their success. The amount of change that you have to go through can't be overestimated. And I think that's what they were going through . . . I mean, you have to remember where they were coming from. When I first met them, they were only a step or two up from being on the street. They didn't have money; they didn't have *anything*. And then all of a sudden they were millionaires."

There was never any question that Rob Cavallo would produce Green Day's fourth album. When the two parties convened at Hyde Street Studios in San Francisco the band were clear about what they wanted to achieve. They wanted their new material to sound harder than anything that had preceded it. They wanted it to be a record that said to their core constituents that they had not sold out and that they were not motivated by success. They wanted the record to be made on *their* terms. Of course *39/Smooth*, *Kerplunk* and *Dookie* had each been made on Green Day's own terms, too, but none of those albums were being born in the shadow of a diamond-certified disc. Rob Cavallo knew the band's latest collection of songs was more abrasive, and he liked that. He also liked the fact that more than anything they wanted the songs to *rock*. "Their attitude was 'Fuck this, we'll show them,'" he remembers. The album quickly assumed the working title *Reactionary Record*.

Rob Cavallo contacted the guitar-rig technician Bob Bradshaw at Custom Audio Electronics to help him and Billie Joe Armstrong find a harder tone for the record. Bradshaw took the Dookie model and added to it a hundred-watt Marshall amplifier and an SE lead modification. "It has more claws on it, and sharper teeth," says Cavallo. On the album's meatier moments, the tone the listener hears is sixty or seventy percent Armstrong's new rig, and thirty or forty percent of the sound produced for *Dookie*. "Billie liked it hugely," remembers the producer. "He thought it worked with the record's unapologetic mindset, which was, you know, 'We're gonna kick you in the teeth with some of these songs.'" "We were like kids in a candy store on that record," remembers Tre Cool. "We just wanted to find the biggest sound that we could. We wanted the biggest guitar sound, the fattest bass sound and the loudest drum sound that we could find. And we wanted to do it properly. We didn't want to use those lame production techniques that a lot of bands from that period were using."

No track better exemplifies this quality than "Panic Song." A track of two halves, the first section begins with Mike Dirnt playing bass notes at such a speed as to sound like machine-gun fire. Tre Cool joins him on the drums at a beats-per-minute ratio that is too fast to discern. Billie Joe Armstrong's guitar hangs in the background. As the introduction builds, so too does the song's sense of tension. The guitar is now being struck with force and with greater regularity. Mike Dirnt and Tre Cool's rhythm section thunders away beneath the chords. Suddenly, like a streak of lightning, Armstrong's guitar is matching the bass note for note. The song shudders on its four-time axis, as if in a spasm. As the introduction gives way to the song it supports, the point of it all becomes clear—*this is the musical equivalent of a panic attack*.

Today both Tre Cool and Mike Dirnt are rather nonchalant about the effort required to record the relentless first act of "Panic Song." "That was as fast as I knew how to play at the time, but I could probably play faster now," says the drummer. The bassist admits that "it took me a long time to get there, but once I got there I stayed there." Rob Cavallo, though, is in no doubt about the energy it took to capture the song on tape. He remembers Tre Cool's hands being "a bloody mess" as the drummer ripped through the calluses on the palms of his hands and how "for every single take, he put one thousand percent into it." The producer remembers being full of admiration for the drummer for his efforts. It was almost as if Tre Cool was an American football player doing pre-season drills in the remorseless heat of summer. Cavallo recalls "Tre going to sit down by the wall on the floor after a take and him being completely spent. I really take my hat off to him for having gone through that."

"I can remember my wife [Adrienne] saying to me when we were listening to the record . . . She goes, 'Wow, this is a lot more aggressive than the last album,'" remembers Billie Joe. "And she says, 'What do you think people are going to think of it?' And at that point I was, like, 'I don't give a shit what people think of it.' The point of the record was to make the hardest record we knew how to make, and that's what we did."

Like Green Day themselves, in 1995 Warner Bros. was also in a transitional state. By now the company's president, Lenny Waronker, the man who had green-lit the twenty-five thousand dollars needed to buy the Bookmobile, had left his post in order to head Dreamworks Records, an arm of the new entertainment conglomerate cofounded by Steven Spielberg. Rob Cavallo recalls a meeting with Waronker's successor, Danny Goldberg, at which the only pressing issue seemed to be the speed with which the producer could deliver *Insomniac* to his paymasters. "My conversation with him had nothing to do with how good the record was, or anything like that, just that I get it to him sooner," says the producer. He had enjoyed a close working relationship with Waronker, a man who didn't seem to mind that the singles from *Dookie* were chosen solely by Cavallo and Billie Joe Armstrong. In reporting to the invariably receptive president and to Ted Templeman, the producer of the David Lee Roth–era Van Halen albums, Rob Cavallo was also given full license when it came to the sound of the music itself. But wholesale changes in the company's personnel led to the running of a tighter ship. The fact that in the space of just six months Rob Cavallo had been promoted from A&R representative to senior vice president did not insulate him from a warning from a newly installed superior that "I'm your boss and I'm senior to you. I'm responsible for the quality of the music that comes out on Reprise Records, and if I deem that your records do not meet up to these standards, then I'm going to be able to make remedy on that."

"There's no way [the company] was as hip as what was happening when Warner Brothers Records was at full force," says Cavallo. "We were a well-oiled machine that partially got dismantled. It was never going to be good."

Immediately prior to its release on October 10, 1995, the ladies and gentlemen of the Fourth Estate were given the chance to bestow *Insomniac* with faint praise or else common or garden variety disdain. In the running for the award of backhanded compliment of the year, Rolling Stone wrote that "in punk the good stuff actually unfolds and gains meaning as you listen without sacrificing any of its electric, haywire immediacy. And Green Day are as good as this stuff gets." *Spin* magazine believed that parts of the album "dawdles [and are] lost in self pity and failed attempts at class rhetoric." It's too bad, the reviewer went on, that "Billie Joe didn't incorporate more of his experiences as a family man or a star—just proof of how much freedom a young band with quick hands can still find within the hallowed changes of the garage-rock jamboree." Whatever that means. "In order to fill the stadiums they were about to play with a full sound, the band bumped up their guitars, streamlined their songs and looked back to stadium rocking power-pop/hard rock acts like Cheap Trick" was *Alternative Press's* take on things, confused tenses and all. It concluded by saying that "if *Dookie* was the band's emotional and intellectual breakthrough, Insomniac is their big rock record." *Entertainment Weekly* was much less ambiguous and much less impressed. "*Insomniac* does make you wonder about Green Day's growth, though," they wrote. "Between albums one and four, The Clash, to take an old-school example, branched out from guitar crunch to reggae, dub, and Spectorized pop. By comparison, Green Day sound exactly the same as on their first album, albeit with crisper production and, ominously, a palpable degeneration in their sense of humor. The few hints of growth are fairly microscopic: a tougher metallic edge to a few of the songs . . . and lyrics that are bleaker than *Dookie*'s."

*Insomniac* is not Green Day's "big rock record." It is, in fact, their coiled, twitching, uneasy and agitated record. And to say that the band "sound exactly the same as on their first album" is plainly daft. *Insomniac* is an exercise in reduction where the songs have been distilled down to such a point that the removal of even a single chord would cause them to collapse in on themselves. The band are so trimmed of fat that were they to become any leaner the body would start to devour itself. *Insomniac* features fourteen songs, of which only two clock out at more than three minutes. Two of the tracks, "Brat" and "Jaded," make their point in under two minutes. It is a master class in buzz-saw efficiency.

A glance at the lyric sheet casts light on the darkness that in 1995 was filling Billie Joe Armstrong's mind. On the brilliant and spacious "Brain Stew" he finds himself "fucked up and spun out in my room / on my own / here we go." On "Jaded," by far the fastest song the group had to date penned, the singer observes that "there is no progress / evolution kill it all / I found my place in nowhere / in nowhere / in nowhere." Every character on "Stuart and the Ave." is "all fucked up." The sight from atop the hill of "Panic Song" sees "the world as a sick machine / breeding a mass of shit / with such a desolate conclusion / fill the void with . . . I don't care." Most impressive of all, and in some ways the most startling, is "No Pride." There's poetry in the lines "hand me down your lost and founds / of secondhand regrets." But the chorus is pessimism unredeemed. "You better swallow your pride / or you're gonna choke on it," Armstrong sings, adding that "you better digest your values / 'cos they count for shit."

found *Insomniac* to be depressing," says Lawrence Liver-more. "There's one song on there ["Brain Stew"] that I can't even listen to. I was even a bit worried for them when I heard it. I'm sort of putting myself out there when I say that because people will get cross with me for even mildly criticizing it—and I'm not criticizing it. But it felt a little too raw. I'd always known the band—again, like the early Beatles—to be full of these great love songs, or adolescent and post-adolescent yearnings. And we now know from the perspective of history that the Beatles' lives weren't all peachy behind the scenes, either. But the music that we as fans heard made you happy and made you want to sing along. It made you think, 'Gosh, the world isn't such a bad place after all.' And that's what Green Day has always been for me. And *Insomniac* was the first record where I thought, 'This music isn't pleasant.' To me, it was kind of their *In Utero*."

When *Insomniac* landed in the record shops and shopping malls of the world, mindful listeners didn't even need to take the CD out of its case to know that things had changed. Whereas *Dookie* featured a good-natured cartoon on its front and a glove puppet of Ernie from *Sesame Street* on its rear, its successor is a piece of work titled "God Told Me to Skin You Alive." A collage constructed by the artist Winston Smith, then best known for his work with Dead Kennedys, the piece features surreal and often macabre images of a housewife holding a gun to the head of a man asleep in a hammock. Elsewhere, Uncle Sam can be found on his knees, hands clasped together in prayer. In an image that might have been dreamed up by David Cronenberg, a dentist drills both the head and the mouth of a prone patient (this image originally appeared on the inner sleeve of Dead Kennedys' reassuringly risqué *Plastic Surgery Disasters*). A human skull sits on a table. A soldier hands a rifle to a toddler in a high chair while to his right another man cuddles a lemur. "I think people should have known what kind of album *Insomniac* was going to be by the fact that the artwork featured a picture of a woman with her hair on fire," Mike Dirnt told the author in 1997.


**M**ark Kohr was at home on the Haight when Billie Joe Armstrong phoned up to pitch him an idea. The director was moving house that day so the call was not well timed. His sister picked up and handed the receiver over to her brother. "Billie's on the phone," she said. Green Day's original intention was to eschew the idea of shooting music videos for any of the four singles that would be released from *Insomniac*. To put it kindly, in the age of MTV this was a radical strategy, not to mention one that would have brought Warner Bros. no joy at all. But Billie Joe Armstrong had an idea about which he wanted to consult Mark Kohr. The lead-off single from Green Day's forthcoming album was the not overly commercial "Geek Stink Breath," a song about the addictive properties of crystal methamphetamine. The musician told the director about a friend who had been led down this path, and of an outcome that had little to recommend it. The friend was booked in to have his teeth removed: would Kohr fancy shooting the operation? "And I was, like, sure," he says. "But I didn't want to push him [Billie Joe]. I didn't want to say, 'Well, are we going to make a video out of it?' So I was, like, 'Okay, yeah sure, I'll see about shooting it.'"

Kohr placed a call to Julia Roberts—not that one—who at the time was the music video commissioner at Warner Bros. He presented her with the terrific news that Billie Joe Armstrong wanted him to film a friend who was having his teeth removed as a result of him being addicted to a particularly destructive and very hard drug. "Shall I draw up a budget?" Roberts was asked. At this time it was still unclear as to whether or not this footage would form the central plank of an actual music video. It is testament to Green Day's power, not to mention the sheer amounts of money sloshing around the music industry at this time, that the commissioner gave the green light to this frankly crazy idea. "Okay, cool," thought Mark Kohr, "this is gonna be great."

"I thought, 'I'll shoot it in thirty-five millimeter with this special lens that's like a rod that has a little optic on the end," says the director. "These days it's really easy to do, but back then it was much harder. You could bring it right in, super close, and it had a tiny light on the end. It was perfect for getting right in there while the dentist did his work. But we were very careful about it. I didn't want to affect the situation and make it [the procedure] a bigger thing than it already was. I didn't want to bring the dentist's chair into a studio or anything like that. So I thought, 'Okay, let me talk to them and figure out how to work it out.'"

Not surprisingly, Billie Joe Armstrong's friend, whose name is Paul, didn't have much money. Because of this, the procedure was scheduled to take place at a dental school in San Francisco. Mark Kohr called the facility and asked if he might set up a Panavision camera, a thirty-five-millimeter probing gizmo, a dolly from which to operate both and studio lights, inside a cramped surgery in which an anesthetized drug addict was having his teeth taken out. The dental school said, "Sure, why not?" The fact that Warner Bros. paid a location fee probably helped sugar the deal. Kohr remembers that the school "adjusted to us to some extent," but also that "we were very clear with them what this was going to be." (By now it had been determined that "Geek Stink Breath" would be released with an accompanying music video). He also remembers that the dentist's name was "Lipscum, which is definitely not a good name considering what he was training to be." The video was shot in real time as the procedure took place. The director and crew were on hand at the surgery in the middle of the day to make the afternoon appointment slot.

As it turned out, Paul only needed to have one tooth removed. He could even have had it fixed, but lacked the funds with which to do so. Also, Mark Kohr cut two edits of the clip, only one of which featured a young man having a tooth pulled. But in North America, only the more graphic video was released and any viewer watching it is privy to an exquisitely excruciating experience. With the patient's mouth agape like that of a monkfish, the dentist pulls the gum back from the tooth and draws blood. Then come the pliers, teasing the molar back and forth until it is loose enough to be extracted. Every shot taken from above the dentist's chair is painful to watch. In two minutes and fifteen seconds, Green Day had repositioned themselves as a band who were not quite as loveable as listeners might have believed them to be. This was news that certainly came as a shock to the many broadcasters faced with the quandary of whether or not to play a video that would stand no chance of making it onto the air were it not made by one of the world's most popular bands. MTV did play the clip for a time, but only with a warning beforehand. After a short while, the channel then quietly removed "Geek Stink Breath" from its schedule.

"We were a little bit bummed out because they pulled it off of MTV," says Tre Cool. "That was the first bit of censorship or criticism that we got from MTV at any point. They were fine with all of the stuff from *Dookie*. But with 'Geek Stink Breath' they said, 'Well, you know, we've been getting a lot of complaints about it and people aren't digging it. They don't want to see that on TV while they're sitting in their houses—it's kind of gnarly, so we're going to take it off.'"

For a punk band that had made a career out of playing caffeinated pop songs, *Insomniac* is glaringly short of singles. In the United States, just three were issued, although the second release featured two songs combined, "Brain Stew" and "Jaded." Both releases nestled briefly in the mainstream top-ten chart, but fared less well on the airplay chart, where only "Geek Stink

Breath" troubled the top thirty. A third single, "Walking Contra-diction," failed to make the top-fifty most played songs on the radio and scraped only top-thirty positions in *Billboard*'s alter-native and mainstream charts. The final release from *Insom-niac* was the only track not to feature either the words "shit" or "fucked."

Within the first year of its release, *Insomniac* sold a blush over four million copies. In the United States it went gold and then platinum on the same day, January 8, 1995, and double platinum on the February 27. But, really, Green Day's fourth album was curiously unloved, and, just as strangely, it remains so. In recent years its authors have excised all traces of its material from their live set—the only one of the band's first eight albums to suffer this fate—with few seeming to mind the omission. By almost any measure, during its initial cycle the album was a commer-cial hit—and in the fullness of time the record would sell seven million copies. But compared to *Dookie*, it paled. The word may have been wrong, but it was in: *Insomniac* had bombed.

"The songs were harder, and I liked that," says Rob Cavallo. "But it was obvious that the album wouldn't be loved by every-one. The people who had bought *Dookie* because it was poppy might not like *Insomniac*. And we knew that, and in a way that was the point. But it didn't really matter because we still went on to sell seven million records or whatever."

"It was so funny because I remember watching a TV show at the time," says Mike Dirnt. "It was a daytime TV show. And they had an item on there that said, 'In other news, one record that's not doing so well is the new Green Day. It's not doing as well as the other record they've done [*Dookie*]'—and blah blah blah—'and its sales are at only four and a half million.' I looked at the TV and laughed and thought, 'You're fucking crazy—it's huge!' But none of that stuff matters. The moment we've written and recorded an album, and put it to bed, it no longer belongs to us. It's out there for other people. But what I do know is that

I'm going to be proud of that record [*Insomniac*] for the rest of my life."

"The fact that that album came out, like, a year and a half after *Dookie* was us trying to cut off the bullshit in its tracks and just keep making music," says Billie Joe Armstrong. "That's all we wanted to do, keep making music. Sometimes I feel that *Insomniac* is the most honest record I ever made at the particular moment that it was written and recorded."

Five hours south on Interstate 5, one of the great feel-good stories of the 1990s was about to be cut to ribbons. A year after becoming the world's most successful independent record label owner, Brett Gurewitz was addicted to heroin, cocaine and crack. Even before becoming a millionaire, he had experience when it came to drugs. He had grown up as a stoner, and then as a young punk had dabbled with more accelerated substances. By the time of his twenty-fifth birthday things were getting sufficiently out of hand that the Bad Religion guitarist took action, the result of which was a period of sobriety and abstinence that endured for seven years. After this, he fell off the wagon with a walloping thump. So clouded was his mind that today Gurewitz questions his cognitive abilities and even his grasp of reality at this time. Finally checking into a rehabilitation clinic, he arranged for friends to throw apples hollowed out and stuffed with cocaine over the facility's walls. Brett Gurewitz hated cocaine, but he didn't half like the smell.

"I kind of got carried away," he says. "I thought I was bullet proof. I think that along with success there are certain stresses that come with getting big overnight. But there's also the feeling that you *are* bullet proof. I thought that I could use drugs and alcohol freely and successfully now because I thought I had arrived. I was successful. So I decided to see if I could do that, which was a famously failed experiment. That period lasted about three years. I don't mind talking about it because it was in the papers in LA at the time. But I did go to jail a couple of times."

In other news, Jim Guerinot was a worried man. As the manager of Trent Reznor and Nine Inch Nails, he had watched helplessly as Steve Gottlieb, the founder of TNT Records, the band's label, sold out to Interscope. Now he was hearing rumors that Brett Gurewitz was taking numerous meetings and testing the waters with a mind to selling part of his company and, by definition, The Offspring, to a major label. As we have seen, Gurewitz emphatically denies this. Guerinot says that "I don't know what was going on in Brett's life, but I know it wasn't going great." This is of course code for knowing exactly what was going on in Brett's life, but being too kind to say. But he did know about the meetings. He would receive calls from those who had attended, or else their lawyers. The sticking point in these alleged negotiations was that The Offspring were contracted to Epitaph for only one more album, after which they were free to sign with any label of their choosing. It was incumbent on any suitor to sign the band for longer than this. Rancid and NOFX were nice pickings, but it was the group from Orange County that was the goose laying twenty-four-carat eggs.

Jim Guerinot and the band wondered why they needed Epitaph if Epitaph planned to sell them out. If they were going to become part of a major label network, wouldn't it make more sense for them to choose their own destination and leave behind the independent label to which they were contracted? The problem again was that pesky third album The Offspring were obligated to deliver to Brett Gurewitz. The band took stock and came to the conclusion that were this contract to prove binding—and about this they had their doubts—as a last resort they could deliver one more record to Epitaph and then depart for pastures new. Hustling as ever, Jim Guerinot called Michelle Anthony and Donny Ironer, the chief executive officer of Sony

Music and the president of Columbia Records respectively, and offered them the band. As he had done with Brett Gurewitz and Rancid, he laid out the lavish terms required to secure their signatures. Columbia Records agreed to these demands.

"Originally, this isn't what we wanted to do," says Guerinot. "It just wasn't what we wanted. Everyone wanted to stay independent. But when it felt like we weren't going to stay independent of our own volition, then we realized we had to go. We realized that we had to leave at a time of our choosing."

"We had a three-record deal," counters Brett Gurewitz. "It's that simple. They'd given me two records and we were in negotiations for the third record when they told me, 'Hey, we signed to Sony for the third record.' This was a surprise to me. I said, 'But we're negotiating to extend our three-record deal—you owe me the third record; you can't give it to Sony.' And they said, 'Well, we don't think your contract is binding, or that we have to stick by it, so this is what we're gonna do.' At this time they were very mad at me for various things. One of the things they were particularly mad at, and which they cite often, was that I cared more about myself than my bands and that I was acting like I was the star and not giving credit where it was due. And there may be some truth in that. I was new to this kind of success so I did do a lot of interviews. As a writer and a musician myself, I don't think I would take credit for another band's success. I don't think I ever took it that far. But I probably did do too many interviews. People were interested in me at that time, but I don't know if they [The Offspring] should have been that mad at me. It seems like a bit of a straw man. But they were mad at me for that."

Dexter Holland concurs. "Us leaving wasn't so much a business decision," he says. "It was a feeling that we had that as things became more successful for us, the more Brett saw this as an opportunity to make Epitaph big. It was becoming more about Epitaph's success instead of The Offspring's success, and that felt backwards to us. It felt hurtful. There was a point where he did an article in *Forbes* [magazine], for example—and I'm not trying to say he did this, he did that; I'm just using it to illustrate the point—and it just started to feel that Brett wanted to become a record mogul. He wanted to show himself that way and it just didn't feel right to us. It felt like it should have been more about the label promoting the artist, not the label promoting the label. That became harder and harder to overcome as we tried to go through negotiations."

What we have here is a failure to communicate. The way The Offspring saw it, they were playing three concerts in New York, not one of which their record label owner could be bothered to attend because he was too busy promoting himself in a magazine. But Dexter Holland admits that he didn't see too much of Brett Gurewitz during this time, let alone sit with him and articulate a resentment that had gone from simmering to a rolling boil. It was that "it was very much the 'Epitaph, Epitaph' stuff that bothered us," but "not so much saying just personally that our feelings are hurt."

Twenty-two years on, the most striking thing about the fracture between The Offspring and Epitaph is that no one seems fully sure if it was worth the candle. Dexter Holland, Noodles, Greg K., Brett Gurewitz and Jim Guerinot all agree that the parting was an awful shame, not to mention the end of a story that is as good as any in the history of punk. All express regret that events turned out this way, and all agree that if time were to be had again, The Offspring and Epitaph Records would have remained united. Also striking is the complete absence of rancor on the part of all of the combatants. Looking back, it appears for all the world like a case of some people acting stupidly and others getting greedy.

Brett Gurewitz asserts that the band asked for a ten percent stake in Epitaph. Dexter Holland can't quite remember, but doesn't deny it. Jim Guerinot vaguely recalls that Gurewitz *offered* the group a stake in the firm, but either way, he says, "That was something that had precedent. I'm not being coy here, but I truly don't remember if we got offered first or if we asked first. If they said that I asked first then I'll accept it as being true. But I know that U2 owned ten percent of Island [Records]. And I thought, 'Okay, what U2 represents as an amount of billing for Island, relative to what The Offspring means for the billing of Epitaph, is not even close.' And if Brett can't compete with a major label offer, he can compete by making the band partners in some way. There has to be some way that Brett can do that, if he had wanted to."

"Epitaph was selling a million records a year," says Brett Gurewitz. "And then along comes The Offspring and they sell three million records in one year. So there were suddenly orders of magnitude bigger than my entire label. And Brian [Dexter] even expressed this to me one day during the tumult of it all [when] he said, 'You know, we should be partners in Epitaph because our sales represent more records than your entire company.' And I said, 'Well, you know, I understand why you would feel that way, but we have a record contract together. I'm a record label. I signed your band, and I was hoping to do a great job and make your band huge. I don't see why I should be punished for exceeding beyond anyone's wildest expectations. I want to be the label and you can be the band and we can work out anything else on that basis.' But he felt that it should have been more than that. He felt that he should have gotten the recognition of getting to own part of my company and of being something more than just an artist." (Here, one might say that Gurewitz's use of the word "just" is rather interesting.) "Anyway, that might not be the reason [that the band left the label] but it was something that he mentioned to me once. And while I understand why he would feel that way, that's not something I was interested in. I thought, 'Well, I'm the record label and if I do a great job for one of my bands, I deserve to benefit from that, as do they. And they benefitted massively from it, and so did I. And after all these years, I think both of us are better for having known each other. There is no ill will on my part."

But it was over, and it remains so. Brett Gurewitz and Jim Guerinot—or "my great adversary," as Gurewitz half jokingly puts it—are now on good terms. The pair reconciled after happening upon each other in Hawaii where Guerinot told his one-time nemesis that despite running A&M Records and having had offers to head up other giant corporations, the person he most wanted to be was Brett Gurewitz. He let him know that he is "the most impressive guy I have ever met" and reminded him that he built an independent record company from the ground up that was able to compete with the music industry's highest rollers. It wasn't, he said, a company founded in the twenties, or the forties, but rather an organization that didn't exist until the teenage guitarist with Bad Religion founded it. "I told him, 'You had a vision, and you made something unique.'"

Brett Gurewitz says that since their fracture, he and Dexter Holland have "never connected." Despite this, Holland says that "it's been way too long to have any hard feelings now. We've turned out great and it seems that he's doing great." Asked if his band would ever consider reuniting with Epitaph Records, he says, "I would be happy to talk with him about anything. I don't foresee us going with Epitaph, but, hey, you never know."

"That's interesting," says Brett Gurewitz, sounding interested.

## CHAPTER TEN

# A PUNK ROCK SONG, WRITTEN FOR THE PEOPLE WHO CAN SEE SOMETHING'S WRONG

In the late spring of 2004, Rob Cavallo convened a meeting at Warner Bros. Records headquarters in Burbank, California. In a tasteful and modern conference room he addressed twenty representatives from the departments who would soon go to work selling Green Day's forthcoming album to the American public. Women and men from the promotions department were on hand; also represented were workers from the sales office, as well as people who staffed the press office. Standing at the head of the table, Cavallo cleared his throat and said, "'Okay, we have an album that we've made. It's a punk rock opera and I think it's the greatest piece of music that we'll put out this year.' And then, to all these people I said, 'We're gonna sell one million records in the first week, and we're gonna sell ten million records by the time it's done.'"

The album of which Rob Cavallo was giving his colleagues advance notice was *American Idiot*. Also on hand representing Team Green Day that morning were Billie Joe Armstrong and Pat Magnarella, at the time the band's manager. Like any artist worth their sodium, Billie Joe was uncomfortable in his surroundings and ill at ease with the hard sell that Cavallo was putting down. The producer, though, knew it was imperative that he capture the attention of his audience. "There are times when I grow a pair," he says. He remembers "looking around the room and people were kind of shocked. It's not normal for someone to say that kind of thing, you know, at least not seriously. And it *was* kind of a crazy thing to say. But I did it on purpose. I wanted to drive home to them just how great an album this was. I wanted them to forget what they thought they knew about Green Day and that band's overall standing at the label." Billie Joe Armstrong told the author in 2005 that "*American Idiot* was such a difficult album to explain to people before it came out. I would be talking about things like nine-minute songs, and the response from Warner Brothers, was 'Okay, they've finally lost their fucking minds.'"

Too much has been made of the commercial slough in which Green Day found themselves in the years prior to the release of *American Idiot*. The response that greeted *Warning*, the band's sixth album, released in the autumn of 2000, may have amounted to little more than a hesitant thumbs-up from its creators' constituents, but the twelve-song set was a top-twenty hit in no fewer than eight countries. It also popped its head into the top five of the British and American album charts. With sales of two million copies, *Warning* was also a commercial success, if hardly a smash. On the tour in support of the record, the author witnessed Green Day play to twelve thousand people at London's Wembley Arena, as well as seven thousand people at what was effectively a hometown concert at the Bill Graham Civic

Auditorium in San Francisco. Even at their lowest ebb, the idea that the band's popularity fell off a cliff in a manner reminiscent of Cheap Trick is not borne out by evidence.

In a fuller context, though, this *was* a difficult period. *Warning* features many fine tracks—of which "Church On Sunday," "Waiting" and "Macy's Day Parade" are just three—but in commercial terms the shadow cast by *Dookie* was long and dark. Rare is the band that follows up a fully blockbusting album with a record of equal commercial stature—Def Leppard are the only exception to this rule—but each Green Day record after *Dookie* sold significantly less than its predecessor, a trend continued by *Warning*. Troubled times, etcetera etcetera. "Green Day were kind of on a downward spiral after *Warning*," admits Rob Cavallo.

"When it came time to getting ready for a new album, there were some things that as a band we needed to work out," Mike Dirnt told the author in 2004. "For one thing, there was the fact that we were being dicks to each other. We'd gotten kind of good at that. We wouldn't let each other speak, and we certainly wouldn't listen to what each other was saying. That led to some communication problems. We didn't go into therapy or anything like that, but it was something that we needed to deal with. Those kinds of things can lead to real problems for a band. Rifts develop, and then suddenly you've got a group of people who aren't happy in each other's company any longer. And we were damn sure that that wasn't going to happen to us."

Upon its release in September 2004, many were the people that viewed *American Idiot* as being a wonderful anomaly, some of whom should have known better. The more hysterical regarded it to be a record without precedent. Given its thematic proximity to The Who's *Quadrophenia*, this is palpable nonsense. A more familiar line was that Green Day's seventh album was wholly and refreshingly out of step with the body of work that had preceded it. But this, too, is wrong. It is in fact the restrained *Warning* that was at this point the anomaly in the band's oeuvre.

*American Idiot* did not fall from a cloudless sky like the monolith from *2001: A Space Odyssey*. In terms of its musical execution, at least, the record had a precedent. In 1997, Green Day released their fifth album, *Nimrod*, and in doing so made the biggest creative leap of their career. *Nimrod* may lack focus in that it features too many tracks, but its high points are dazzling. Songs such as "Nice Guys Finish Last," "Hitchin' A Ride," "Uptight," "Scattered" and "Redundant" herald the points at which the modern Green Day was born. In comparison to the reductive and abridged *Insomniac*, the progression is startling. The band were even able to find house space for the beautifully bittersweet ballad "Good Riddance (Time Of Your Life)," originally written at the time of *Dookie*. "Can you imagine all those housewives in the Midwest buying the album because of that one song?" says Rob Cavallo. "And then taking it back to the store, saying, 'What the *fuck* is this?'" With its more expansive form, *Nimrod* may not have been a sound check for *American Idiot*, but it is its forebear. Presented with this theory, Rob Cavallo concludes that "it's probably right." He says that "I loved *Nimrod* because of the fact that there are a lot of songs on there, and they're so interesting and diverse . . . It had a lot of songs that sounded very different for Green Day. It was an experimental record. We were testing some of the limits and the boundaries of what a punk rock band could do. So in a funny way, unconsciously [*American Idiot*] might have started with *Nimrod*."

Following this high point, it appeared as if Green Day's finest hours may have been behind them. There were even whispers from those not in the know that the band could be dropped by Warner Bros. In fact, this was far from the truth. Despite it having been a while since the goose had laid a golden egg, the record company did not reckon it ripe for the cooking. Instead, a slow and thoughtful campaign was set in motion to bring Green Day back to prominence. In 2001, the release of the compilation album *International Superhits!* reminded listeners that when it came to seven-inch singles the band were nothing less than a punk rock ABBA. With sales of more than three million copies, the album was a hit. The following year, Green Day embarked on the two-month Pop Disaster Tour of the United States and Canada. A co-headline caravan with Blink 182, the shows were mostly staged in the kinds of sheds in which the band had last appeared eight years previously as part of the Lollapalooza package. Billie Joe Armstrong, Mike Dirnt and Tre Cool were the least popular trio on the Pop Disaster Tour and as such did not close the show. The result of this meant that damage was caused to Blink 182's reputation as a live band. "I quite like being thought of as *that*," Billie Joe told the author in 2004. "As in, how is anyone going to follow *that*?"

If nothing else, for Green Day the opening years of the twenty-first century proved there was life in the old gods yet. "I never lost my faith in rock 'n' roll music," Billie Joe Armstrong told the author in an interview for *New Musical Express.* "And one thing we've never done is to kid ourselves about shortcuts. It's easy for a band to go out and make a cheeky song that's sort of a novelty, or do a cover or appear on a reality television show. But we didn't do that. We chose to take the hardest route possible as far as a career plan . . . Our approach was working really hard and doing things the right way. We set out as a band that wanted to give rock music a kick in the ass, and we've achieved exactly what we set out to do."

There were times when this took a while. In November 2002, a story was put about that the band had recorded an album, *Cigarettes and Valentines,* the master tape of which was stolen from Studio 880 in Oakland. If this tale is true, the band seemed remarkably sanguine about having been robbed of four months' worth of recorded material. Unusually, Rob Cavallo himself is less than clear on the subject of this ripping yarn. "I might have to go off the record on this one," he says. When asked about the matter, after a pause Tre Cool answers, "Er . . . let's move on." Rather than rerecord the material they had "lost," Green Day instead decided to cook up a new batch from scratch. Billie Joe Armstrong described the misappropriated music as being "good stuff." But in the absence of all intended output, the band transformed themselves into a phoenix that elevated itself gracefully from the ashes of *Cigarettes and Valentines*.


I t was a slow start. Rob Cavallo remembers going to see Billie Joe Armstrong at his home in Oakland and seeing a man short on hunger and long on uncertainty. Following what seem like minor communication problems, Green Day had sat down for *the conversation* about whether or not each man wished to continue making music with the others. As it turned out, no one was in any doubt that they did. The next logical step, then, was to make an album. But if one leaves aside the story about *Cigarettes and Valentines*—and one *should* leave it aside—it would likely be four years until the band were ready to release a twelve-inch record's worth of new material, a duration that would constitute their longest fallow period to date. In itself, this was not a problem; what *was* a problem was that Billie Joe Armstrong was acutely lacking in appetite. As Kurt Cobain put it a decade earlier: "What else should I write? / I don't have the right."

"I remember one conversation that I had with Billie where he said to me, 'You know, I've had this amazing career,'" remembers Rob Cavallo. "He said, 'I've played some big shows and written some big songs, and, frankly, I've made a lot of money. And I have a big house that looks over the bay.' And he goes, 'What right do I have as a punk rocker to sing about what's going on?' And I said to him, 'It doesn't matter what house you live in. It doesn't matter how much money you have. You'll always be able to write about how you feel. Let me tell you that your fans out there, they could care less about how much stuff you have.' And this is really important to write—I said, 'You have a life and you live it true. You're not a faker in any way what-soever. It doesn't matter what your music might have earned you. You live a real punk rock lifestyle and that's who you are. Your fans want to know how you feel, so you've got to write about whatever it is you're feeling. As long as it's real and true, I think people are gonna respect it and I think they're gonna like it.' And I guess he agreed with this, because over the course of weeks and months the conversation went from this, to what he was feeling, and also, finally, 'What are you angry about?' Because we wanted to make a record that had traditional punk rock values, and anger is a part of that. I know that Billie, Mike and Tre wanted to harness their frustrations and basically stick it to the Man while shouting from the rooftops."

One morning, Billie Joe Armstrong was driving his car while listening to the radio. For reasons unknown, the station played the song "That's How I Like It" from Floridian throwback rockers Lynyrd Skynyrd. One of the Jacksonville group's lesser known songs, "That's How I Like It" seems to be comprised entirely of things guaranteed to agitate the nerves of any punk who hap-pens not to be a member of the John Birch Society. To a beat that is all swagger and no thumbs, the band sing of how the menfolk in their corner of the United States like their "women hot and my beer ice cold / a real fast car and my whisky old." Continuing in this vein of lyrical panache, the listener is also informed how "there's nothing better than the sound of a crowd"—perhaps at a lynching—and that "the American flag makes me proud." Thanks are also given to God, obviously; or, as Lynyrd Skynyrd know him, "the man above." Billie Joe Armstrong might also have given thanks to the same entity for polluting his car with the music of a band who, as Fat Mike would have it, are "from the heartland, not very smartland." In response to "This Is How

I Like It," Billie Joe wrote his own song. He called it "American Idiot."

Perhaps surprisingly, Green Day remained one of Warner Bros.' priority acts. Rob Cavallo had just returned to the company after stints with Hollywood Records and the Walt Disney Company, and, having swapped Mickey Mouse for Bugs Bunny, was told by Warner Bros. Records chairman Tom Whalley that "you know, this Green Day record is really important. Why don't you take the whole year off to work on it? Don't concentrate on anything else." From the middle of April 2003, each Monday morning Cavallo would fly to the Bay Area and spend five days at Jingletown, Green Day's rehearsal space and studio in Oakland. Each working day, the producer would sit in as the band wrote and played music. No idea was too outré to preclude consideration, and pieces of music lasting no more than a minute were pushed through, seemingly at random. In search of lyrical inspiration, Billie Joe Armstrong flew to New York and consorted with the songwriters Ryan Adams and Jesse Malin. He walked the streets of the Lower East Side for hours on end in the night's slimmest hours. From these experiences, the lyrics to the songs "Boulevard Of Broken Dreams" and "We Are The Waiting" were harvested.

At Jingletown, over the course of four and a half months, music began to coalesce. Songs such as "American Idiot" and the dynamic "She's A Rebel" were relatively straightforward and might have found a home on *Nimrod*. Others were startling departures. Two songs emerged from the sessions that comprised ten sections. These pieces were titled "Homecoming" and "Jesus Of Suburbia" and featured recurring characters and a narrative that was thematic, if not conceptual. The settings moved from the Bay Area to New York City, while elsewhere a hat was tipped in the direction of "the kids of war and peace / from Anaheim to the Middle East." Billie Joe Armstrong even found the chutzpah to subvert one of punk rock's founding principles. "Don't ask to attend / 'cos we're not all there," Johnny Rotten sang on "Pretty Vacant." "Oh don't pretend, 'cos I don't care." This was fine in 1977, but by the twenty-first century the repetition of this statement by punk rock bands down the years had become just that bit too easy. Aware of this, Green Day remolded the rhetoric into a question: "Does anyone care if nobody cares?"

"The whole point of doing this, of making new music, is to push ourselves to do something that we'd never imagine ourselves doing," Billie Joe Armstrong told the author in 2004. "The lyrics are definitely an example of that, but then so is the music. It's not always easy doing it this way, but that's the only way of doing things for me. Otherwise we're just making the same album that we did last time, and that's not something I want to do."

"[American Idiot] has been quite difficult to make," said Mike Dirnt in the same interview. "We pushed ourselves so hard on it, you know? On 'Jesus Of Suburbia' we were doing something that we'd never attempted before. We had great individual sections but we needed to get them to fit together. At times it was a case of writing almost anything just to see if it would work. It was a question of finding a way to get from one part to the next. It was grueling."

As American Idiot began to take shape, the band and their producer talked about what surely neither party referred to as their mission statement. One of their shared aims was that the music be ambitious and adventurous. Mind was paid to The Who's expansive A Quick One While He's Away, a precursor for the storyboard-sprawl of Quadrophenia. Also important was the changing nature in which music was being heard. With iTunes on the rise, listeners were now able to buy single songs from any given album that they pleased. The long play record had been the music industry's dominant form since the release of the Beatles' Sergeant Pepper's Lonely Hearts Club Band in 1967, but as this landmark set approached its fortieth birthday the future of the format it represented seemed to be in doubt. Green Day reacted to this development with opposition rather than acquiescence. They liked the idea and the habits of albums and didn't want them to die. Viewed in this context, *American Idiot* was their skin in the game. "One thing you can definitely say is that we hated the idea of iTunes selling singles," says Rob Cavallo. "We hated the idea that music was being listened to in this way; that people could pay a dollar twenty-nine, or whatever it was, and come away with a single song. We didn't want people cherry-picking singles, so we tried to make the music work as a complete body of work. We liked the idea of it being *an album*."

On the first day of recording, the studio caught fire. By now the band had moved from Oakland to Los Angeles, and it was now they who were spending their working week away from home. The initial sessions were undertaken at Ocean Way Recording, the location at which Frank Sinatra had recorded each of the albums released on the Warner Bros. subsidiary to which Green Day were signed. Toward the end of the first session, Billie Joe Armstrong said that he could smell smoke, and indeed he could. While the fire was being extinguished, the band called it a night and, according to Tre Cool, "went and partied" at the Hollywood hotel at which they were staying. Over the course of their stay, the band's exuberance drew complaints from fellow residents who wished to sleep rather than listen to X and the Kinks at skull-denting volume.

The next day, Green Day returned to Ocean Way Recording to try again. This was the point at which the drums were recorded, a stage that many musicians dread. But even here, *American Idiot* was throwing out sparks. "The drums sounded incredible," remembers Tre Cool. "I remember thinking, 'Yeah, we're nailing it—this is awesome!' There was just such energy to it. I felt like Frank Sinatra was in the room with us. I wouldn't say that what was happening was effortless, but it was really natural. I think all the stars were aligned. It was just coming together. I really liked the way the music was going, I really liked the way the story was going, and I loved the way we were getting our heads around it all. It was like holding on to a new-born baby. It was just really special . . . And I knew it was going to be special from the first. I pretty much knew that this was going to be amazing. I think we all knew that we were really onto something."

Rob Cavallo remembers loving the phrase "punk rock opera," and loving the fact that he could head into Warner Bros. marketing meetings and use the term to grab the attention of his colleagues. He remembers being in the studio and having "my mind blown" by the song "Homecoming." He recalls Billie Joe Armstrong challenging Mike Dirnt and Tre Cool to come up with sections that might be used in what was not yet called "Jesus Of Suburbia." He remembers there being numerous sections that no one could quite figure out how to link together. "We'd have section A and B, E and F," says the producer, as if describing an obscure alchemic formulation. "But what we didn't have was parts C and D. Plus, some of the time we hadn't figured out a way to put these parts together." As the pieces began to slot into place, Rob Cavallo realized that "Jesus Of Suburbia" should be *American Idiot*'s second track. He listened through Ocean Way Recording's expensive speakers and thought, "What a journey this is." "You listen to that as the second song on an album and you think, 'What the fuck is happening? This is unbelievable! This is amazing!' And no one had done this before, either with a punk record or in a pop song."

With each of *American Idiot*'s thirteen tracks recorded, Green Day and Rob Cavallo then decided to drive themselves mad in determining a running order. They knew that the title track would be first up, and that "Jesus Of Suburbia" would bat at number two; but that's all they knew. The titles of "Holiday," "Boulevard Of Broken Dreams," "We Are The Waiting," "St. Jimmy," "Give Me Novocaine," "She's A Rebel," "Extraordinary

Girl," "Letterbomb," "Wake Me Up When September Ends," "Homecoming" and "Whatsername" were written several times on pieces of three-inch-by-five-inch cards, which were then placed on a table and on the floor. The band then played song-title Twister until every computation was exhausted and *American Idiot*'s track listing had been decided. The album was then mixed by Chris Lord-Alge, whose past credits included Bruce Springsteen and Joe Cocker, and mastered by Grammy Award–winner Ted Jensen.

After a gestation period of almost eleven months, Green Day's seventh album was ready to drop. Already, a flare had been propelled into the air with the release of the LP's lead-off single, "American Idiot," in August 2004. The track would sell more than one and a half million copies and serve as the ideal *amuse-bouche* for the body of work that followed. By the time the parent album was released on September 21, Green Day were in possession of a quality that had eluded them for more than five years—buzz.

"I just had a *feeling* about *American Idiot*," says Rob Cavallo. "I don't know, when you hear a record that is important and that is resonating, it's almost as if a bell goes off inside your head. It's just a funny feeling that I get. You can feel it in your body. I just knew that when we released it, people were going to respond and explode. I had this feeling of electricity in my body that was as intense as any I'd had before. The only time I had it like that was on *Dookie*."


**A**t a time when Green Day were playing theaters in the United States, The Offspring were performing in arenas and sheds. On May 6, 2000, more than sixteen thousand people gathered on a spring day without blemish in the open air of Irvine Meadows Amphitheatre in Orange County for a celebration of Southern Californian punk rock spanning four decades. On a bill headlined by The Offspring, an audience of punks both urban and suburban—not to mention thousands, surely, who would define themselves as neither—were also offered entertainment from Social Distortion, X, Pennywise and T.S.O.L. Just six years earlier, a punk rock concert on this scale would have been unimaginable. As well as this, the older bands on the bill could well remember a time when shows in their name were often dangerous and violent events that no mainstream promoter would touch and which no insurer would underwrite.

In 2000, The Offspring were the world's most popular punk rock group, a title they had wrestled from Green Day two years earlier and which they would not surrender until 2004. This is a statistical fact that today tends to be overlooked. Green Day's *Nimrod* sold in tidy numbers, but a year later The Offspring released *Americana*, their fifth full-length collection, and shifted nine million units. This is worth mentioning not because numbers in themselves are important, but because the arrival of *American Idiot* cast a shadow so enormous that it obscured the past achievements of other bands. No group was more affected by this than The Offspring. At the time of their more or less hometown show at Irvine Meadows Amphitheatre, the Orange County quartet were performing on the back of an album that had sold more than five million copies in the United States alone. *Americana* may not be the band's most celebrated release—as it always will, and should, this honor goes to *Smash*—but it is one of their most popular.

That afternoon, Social Distortion played in daylight. Fortified with a Les Paul guitar, an access all areas pass and a headful of grizzled-veteran skepticism, mainstay Mike Ness viewed the rapid reversal of the fortunes of punk rock in the same way an alcoholic barfly views the transformation of his favorite hostelry into a health spa. He wasn't, and still isn't, convinced that the sale of *Never Mind the Bollocks . . . Here's the Sex Pistols!* T-shirts in Hot Topic chain stores is an entirely good thing.

It's not that he believes that punks today could learn a lot from being beaten up by construction workers and cops, as he and his friends were—but schooling to a curriculum of hard knocks *does* build character. Predictably, The Offspring count Social Distortion as being one of the key reasons they were moved to make music in the first place. Even more predictably, Mike Ness cites bands such as The Offspring as one of the key reasons he doesn't much like punk anymore.

"Let's just say I had mixed feelings about what happened when punk rock became huge," he says. "I remember opening for The Offspring [a number of times], I guess it was around the late 1990s, and I guess I thought they were nice guys who had a couple of good songs. But we just didn't have very much in common. They had sold many millions of records and had become millionaires and for a while I honestly think I was a little bitter . . . But here's the thing about bands like The Offspring—it's not their fault that they hit the mainstream. Nirvana never set out to be a mainstream band that would be selling out arenas in Alabama. It just happened. So you can't fault the bands for that. Even in the early days I never subscribed to the idea that it wasn't cool to be successful. I never believed that."

At Irvine Meadows Amphitheatre, The Offspring played songs that had become *very* successful indeed, some of which have been wildly misinterpreted. The spoken-word line "You gotta keep 'em separated" in "Come Out And Play" deliberately detracts from the seriousness of the song's subject matter. The band's 1998 blockbuster "Pretty Fly For A White Guy" goes yet further in flirting with the idea of becoming a novelty song. Everything is set up in this manner. It has a groove and a riff that to the casual ear sounds as dumb as a stump. It has a cheeky and catchy female-voiced refrain that sings the nonsense lines "Give it to me baby / uh-huh, uh-huh." It has goofy spoken-word sections in which a hapless narrator announces, "All the girls say I'm pretty fly for a white guy." An interesting facet of Dexter

Holland's lyrics is that the characters about whom he writes are often rather dim. Usually, Holland views these lives not with contempt or condescension, but with the eye of a scientist.

"Pretty Fly For A White Guy" is an observation of the social phenomenon of wealthy young suburbanites longing to share the authenticity of poor black kids from the dangerous inner city. The song's protagonist goes to a record shop to buy CDs. "They didn't have Ice Cube / so he bought Vanilla Ice," sings Holland. He plays this fraudulent slop while behind the wheel. "Now cruising in his Pinto, he sees homies [walking] past / but if he looks twice they're gonna kick his lily ass." This is decent satire, not to mention a modern take on Tom Wolfe's definition of radical chic: black rage, white guilt. It is not the fault of The Offspring that people not listening closely identify "Pretty Fly For A White Guy" as a novelty song, just as it is to their credit that the band assumed a measure of intelligence in the listening public that was not wholly justified. Unfortunately for them, many are the people who *despise* The Offspring for writing songs they so casually misinterpret.

"I think we can be labeled as a novelty act," says Greg K. "People might not listen to the lyrics, or else they might just listen to the hook or something like that. And because they don't listen to the lyrics, they don't get what the songs are about. They don't get that "Come Out And Play" is about gang violence. They hear the chorus line and that's about it."

**W**hile Green Day were not seen as a novelty act, neither were they viewed as a band of any great substance. Even when evidence to the contrary was presented in stark detail, many were deaf to the signs. Karaoke singers the world over quickly learned the words to "Good Riddance (Time Of Your Life)" as if it were the modern-day equivalent of "Mull Of Kintyre," rather than a song so bittersweet as to be almost mournful. If one accepts that *Nimrod* heralded the birth of the modern Green Day, it follows that this is also the point at which Armstrong developed into a superior lyricist. On "Redundant" he speaks of a dying relationship, noting how it embodies something "choreographed . . . [a] lack of passion / prototypes of what we were / went full circle 'til I'm nauseous / taken for granted / now I wasted, faked it, ate it, now I hate it." "On Hitchin' a Ride" he tells the listener that "tonight I'm eating crow / augmented salmonella poison oak, no." Admittedly, Green Day didn't always help themselves when it came to obscuring their more nuanced qualities. Listeners removing the CD from the diamond case of *International Superhits!* were greeted by the sight of Billie Joe Armstrong dressed in his underpants.

With the release of *American Idiot*, this changed overnight. The advance word was that the band had made a political album, a theory that holds true so long as one doesn't listen to it. But despite the fact that only two of the set's songs are explicitly political, Green Day *were* strident in singing like canaries in a coal mine. Their crosshairs were trained on the smirking face of president George W. Bush—America then being a dozen years away from electing a president that made Bush look like Archbishop Desmond Tutu. In this, Green Day weren't the only people to form an offensive. Fat Mike, that most reliable of irritants, issued compilation albums titled *Rock Against Bush* that featured songs by, among others, Foo Fighters, Bad Religion and of course Green Day. The NOFX frontman also marketed a T-shirt that pictured Bush's face and the words "Not My President."

But while Green Day were not alone in their opposition to the forty-third president of the American republic, they were one of the charge's more surprising participants. Prior to 1994, the band had, at a push, written two songs that could be described as being political—"Minority" and "Maria"—and then only implicitly so. Suddenly, as Billie Joe Armstrong artfully put it, they were "the needle in the vein of the establishment." Rob

Cavallo admits, "It was scary to put out a record like *American Idiot* [because] it might sound as if you were saying something un-American. We heard that the Dixie Chicks had gotten into trouble for something like that." (At a concert at London's Shepherd's Bush Empire in 2000, singer Natalie Maines had said, "Just so you know, we're on the good side with y'all. We do not want this war, this violence and we're ashamed that the president of the United States is from Texas," as were the band themselves.) Although if Green Day did have concerns about being seen as a hothouse of un-American activities, these fears had clearly been calmed by the time they were on the stump promoting *American Idiot*. Speaking to Britain's *Q* magazine, Mike Dirnt said of his nation's flag, "It means nothing to me, let's burn the fucking thing."

Away from this noisy hyperbole, the manner in which *American Idiot* melds the personal and the political is exquisite. "Cigarettes and ramen and a little bag of dope / I am the son of a bitch and Edgar Allen Poe," sings Armstrong as the character St. Jimmy in the song of the same name. A product of his environment, St. Jimmy will later die at his own hand, as "he blew his brains out into the bay." There is death elsewhere on *American Idiot*, too. "Can I get another 'Amen'?" is the question posed and answered on "Holiday." This call and response is followed by the image of "a flag wrapped around a score of men / a gag, a plastic bag on a monument."

Those who describe the album as a "punk rock opera" are not far away from the money; but those who believe it to be a concept album are streets away. Rather than a concept, *American Idiot* has themes and characters that pop up like faces in a dream. Along with the doomed St. Jimmy, the Jesus of Suburbia roams restlessly through some of the songs, keen to become the savior of the city. You can see why. The town in which he lives is a place where all one needs to do is "strike the fucking match to light this fuse." These words are from "Letterbomb," which

Billie Joe Armstrong believes to be the finest song to which he's put his name. Here, he might be onto something. Furious and focused, the track is a punk master class, a thing both propulsive yet deeply complex. Its setting is a dwelling in which the neighbors are "collecting unemployment checks." Authority figures are people such as the town bishop, who "is an extortionist / and he don't even know that you exist," and a citizen's paperwork reveals "once in love is now debt / on your birth certificate." It can't end well, and it doesn't. "She said I can't take this place / I'm leaving you tonight" is the closing refrain. This "she" is Whatsername, an elusive presence whose image, come the final song, has been forgotten even by the album's narrators. This is a surprise, seeing how in the LP's middle section she is "the mother of bombs [who is] gonna detonate." Come the final reckoning, even this most combustible of characters "seems to have disappeared without a trace / did she ever marry old Whatisface?" The question is asked with a shrug, as if everything that preceded it is fit only to wither on the vine, as if everything here is temporary.

*American Idiot* is a State of the Union address for a turbulent nation. As well as this, it's a study in relationships, hope, frustration, defiance and longing, not to mention an examination of one's inner self. "My shadow walks beside me / my shallow heart's the only thing that's beating," sings Billie Joe in "Boulevard Of Broken Dreams." Whatever the line of attack, the news from *American Idiot*'s numerous front lines is not always encouraging.

"It was very important to me when I was writing the lyrics for this album that the things I'm singing about are personal," Billie Joe Armstrong told the author in 2004. "So the things that are political have to have that personal element to them. If they don't, it just doesn't work for me. There are bands who can do that kind of thing—a band such as Rage Against the Machine would be a good example—but I know that it wouldn't work for us. I'm not saying there's anything wrong with what a band like that does, but it wouldn't suit us. So although parts of the album deal with political subjects, it's still a very personal thing for me."

Warner Bros. Records' marketing campaign in support of *American Idiot* was a study in corporate ingenuity and effectiveness. The result of this was to reposition Green Day from a trio of loveable scamps, often spoken of in the past tense, to a band with agency and authority. It isn't an exaggeration to say that in 2004 the group were reborn.

Director Sam Bayer's quintet of videos were particularly effective. "American Idiot" sees the band performing in front of a vertically hung American flag of corrupted colors that bleed behind them and eventually flood the space in which they appear. "Boulevard Of Broken Dreams" finds the musicians wandering through what looks like a post-apocalyptic wasteland, windblown and ruffled. There is a fleeting moment of particular loveliness as Mike Dirnt places a protective arm around Tre Cool's shoulder, as if to shelter his friend from the news of the world. Even more evocative is the clip that accompanies "Wake Me Up When September Ends." In its recorded form, the track is a paean to Billie Joe Armstrong's father, who died when the songwriter was a child. On video, the song is sufficiently supple to carry a narrative about a young man's decision to leave his lover and undertake a duty by joining the armed forces. With spacious spoken-word sections, the English actor Jamie Bell plays the teenager, while Evan Rachel Wood takes the female lead. The conversation the characters share at the start of the clip will be their last.

"*American Idiot* could have been a mess; in fact, it is a mess," wrote *Rolling Stone* in a sentence that doesn't quite make sense. The magazine did, though, grudgingly concede that "against all odds, Green Day have found a way to hit their thirties without either betraying their original spirit or falling on their faces." Elsewhere, the initial reviews were more positive, although many featured a measure of surprise. In *The Guardian*, England's best music critic, Dorian Lynskey, wrote that "this is a fully fledged rock opera—which is almost as chilling a concept as a second Bush term, although Green Day's muscular grasp of pop verities steers them safely away from conceptual meltdown." "In the tradition of The Who and Pink Floyd, *American Idiot* is a pompous, overwrought and, quite simply, glorious concept album," wrote Sal Cinquemani in *Slant* magazine. None of these or any other reviewers could have predicted the album's dominant commercial success, or, indeed, the fact that it now stands as rock music's last true blockbusting release. In this, it is the final heavyweight champion of the world, a title it will retain forever.

As 2004 ticked over into 2005, *American Idiot* refused to go away. "Boulevard Of Broken Dreams" made itself at home in the UK top forty for *three months*, selling more than half a million copies in the process. By now people in high places were beginning to take serious notice of Green Day. *American Idiot* won gongs at the American Music Awards, the Japan Gold Disc Awards, Canada's Juno Awards, MTV Music Awards and the United Kingdom's BRIT Awards. It also scooped up the prizes for best rock album and record of the year (for "Boulevard Of Broken Dreams") at the Grammys. It is worth noting that *Warning* earned not a single award from any of these bodies (or from any others, for that matter).

"I think what *American Idiot* has done for us is really change our history in a lot of ways," Billie Joe Armstrong told the author in 2005. "It created a new future for us. It's made all of our albums since *Dookie* make sense for people who weren't really up to speed with what we were doing. Obviously having all this critical acclaim is a first, but that's all."

Ten years prior to the arrival of *American Idiot*, as young twentysomethings, Green Day and *Dookie* ruled the world. At the time, the band weren't entirely sure they liked this prize and, in its slipstream, made music that rebelled against the disorientating side effects of international success. A decade on, Billie Joe Armstrong, Mike Dirnt and Tre Cool were better equipped to both enjoy and process the good fortune flooding their way. Suddenly they were that rarest of things: a band who on two occasions had become the biggest in the world. In 1994, there was vertigo and nausea. Ten years on, the view was nothing shy of spectacular.

"Back then success was so new to us that we didn't know what to do with it," Mike Dirnt told the author in an interview for *New Musical Express*. "We just wanted to prove that we weren't a flash in the pan. We've proved that. Back then I thought we had something to prove; now, I think we've proved something."

"The difference between *Dookie* and *American Idiot* is pretty simple," says Tre Cool. "The first time, the success was an accident; the second time, it was on purpose."

The author was the first person from the United Kingdom to hear *American Idiot*, although I wasn't in the United Kingdom when I did so. And I didn't hear all of it; I heard half of it, mostly the first half. On a sunny late-summer day, I was shown to an empty chrome and glass office at the Warner Bros. Records headquarters in Los Angeles where a CD was inserted into a stereo system that cost more than a studio apartment. I was kindly asked that I not try to tape the half an album on my Dictaphone and was then left to my own devices. Feel free to turn up the volume, I was told. Feeling sufficiently at liberty, this I did.

From scribbled notes, I wrote up the accompanying article like a hysterical teenager. "You can lose those gags about progressive punk rock—pronk?—and listen to what Green Day have learned to do [on 'Jesus Of Suburbia']" was one of the more restrained sentences. "'St. Jimmy' arrives like a punk rock shitstorm, a beautiful piece of swagger and roll that manages to be both rollicking and entirely irresistible" was one of the less restrained.

Really, though, I was wasting my time. The verdict on *American Idiot* can be distilled down to one sentence. It is a popular punk album so good that it's hard to imagine it being bettered. It won't be bettered by Green Day, certainly, or The Offspring, or by any other act that bloomed in the glorious summer of 1994. All of these groups continue to exist, and even to prosper, but the musical high-water mark has been reached. As is only right, it's now time for younger hands to have a go.

In 2016, Billie Joe Armstrong was at 924 Gilman Street with Lawrence Livermore. The man who had helped bring the club into being and the musician who, up until his painful expulsion in 1993, had played there almost from the start, realized that they were among the oldest people in the room by at least twenty years. They listened as young people made music on the stage and watched as teenagers took ticket money. They looked on with paternal grace as they realized that they had been replaced. Both men understood that it was only right that they were no longer needed.

"We were both standing watching what was going on," remembers Lawrence Livermore. "Billie said, 'Wow, this is amazing. These kids have taken over and are now running the place better than we ever did.' Before then, people who ran Gilman were following the traditions of the eighties. The kids there would look like they were at a dress-up party where they could reenact the costumes and the music and everything from the eighties and nineties. But these kids were doing twenty-first-century music using the mechanisms that we had created and left for them. Right after we walked out of the sound booth, this tall guy came up to us. He was about fifty or something and he said to me, 'Excuse me, I've never met you before but I used to read your column [in *Maximumrocknroll*]. At the time Gilman was just getting started,' he said, 'but I was living up in the far north of Canada and it wasn't possible for me to get down to the States at all. So this is my first time here.' He'd also brought his son, an eleven-year-old who was looking around wide-eyed, as you can imagine, at this wonderland of chaos. I don't know why this popped into my head but I said to this little boy, 'Welcome to your club. We built this for you.'"

# HOME, WE'RE COMING HOME AGAIN

Brett Gurewitz was in jail for possession of cocaine and heroin when Greg Graffin called with good news. The singer was at home in upstate New York, and was calling his erstwhile bandmate to tell him that two years after its release, *Stranger Than Fiction* had gone gold.

Gurewitz had taken some finding. Eventually, Graffin reached his friend's parents who told him where their son was staying for the next couple of nights. "I pride myself on not being a judgmental person," he says. "I think that's attributable to my midwestern upbringing." Brett Gurewitz doesn't dispute that his old comrade called the prison, though he doesn't remember receiving the call. He is, though, quick to point out there are more than a few things from this period that he no longer recalls with any great clarity. Graffin is adamant that the authorities allowed their guest to speak on the phone. "I don't know if he's ever told anyone this, but he was so filled with joy," says the singer. "He was screaming on the other end of the phone about how excited he was."

Unusually for a member of a punk rock band, Greg Graffin's head has never been turned by any class of drug. This is especially unusual when one considers that the band of which he is a member is Bad Religion. Since Brett Gurewitz's departure on the eve of the release of *Stranger Than Fiction*, Graffin had steered his band's creative course alone. In this, his workload had doubled. He was now responsible for every lyric and each note of music that appeared under the group's name. He was also denied the guitarist's ear for what is and what isn't a good fit for their highly identifiable punk rock songs. Without much rancor, the two men were no longer speaking.

Greg Graffin met these challenges with a large degree of success. *The Gray Race*, 1995's successor to *Stranger Than Fiction*, is one of the band's finest albums. But as the twentieth century began to pack up its tent, so too were Bad Religion. A live LP, *Tested*, gathered from sound desk recordings from the tour in support of *The Gray Race*, ranks as one of the worst concert records of all time. The creative success of 2000's *New America*, on which Greg Graffin realized a childhood dream of working with producer Todd Rundgren, did nothing to arrest the decline.

By this point, Atlantic Records regarded the band with disinterest, although it was nothing personal. Whenever he was in New York City, Greg Graffin went to the company's Manhattan offices simply to say hello to the people who toiled for his band. The relationship with these shop-floor workers was good; both parties were of a similar age and mindset. But upstairs in the corridors of power, decisions were being taken in Bad Religion's name. Atlantic Records were unhappy that *New America* had limped onto the *Billboard* Hot 200 at number eighty-eight, while Greg Graffin was displeased that a lack of promotion had hampered the record's chances. When Atlantic decided against picking up the option on the group's next album, the four-record deal to which they were signed had run its course. "Really, by that point, Atlantic Records didn't know what to do with us," says Graffin. "And that's kind of the history of major labels when it comes to bands who aren't a comfortable fit for their marketing departments. But I don't think they wanted to drop us, because we were looked at and respected, and that might impact their ability to sign other bands. So they kept giving us exorbitant advances to keep us on the label, which of course was merely a drop in the bucket to them. You'd have to ask other people in the industry about this, but I have a hunch that they kept us so we'd act as some kind of a magnet for other bands. And the money didn't mean much to them, anyway, because they were selling so many records by Hootie & The Blowfish."

Greg Graffin wonders if the decision to ask Brett Gurewitz to contribute a song to the sessions for *New America* might have come from Atlantic's marketing department. It might have had something to do with Japanese B-sides, he thinks, or else be something the label could use as a selling point, alongside Todd Rundgren's production credit and Bob Clearmountain's involvement as the album's mixer. On a visit to New York City, Graffin remembers playing Gurewitz, who was also in town, some of the songs from the sessions for the album. The pair discussed collaborating, and both seemed keen on the idea. Later, the pair had dinner at Daddy's, a restaurant in Silverlake, Los Angeles. Over broken bread, Mr. Brett agreed to contribute a track to *New America*.

Given that "Believe It" is the first song he had written in four years, and the first Bad Religion song he'd authored in six years, it can be counted as a remarkable success. While not likely to pester the top-twenty chart of the band's finest tracks—or even the top fifty, for that matter—it does feature enough effervescence and bounce to cover the rust of its writer's creative engine. A demo was dispatched to Hawaii, which the band duly recorded. Jay Bentley called and asked his former bandmate how he would like to be credited on the album's booklet. "Mr. Brett appears courtesy of Mr. Brett" was the agreed wording.

For anyone in the market for a Hollywood ending, what happened next is as good as any. With LA's best and most important punk group now without a label, Brett Gurewitz invited his former bandmates to close the circle and return to Epitaph. In turn, Bad Religion invited Gurewitz to return to the flock. One of the guitarist's stipulations for this was that Brian Baker, his replacement in 1994, remain part of the lineup. (Another newer recruit was the drummer par excellence Brooks Wackerman.) It was also agreed that Mr. Brett would not tour with the group. He would, though, write and record as a permanent member and equal partner. "I was in no way certain that I *could* write half an album," he says. Also, "Not to sound cynical, but wearing my record label hat, I knew that Bad Religion's reputation had lost some of its luster. I knew that the band coming back to Epitaph would be something that people would pay attention to. I knew that creating that talking point would be helpful to the band. Because once a group is on a downward trend, it's hard to turn around. It's really hard to reverse that."

Here, Brett Gurewitz is right; by realigning with Epitaph, Bad Religion didn't need much by way of marketing. Released in January 2002, *The Process Of Belief* was the first of the band's albums to appear in the US top fifty. "Sorrow," the first of two singles, was also a top-forty hit on *Billboard*'s modern rock tracks chart. With typical panache, the song is narrated from the point of view of God, albeit a deity wracked with uncertainty. Elsewhere, the band showed that when it came to playing fast, few punk bands could touch them; and when it came to harmonies, no one could. Most fitting of all, on "You Don't Belong," Brett Gurewitz writes a touching love letter to a punk heritage of which he and his friends are a crucial part. In it, Graffin sings,

"You know we've been here all along / like a confederacy of the wrong / and I confess it could be prejudice / but to you, I dedicate this song."

R eunited with Bad Religion, Brett Gurewitz played a smattering of shows on the tour in support of *The Process Of Belief*. One of these was an appearance at the Hollywood Palladium on the last Saturday of March in 2002. It was the guitarist's first appearance at the venue for nine years. In 1993, that evening's support act, Green Day, were a band unheard of by the mainstream, while Epitaph Records was a quietly successful independent company that had yet to trouble the American album charts. One of the label's artists, The Offspring, had not yet sold fifty thousand records and thus had yet to have an ice cream cake party thrown in their honor. Rancid were yet to be in receipt of risqué photographs of Madonna. Most of these events, and perhaps all of them, would not have happened without Bad Religion.

Reunited with Brett Gurewitz, onstage in front of thirty-seven hundred people, Greg Graffin tells a story of his teenage years. The tale ends with his father admonishing him for being a punk. Graffin tells the crowd that his parent meant this in the Dirty Harry sense of the word. At the Palladium, the memory of this causes the singer to smile.

"I was a punk then," he says. "And I still am."

# THE AUTHOR PLAYS POOL WITH THE OFFSPRING

*The following is an article written by the author that appeared in*
Kerrang! *magazine in December 2003.*

Right, let's get the usual stuff out of the way first, shall we? The
Offspring have a new album coming, *Splinter*, which they're
delighted with and which sounds excellent. They have a new
drummer, Atom, who looks like a psychopathic Buddy Holly but
seems like a nice man. The band seem to think so; they like
his playing and they like him. Next year they'll be touring the
world, no doubt passing by somewhere near your house. They
love doing this, seeing their friends and that. Check local press
for details.

Everybody got this, yes? No questions, no?

Good. Because we've got some pool to play.

The Elbow Room on Westbourne Grove is the original modern London pool hall. The felt on its numerous tables in its
L-shaped main room is purple. Balls are handed out from behind
the bar. The beer is imported and the music comes loud with

the pulsating rhythms of the dance world. Attractive waitresses bring shiny food to players who stand beneath speakers pumping at such a volume that it's tempting to answer any questions asked with a glance at the watch and the words, "About twenty past six." It's Saturday afternoon, halfway through November. The balls are racked. The chalk has been applied. Cues are rolling and bouncing in anticipation.

Because it's Match Time—Team Offspring (Dexter Holland and Noodles) versus Team Kerrang! (Paul Brannigan and Ian Winwood). Team Offspring arrive bang on time. Resisting the urge to sing a few bars of the popular English folk song "You're Going Home in a Fucking Ambulance"—with the European pairing gallantly not making up new ones, on the spot, and, naturally, to their own advantage.

To give a match between two American millionaires and two poverty-stricken writers even more of an edge, we decided to place something at stake. And so it is decided that if they— the ultraviolet-toothed rich boys of Team Offspring—win, they will each receive a year's subscription to this very magazine. If Team Kerrang! win, we will be sent every piece of Offspring merchandise issued in the next twelve months. Despite hoping for a house, a car, or, at the very least, Noodles' Ibanez American flag guitar, we manage not to appear too disappointed.

A coin is tossed. Heads or tails?

"What's heads?" asks Dexter Holland. He is shown the side of a fifty pence on which features the head of the Queen.

"Yeah, okay. Heads."

Tails.

"Damn."

To show there's no hard feelings, Team Kerrang! greets this small victory by making with the hand insults. To display an understanding of both the status of our new friends as guests, and also our grasp of matters multicultural, Team Kerrang! display both the American-style single-finger gesture as well as its mid- and forefinger British equivalent.

By which point, The Offspring and their opponents are very much ready to rumble.

**A** quick word about the players, and about the form. As photographs are taken, bassist Greg K. plays a frame with Atom. This he does with so much skill that it's clear he has an innate natural ability for the game, or else as a child his best friend was a pool hall. Noodles says that Greg bought a table at a garage sale just after The Offspring formed.

"That must have been . . ."—Noodles now pulling the pose of a thinker—"what? . . . 1986? Yeah, I think that was it."

He shouts over, "What year did you buy your pool table, Greg?"

"1989."

Fortunately for us, Greg K. isn't playing in The Match. Dexter and Noodles intuitively understand the idea of this feature, thus avoiding the sticky matter as to why none of the questions are about their music, or even, really, their band. Also, they can't play pool very well. So far, so good. But Team Kerrang! can't play pool very well, either. Brannigan is the better of the two, but only intermittently. His playing is fueled by the kind of conviction that sees people blow themselves up outside tourist attractions. His partner is much less focused, much more reckless and impatient. Both are capable of missing anything.

The Offspring break and pot. They're playing stripes. Only one ball is sunk. Brannigan steps to the table and pots four balls in four shots. The ascendant Team Kerrang! somehow resists the urge to begin singing the popular English folk song "Can We Play You Every Week?"

A young man from another table wanders over.

"You're that guy Crazy Noodles, aren't you?"

"Erm, sure."

"It's my friend's birthday. Can we have a photo taken with you please?"

So Dexter Holland and Crazy Noodles go and have their picture taken. As the guitarist forces the birthday boy to wear his glasses, we resist the urge to fist a couple of spot balls into corner pockets.

For his first three visits to the table, Team Kerrang!'s weaker player pots three balls. This will be the last example of good pool playing he'll display all afternoon, and possibly for the rest of his life.

"Noodles?"

"Yeah, what?"

"If we win, are you going to beat us up like you did that guy at the Kerrang! Awards party last year?"

"No," he says, all pout seriousness, "I'm not like that."

"What happened there, then?"

"Well, I was in the toilet and this kid was talking shit about my band. And it just kind of went from there. I wouldn't say I beat him up, exactly. Although I did land about six shots, and he didn't land any."

"He beat him up," says Dexter, with a quick nod of quiet satisfaction.

"You must have thought, *That's my boy!*"

"Yep, I did."

Unfortunately—fortunately—the punk rocker's quickness of temper isn't put to the test, as Team Kerrang! manage to hoof and spoon their way to defeat in the first frame. With the game resting on the black ball, Winwood confidently thrusts a finger of prediction toward the top right-hand pocket. Seconds later, the eight ball rolls regally into the center-left—with the white ball following it.

Time flies when you're getting fucked, and we only have time for one more frame. The two options facing us are a noble tie or else grave upset and the possibility of a fight. The Offspring have to head over to Hammersmith to film a performance for CD:UK. Team Kerrang! are holding their cues with such force that the wood can be heard creaking over the throb of the Elbow Room's music system. A measure of focus is now required.

Team Offspring are beginning to circle the table like big cats stalking their prey. Too tall to be trusted, Dexter Holland takes a split second longer than his bandmate to understand that the now torrential volley of insults flying his way is what passes for humor here in England. For a second, he'll look confused— outraged, even—before realizing that he has 47 credit cards, whereas the only cards his opponents hold have the words National Union of Journalists stamped across them. This is the reason why the air is blue with language and black with the temper of two grandly sore losers to be.

Since we're not playing cricket—now *there's* an idea—it's time to throw Dexter and Noodles off their game.

"You know, when Green Day played in London a few years ago they got a fan up onstage to play a song with them. The kid was wearing an Offspring t-shirt, and Billie Joe Armstrong said, 'You can take that fucking shirt off for a start.'"

"That's fantastic!" Noodles says, laughing.

"I like Green Day," says Dexter. "I talk to Billie Joe on the phone. That stuff used to bother both our bands in the early days, but not any more."

Bollocks. Still, they might be bluffing. Just in case, Team Kerrang! begins to sing Green Day songs each time The Offspring pot a ball.

"Do you have the time . . ."

Thunk.

"To listen to me whine . . ."

Thunk.

We have no chance at all of winning the game. Team Off-spring have two balls to pot before the black; their opponents have five. Winwood takes a shot wearing Noodles' glasses. This is an experience. The guitarist's prescription is of such an advanced intensity that dizziness and nausea will greet anyone who ventures to place the things anywhere near their face. Sporting his eyewear, it is impossible to see the balls on the pool table, the table itself, or even the hand held up in disbelief in front of your face. The only thing that remains visible is Noodles' haircut, which still looks as if it were fashioned by someone who was trying to give up smoking.

Brannigan steps toward the table, not looking happy. His teammate steps away from the table, scouting the exits. And then it happens; our little miracle. Actually, no, our major miracle, our garden of four leaf clovers that flower as Jesus Christ rises from the dead, atop a unicorn and singing a Nickelback song that sounds fantastic. Brannigan pots a ball. He then pots another, and then another. Team Offspring and Team Kerrang! are now facing off over the single remaining ball. They shoot, and miss; we shoot, and miss; they shoot, and miss.

We shoot.

We pot.

Goal.

Team Kerrang! are gracious about it. There are just a few bars of the popular English folk song "You're So Shit It's Unbelievable," plus noisy demands for t-shirts. Noodles, hopelessly submerged by now, has taken the rack down from the light above the table and is shepherding balls for a deciding frame. Actually, it might be that he's not even thinking of a deciding frame—just another game. Then another, then another, then another. Because Noodles—as well as his friend and bandmate, but *especially* Noodles—has enjoyed himself. He wants to carry on. He's forgotten that a people carrier is waiting outside to take his band to Riverside Television Studios. He's probably also forgotten that his name is Noodles. All he wants to do is rack 'em up and cue 'em off.

Instead, it's goodbye. It's warm words and warm smiles harvested from an afternoon thick with strong and unexpected pleasures. Team Offspring are off to appear on television. Team Kerrang! are off to the pub. They'll be off to the pub for years to come to tell the glorious tale of the time they thrashed two members of a world-renowned punk rock band 1-1 in a pool competition.

# ACKNOWLEDGMENTS

Congratulations, you made it. It is at this point in the process that authors tell the reader that writing a book is a collaborative exercise. This is something we do because it's true. Certainly, this is by a street the most collective piece of work with which I have been involved. At the book's outset, I believed that I knew this story inside and out. After conducting forty interviews, I realized I knew nothing of the kind. Many people helped enrich my text with details that otherwise would have remained hidden, and for this I am deeply grateful. A busy man with better things to do, Brett Gurewitz consented to be questioned no fewer than six times. Greg Graffin picked up the phone five times, and answered numerous emails. Lawrence Livermore and Rob Cavallo made themselves available on three occasions, as did Dexter Holland.

My thanks go to this book's interviewees. These are Jeff Abarta, Billie Joe Armstrong, Brian Baker, Rob Cavallo, Tre Cool, Mike Dirnt, Fat Mike, Jon Ginoli, Mike Gitter, Greg Graffin, Brett Gurewitz, Jim Guerinot, Greg Hetson, Dexter Holland, Veronica Irwin, Lisa Johnson, Greg K., Mark Kohr, Jim Lindberg, Jon Montague, Mike Ness, Noodles and Chrissie Yiannou. Chrissie now owns and runs a sweet treats shop on the Holloway Road in London called Cookies and Scream, which comes highly recommended. Tell her I sent you.

Other people helped me find obscure interviewees. My thanks go to my dear friend Frank Turner, hardcore troubadour and right-wing cracker. Alex Burrows, by far my favorite grump, helped uncover hidden gems such as Jon Ginoli and Jon Montague, and also cast an expert eye over a near-finished draft. Bill Schneider, Pat Magnarella and Susan Leon of Team Green Day helped in getting the three members of that band on the trumpet for me. Alma Lilic and Chantal Neetan from Epitaph's European office in Amsterdam deserve thanks for steering me in the direction of The Offspring. I am also indebted to Larry Tull, the band's manager, for going the extra mile in helping me speak with the group.

Profound thanks go to Kathy Winwood, my mum, for helping with the at times overwhelming task of transcribing hours of interview tape. Without her help, this book would have been filed many months over deadline (as opposed to many weeks).

My thanks also go to Paul Brannigan and Dan Silver for reading back parts of the text and making astute and helpful suggestions. James Sherry proved himself to be a font of all punk knowledge in providing dates and details of even the most obscure of this book's happenings. In Los Angeles, Susan Lucarelli was always a pleasure to speak to in the minutes prior to being connected to Mr. Brett Gurewitz. Victoria Durham was there at the start, and deserved better. Freddie "Metronome" McCall helped a little bit, too, I suppose. Dorian Lynskey was kind enough to send me his excellent feature on Green Day, published in Q magazine. My dear friend Jen Walker was kind enough to find The Offspring feature from Kerrang! reprinted above, and for her help with all manner of technical issues. Thanks also go to Scarlet Borg, Paul Harries and Lisa Johnson for their help with the photographs that partner with these words.

Some of the information regarding Operation Ivy and the early life of Lawrence Livermore relies heavily on Larry's own written work. I am indebted to him for steering me toward it. Without this guidance, the book's second chapter would be a dud. His fine writing can be found at larrylivermore.com.

Finally, praise goes to Ben Schafer, my editor at Da Capo Press, and my agents Matthew Hamilton and Matthew Elblonk. All three helped me through this book with patience and grace.

# INDEX